# the library
## in the twenty-first
## century

# the **library** in the **twenty-first century**

## new services for the information age

PETER BROPHY

LIBRARY ASSOCIATION PUBLISHING
LONDON

Published by
Library Association Publishing
7 Ridgmount Street
London WC1E 7AE

Library Association Publishing is wholly owned by The Library Association.

First published 2001


British Library Cataloguing in Publication Data

A catalogue record for this book is available from the British Library.

ISBN 1-85604-375-4

1203743 5

Learning Resources
Centre

Typeset from author's disks in 11/13 Elegant Garamond and Humanist 521 by Library Association Publishing.
Printed and made in Great Britain by MPG Books Ltd, Bodmin, Cornwall.

I have always imagined that Paradise will be a kind of library

Jorge Luis Borges

This book is dedicated to the staff – past, present and future – of the Centre for Research in Library and Information Management (CERLIM)

# Contents

# Preface

Libraries are one of the marks of civilization. A nation uninterested in the truth of its past, unconcerned with developing its citizens' potential and inimical to freedom of expression, does not need libraries. Libraries may be maintained in the collective mind, as in oral traditions, or may have physical presence in the city, town or village. They may be large or small. What they contain may, indeed should, be contradictory, puzzling, at times shocking, frequently outrageous. Above all, their contents must stimulate the mind, provoke original thinking and suggest new ways of looking at the world.

But libraries are under threat. If the world is really being built on information and knowledge, transmitted almost instantaneously from any place to anywhere, what role is left for yesterday's fusty mausoleums of print? Perhaps they will survive as museums, becoming just one stop on the country-house tour, preserved in the state in which they were left as the world moved on and now trampled through by thousands of feet on their way to the teashop. And what of the profession of librarianship, is that any better? It bemoans the poor public perception of librarians, yet never quite shakes it off. As a House of Commons Select Committee put it recently, 'The image of an imposed silence has been perpetuated, and the most pervasive image . . . is the hissed "shh" in response to the slightest noise' (House of Commons, 2000). Already the library seems to belong to a bygone age.

This book was conceived because, after years of working in libraries, I have come to believe that there is a real danger that libraries and librarians will be left behind. I believe in libraries, but I fear for them. They have so much to offer, yet could so easily become backwaters.

I do not intend to engage in polemic or special pleading. Rather this is an attempt to understand what a successful, relevant, dynamic library must be in the Information Age and to communicate that, inevitably partial, understanding to others. It concentrates on technological change, because that is where the biggest challenges lie. No one needs reminding that we live in an increasingly digital world or that information is at the heart of economic and social development – however defined, the Information Age is now very much a reality. While all organizations, from manufacturing firms to voluntary support groups, are rethinking their strategies and approaches, it is surely stating the obvious to claim that those that have long been involved in information processing are likely to be among the most profoundly affected. Libraries, among the most information-intensive organizations in existence, will have to change. Although there continue to be numerous differing views as to whether or not libraries will be transformed or even destroyed by the changes taking place around and within them, there are relatively few publications that have taken a broad and systematic approach and attempted to set out the challenges to libraries across the different sectors. As Greenberg (1998) has put it, 'We have not thought as systematically as we should about the characteristics of the print library and how and whether they can, or should be, duplicated, transformed, or abandoned in a digital world'.

This book is the result of an attempt to think systematically and strategically about the future of libraries. That it is partial and ultimately inadequate is inevitable given the breadth of issues that must be considered and the rate of change in the information arena.

The perspective from which it is written needs stating in order to explain its starting points and concerns. For the last two years I have occupied the Chair in Information Management at the Manchester Metropolitan University, a position that has enabled me to reflect on and engage in some of the more theoretical and strategic debates that are ongoing. Prior to that I spent 15 years as the 'chief librarian' (with the usual variety of job titles) of academic libraries, having also worked as a systems librarian and as a subject librarian. By the time I moved on from such positions, in 1988, I had also experienced the challenges of responsibility for cross-university IT services and for a Learning Technology Centre. In 1998–99 I was privileged to serve as President of the UK's Institute of Information Scientists, to which body I am grateful for giving me insights into a number of other sectors, including in particular commercial and industrial information service concerns. I am grateful also for the knowledge that colleagues from other disciplines have shared with me down the years. Finally my involvement in international research and development projects, primarily although not exclusively in Europe, has broadened my horizons and given me some inkling of different cultural and societal concerns and approaches.

In Part I of the book (Chapters 1 to 6) the aim is to analyse the changing environments in which libraries operate and to answer the fundamental question, 'What *is* a library?'. In Part II 'Future libraries' the emphasis switches to synthesis, presenting first a model of the 'library' in Chapter 7, and then considering the major issues that need to be addressed in building such libraries in Chapters 8 to 10. Finally, Chapter 11 suggests emphases beyond technological and operational competence that will help to shape tomorrow's libraries within their societal and individual contexts and draws general conclusions.

I remain a believer in the importance of libraries to societies and individuals. Of course I am biased: I haunted the public library as a child and I have relied on academic institutions for employment since graduating from one in 1971.

But it is more than that. To repeat the sentiment of the first paragraph above, for me libraries are symbols of civilized societies. The burning of the national library in Sarajevo was not just the loss of a fine building and a unique collection: it symbolized a decline into barbarism. A library makes a statement about the value that a society places on knowledge and learning, and thus on truth. It is no accident that in the past, and hearteningly in recent years, library buildings have been designed to make statements about their parent bodies – whether it is the Ruskin Library at Lancaster University, the SCONUL-Award-winning Aytoun Library at Manchester Metropolitan University or the public libraries in Vancouver or the London Borough of Peckham.

But symbols are not enough. Without descending into technological determinism, we must acknowledge that information and communications technologies have started to change the whole nature of publication, transmission and use of information. The world wide web is, as a public resource, less than a decade old, yet has utterly transformed information behaviours. It is not obvious or inevitable that libraries, even if transformed from their present state, have a future. While some initiatives are positive – the UK's New Library process for example – the public image of librarians remains poor and distinctly old-fashioned, while technologists lay claim to so-called digital libraries that will apparently replace traditional place-based libraries with a few simple keystrokes.

For everyone involved in libraries these are confusing times. If this book helps to elucidate some of the foundations on which future libraries can be built it will have more than served its purpose.

**Peter Brophy**

# Part I
## What is a library?

# 1

# The end of libraries?

The traditional library, consisting of books and work tables, may give way to a cultural monument, largely unused but maintained at public expense out of collective guilt.

(Shuman, 1989)

## Introduction: The onward march of technology

Hardly a day goes by without further evidence emerging of the revolutionary changes across all sectors of society being introduced by the impacts of information and communication technologies (ICTs). The word 'revolutionary' is used deliberately to convey the idea that this is not a process of gentle evolution, nor even one of carefully planned change. Revolutions involve massive change, the adoption of totally new paradigms, the loss of much that has been taken for granted and the introduction of innovations that were never thought possible. Instant, pervasive access to the world's information from the home, from the workplace and even while on the move raises questions about the structures that have been developed to organize and make available information in the past. Why does the world still need libraries? Are they not the 21st century's equivalent of the 19th century's canals – an intermediate technology to be consigned to near oblivion, canals by the railways, libraries by the world wide web?

Daniel Bell's *The coming of the post-industrial society* (Bell, 1973) is often cited as the foundation text for this view, the first comprehensive analysis of the changes that are destroying industrial society and are replacing it with the post-industrial, variously described by epithets such as 'information', 'knowledge' or 'learning'. Bell wrote that 'knowledge and information [have] become the strategic and transforming resources'. His contribution has been recognized as 'the dominant context for thinking about information and society' (Schement and Curtis, 1995) and, while some have criticized the coherence of his theories – Duff (1998), for example, concludes that 'his theory fails as a synthesis . . . failing to assimilate each of the elements properly (and leaving) some parts of the theory overblown and others underdeveloped' – his place in information society development is assured.

Many writers since Bell have echoed his theme, and many have stressed that what is happening is not simply the effect of a single new technology but the convergence of a variety of technologies – which together may be termed 'digital' – that provide the opportunity to develop new forms of relationship between people and organizations, largely independent of time and place. It is little more than a century since the telegraph displaced the ocean liner as the fastest way to do business across the Atlantic. De Kerckhove (1997) writes thus:

> Whether we call it the Net, the Internet, or the Information Highway, the growing synergy of networked communications is, with the exception of language itself, the communication medium par excellence – the most comprehensive, the most innovative, and the most complex of them all. . . . In the mega-convergence of hypertext, multimedia, virtual reality, neural networks, digital agents, and even artificial life, each medium is changing different parts of our lives – our modes of communication, entertainment and work – but the Net changes all of that and more, all at once. The Internet gives us access to a live, quasi-organic environment of millions of human intelligences perpetually at work on anything and everything with potential relevance to anyone and everybody.

Castels (1998) echoes these thoughts:

> Networks constitute the new social morphology of our societies, and the diffusion of network logic substantially modifies the operation and the outcomes in processes of production, experience, power and culture.

Libraries can seem to be falling victim to these pressures, casualties of the revolution as their role changes beyond recognition and the appropriateness of keeping such an antediluvian term as 'library' is called into question. After all if 'connected intelligence' (the title of de Kerckhove's book) underpins the future, is there any place for old ways of recording and organizing intelligence, knowledge or human memory? Would it perhaps be best if librarians and information scientists bowed to the inevitable and found themselves new skills and new niches in the information society?

> Five years ago, the library at my laboratory used to occupy several large rooms and employ 30 people. It has been replaced by a digital library that is now ten times bigger – and growing fast. This digital library is staffed by only 12 of the original librarians who are now amongst the best html programmers in the company. This digital library has become an essential part of our lives and the work output has gone up tenfold in 10 years.
>
> (Cochrane, 1999)

That this is a time of rapid change is clear, and people throughout the world are becoming used to a plethora of information, presented to them by multiple channels (TV, cinema, radio, telephone, print in various forms) and in a variety of formats. 'Information objects' – a convenient term to describe books, journals, newspapers, electronic documents, multimedia packages and so on – can be accessed in many different ways. Increasingly they are being delivered direct to the user either using telecommunications for electronic objects or more traditional – but notably non-library – methods such as post for objects ordered online or over the telephone.

So, at the outset, it should be stated that libraries as we have known them are under threat. It doesn't look like it. To enter any academic or public library in almost any part of the world is to be greeted by a scene not that different from that which would have met a visitor half a century ago. Admittedly the serried ranks of card catalogue cabinets have been replaced by computer screens, but the bulk of the space is still occupied by books and journals on shelves, by reader tables and by staff areas where books are issued and returned, new books acquired and added to the collection, and reader enquiries answered. What is more, despite some decline in usage statistics in some sectors, libraries remain overwhelmingly popular. The public library, we are constantly told, is among the most heavily used of local public services, while the academic library attracts ever-growing numbers of student users. But underneath all this activity the ground is shifting and it may be opening up. Hardison (1989) put it this way:

> We are coming to the end of the culture of the book. Books are still produced and read in prodigious numbers, and they will continue to be as far into the future as one can imagine. However, they do not command the center of the cultural stage. Modern culture is taking shapes that are more various and more complicated than the book-centered culture it is succeeding.

## The loss of the core business

Yet even that analysis may be too complacent. Change is incredibly fast – the PC is little more than 20 years old, the world wide web less than ten. The threats are significant, and their impact on libraries as they currently exist could be devastating – their core business could be about to disappear. Consider the following ten points:

## 1 Electronic paper

Experiments with electronic paper have reached a stage where commercial exploitation is about to occur. Undoubtedly the first attempts will be rather crude – as were the first attempts at manufacturing paper itself – but improvement will be rapid. Electronic paper will look like ordinary paper to the naked eye; it will be read by reflected light; it will require little power, so that battery life will not be an issue; its content will be rechargeable by download from the Internet; it will be used to create personalized books, the 21st-century equivalents of the Filofax. Xerox announced in 1999 that its version of electronic paper, based on a display technology called 'gyricons' – thin layers of transparent plastic containing tiny beads that change from black to white when subject to a charge – was ready for its first commercial exploitation (Xerox Palo Alto Research Center, 1999). Each sheet can be re-used thousands of times, and applications will include use in place of normal paper through printer-like devices, use in place of traditional computer displays and use for portable devices, where the image's stability – meaning it does not need to be refreshed constantly – will greatly reduce the battery power needed.

## 2   New publishing models

Scientists, engineers, social scientists and researchers in the humanities, who together provide the vast majority of content for academic journals, are now making serious use of alternative publication methods, based on electronic archives and pre-print services. The Open Archives Initiative, set up to encourage self-archiving systems, has developed the 'Santa Fe Convention', a base of standards and principles that enable scholars to publish their research immediately in electronic archives which, in effect, they control and which do not need intermediaries like libraries. As Van de Sompel and Lagoze (2000) state, 'the explosive growth of the Internet has given scholars almost universal access to a communication medium that facilitates sharing of results', while 'the slow turn-around of the traditional publishing model (is) an impediment to collegial sharing'.

## 3   Online bookshops

Bookshops are more successful than ever before. They fall into two types. The high street bookshop is taking business away from the public and academic library – by providing a wide range of *new* books that customers are encouraged to *own* as opposed to the grubby specimens libraries reluctantly allow them to borrow, by providing pleasant surroundings including comfortable armchairs where customers can linger and by providing ancillary services like coffee shops with a large choice of lattes, cappuccinos and espressos to attract an affluent clientele. At the same time, Internet bookshops are providing access to an enormous range of discounted stock that they deliver direct to the customer's door.

What is the lesson for libraries from the idea that Amazon.com's founder implemented? Jeff Bezo realized that not only does the Internet allow a retailer to interact directly with a customer wherever that customer happens to be – and particularly in the comfort of home or office – and not only can an online retailer offer stock before acquiring it from the wholesaler, but as the business grows it does not have to invest more in bricks and mortar: 'If a chain of 1,000 stores wants to double sales . . . it has to open *another* thousand stores, with all the land and manpower costs that that entails. But once an online operation gets past the fixed cost of its Web site and distribution channel, it can handle bigger sales with very few extra expenses' (Levy, 1999).

## 4 E-commerce

What is true of online bookshops holds good for the wider world of e-commerce. Of course, as yet it represents only a fraction of the total economy, but it is growing rapidly and it is reasonable to suppose that once people become used to e-shopping for one commodity they will have few inhibitions about adopting it for others. Given the efforts being made by banks to switch their customers to electronic accounts, which are far cheaper to service than either high street or postal accounts, the knock-on or trickle-down effects are unlikely to be much delayed. But even more important than e-shopping by consumers is business-to-business e-commerce. There are clearly problems with selling some goods to consumers over the Net – limited take-up of online grocery shopping is at least partly due to people's natural desire to be able to examine the product before buying – how many people want their fruit and vegetables selected by a spotty teenager? But where e-commerce does seem to score heavily is in the service sector, the very sector that most libraries occupy. Finance, travel and, of course, information are particularly suited to transactions in cyberspace. The demise of bank branches in villages is at least in part due to this trend.

## 5 Digital television

As yet digital television has made only a limited impact. If it becomes truly interactive, and e-mail via television services was launched in the UK during early 2000, then again people will build up a habit of accessing information through this medium. The range of applications for digital TV is limited only by our imaginations. Once the set-top box is linked to a telephone line to achieve interactivity, with the downpath having vast bandwidth, the whole nature of television programming could change. No longer would there be 'channels' broadcasting programmes at set times; instead there would be a data-bank of available programmes for each viewer to choose from at will. The video recorder could become just one more piece of discarded intermediate technology. Where will libraries fit into such a world – if at all?

## 6   Integrated learning environments

Learning environments are being developed that deliberately integrate all kinds of learning support. Whether these are to be found in schools, in colleges, in universities, in local learning centres or in cyberspace, they are built on the foundations of modern pedagogical principles which imply that the student is at the centre and is learning actively rather than absorbing information passively. Support no longer means a separate library but rather the integration of largely online, multimedia resources into the learning experience. The role of the librarian, as expert in information sources, becomes an integral part of the role of the tutor. Librarians may, and do, claim that they have a vital role to play as a part of the tutorial team, but remarkably few teachers are on record as stating a similar view. And how many librarians are qualified teachers? Is it not more likely that teachers will develop their own information expertise?

## 7   E-universities

E-universities are now being pushed hard by government with all sorts of experiments under way. The University of Phoenix (**http://www.uophx.edu/**) is usually cited as the first large-scale example of a virtual university, but there are many more examples around the world and most traditional libraries and colleges are experimenting with online delivery. An advantage is seen in the ability to remove many of the barriers of time and place – advocates of this route suggest that each student will be able to choose to study at his or her own time, place and pace – that in effect the student will be in control, and in control remotely.

> Thirty years from now, the big university campuses will be relics. Universities won't survive. . . . Higher education is in deep crisis. . . . Already we are beginning to deliver more lectures and classes off-campus via satellite or two-way video at a fraction of the cost. The college won't survive as a residential institution.
> (Drucker, 1997)

Libraries have a very poor record of supporting distance learners (with a few honourable exceptions, which will be discussed later). They are expensive edifices that university leaders may be tempted to regard as no longer central to their institutions' missions. Hardesty (2000) reports from the USA:

Access to electronic information is now so ubiquitous in higher education that this past summer an officer of a regional accreditation association sent a letter to academic library directors in his region posing this question: Is a library an absolute prerequisite for a degree-granting institution of higher education, or is it, instead, an indicator of some increasing level of quality above an accepted minimum?

And MacDougall (1998) has observed:

... the worst threat will be that of the unenlightened senior administrators and managers who completely ignore the importance of information provision in the rush to register students and minimise or reduce the unit cost. The impoverishment to the student and society will be immense. It is sad to report that there is some evidence to suggest in Europe that this has already happened. In the headlong rush to provide economical distance education courses there has been some lack of interest in providing the student with a clearly costed quality information support environment. In such cases the packs of information and spoonfeeding as substitutes for rounded information services seem to be accepted.

Will the e-university in effect spell the end of the university library?

## 8   Mobile communications

The explosive growth of mobile telephone usage can be seen as an indicator of one of the most likely technological developments of the next few years, namely the replacement of place-based by place-independent telecommunications. Without suggesting that fixed-line and wireless technologies will not have a future, what is clear is that more and more products – by which we must mean information products – will be delivered over mobile communications channels. WAP (Wireless Application Protocol) devices were launched in the UK in late 1999, enabling access to the Internet albeit with relatively low bandwidth and a requirement for specially marked-up content (using WML – Wireless Mark-up Language). However, once XML (eXtensible Mark-up Language) becomes widely adopted it should be possible to extract data from standard web pages for delivery to WAP devices. The expectation is that WAP phones will be used for online news and financial information, some e-commerce applications, e-mail and specialist information services. It is quite likely that WAP phones, or rather their successors (GPRS – General Packet Radio Service – is probably the next technology in line although the Japanese *i-mode* technology, which allows continuous Internet access, is another contender) will become the main way in which users surf the Internet. In April 2000 major global telecommunications companies bid £22 billion – something approaching 10% of the size of the UK's total national debt – for the next generation of mobile communications licences, equivalent, on optimistic forecasts, to about £14 per month per expected subscriber over a ten-year period. This illustrates the anticipated value and anticipated market penetration of the services to be delivered. The major limiting factor for some time will be the size and other constraints of the screen on which information can be displayed, although of course it will be possible to store data and copy it on to a desktop device and no doubt new technologies will remove even this limitation.

## 9   Print on demand

There has been a trend among publishers in recent years towards 'print-on-demand' approaches, especially where titles are expected to sell slowly and/or in small numbers. Digital printing technologies are now mature enough to enable a book to be printed from an electronic file when it is required, rather than in anticipation of demand. The technology is not entirely stable yet, of course, and the products do not have the sophistication of full-colour reproduction and designer bindings – otherwise presumably there would be no one left publishing 'just in case'. However the economics of this approach are attractive:

- Cambridge University Press estimates that it loses sales of well in excess of £1 million a year, and possibly several million pounds, by being unable to fulfil orders for books that have gone out of print but are unlikely to justify a new print run (Holdsworth, 2000).
- Dorling Kindersley is reported to have lost £14 million on unsold stock produced as tie-ins to the Star Wars 1999 epic *Episode One: The Phantom Menace*, believed to be a major contributory factor in the company's takeover (Bury, 2000).

While the implications for libraries are as yet unclear, it does look as if serious competition could arise from this source. Some booksellers are currently able to offer a limited service of this type and it must be expected that this will increase. A major factor in determining the impact on libraries could be the penetration of this approach in the student textbook (academic libraries) and popular fiction (public libraries) markets.

## 10   The unknown

Finally, there is the threat of the unknown. In the 1960s, when it became apparent that libraries could use mainframe computers for their administrative processes, few were predicting that within 30 years computers with greater power would be on every user's desktop and in every user's briefcase. In the 1970s few recognized that the future lay in end-user searching of remote databases. In the 1980s no one predicted the impact of the web, with its matter-of-fact interlinking of users and information sources, based on the principle that, in the words of its inventor, 'once someone somewhere made available a document, database, graphic, sound, video or screen at some stage in an interactive dialogue, it should be accessible . . . by anyone, with any type of computer, in any country' (Berners-Lee, 1999). It is (by definition!) impossible to know what the next unexpected, ground-shifting invention will be; all that can be said with certainty is that there will be one. However, given that all the other inventions in this sphere have posed at the least challenges and more usually threats to traditional libraries, it would be surprising if the unknown did not follow the same course. Will libraries respond by installing the technology and marketing these as yet unknown products themselves? Past experience would suggest that they are more likely to allow another player to capture the market.

These ten points are deliberately presented as threats and are deliberately couched in provocative terms. They are presented in this way to reinforce the point that there is a real crisis for libraries and it is very close. They could also be reinforced by the observation that they are in essence step changes and qualitative effects, while what may be of even more importance are the gradual quantitative effects which, because they have become familiar, may appear to have been allowed for already. Internet usage is doubling every six, nine or 12 months – depending on how it is measured and who is doing the reporting, although the period doesn't really matter. The fable of the Chinese emperor who managed to lose his kingdom by offering to give away a grain of rice on the first square of a chessboard, two on the second, four on the third and so on – before realizing that by the end of the first half of the board he would have given away more than a billion (thousand million) grains – is a useful reminder of how doubling can have unexpected large-scale impacts.

## Libraries: unprepared for change?

But these are not the only threats; others are of librarians' own making:

- The technology is complex and librarians have not developed the skills to understand it, exploit it or create it. Those few who do have such skills find they have a very marketable commodity and can make a much better living elsewhere.

- Libraries are expensive and becoming more expensive. The competition, at least in some of its forms, is cheap: the whole of the world wide web is just a local phone call away. What is more, web content looks good even if in the end much of it is disappointing. In the glamour stakes, libraries haven't yet reached the starting gate.
- Libraries are their own worst enemies. While the competition hots up they find themselves closing branches and reducing opening hours. Grandiose claims to be 'the people's universities' are simply not borne out by the facts: in this case it is the emperor without any clothes that provides the apposite fable.

Over 15 years ago Lancaster (1983) wrote:

> Ultimately . . . libraries as we know them seem likely to disappear. Facilities will still exist to preserve the print-on-paper record of the past, of course, but they will be more like archives, or even museums, providing little in the way of public service. As for the electronic sources, libraries may have an interim role to play. . . . In the longer term, it seems certain that the libraries will be bypassed. That is, people will have very little reason to visit libraries in order to gain access to information sources.

## Beyond technology

And yet. One is left asking whether all this technology-based analysis is adequate. Is it simply a case of the now discredited 'technological determinism', the belief that technology will determine the future? Is what we are seeing simply another step in a process of human and societal evolution that is far less pervasive and far less influential than technology acolytes would have us believe? The demise of paper as a medium of communication, to take one example, has been prophesied again and again. Not only has it failed to happen but world consumption has in fact increased many times over. In their extensive treatment of this issue, Harris and Hanna (1993) remark:

> While it seems undeniable that we are dealing with a new 'social framework' in Bell's sense, it also appears clear that we must find some way to transcend the two most common reactions to the information society – 'the complacent (yet delirious) camp-following celebration' or the 'moralizing condemnation' so common in our literature . . . we must find a way to confront critically and intervene intelligently in the process of change sweeping our society and, more explicitly, our profession.

Toffler (1980) commented, in his influential volume *The third wave*, that even today we cannot reach agreement on the causes of the first Industrial Revolution over 300 years ago:

> Each academic guild or philosophical school has its own preferred explanation. The technological determinists point to the steam engine, the ecologists to the destruction of Britain's forests, the economists to fluctuations in the price of wool. Others emphasize religious or cultural changes, the Reformation, the Enlightenment, and so on.

The sociology of the information revolution is a massive subject with its own extensive literature that goes far beyond the scope of this book. But it is right, at the outset, to acknowledge that the forces shaping the profession of librarianship and the design of libraries are not solely technological. There are massive cultural, social, psychological and philosophical forces at work: our views and understandings of the world are very different from those of our predecessors. The users of libraries come now with expectations far removed from those of their forebears, and technology is only partly the explanation. It is also true that a proportion of our understanding of the foundations of librarianship is based on myth: libraries have never given access to anything more than a small proportion of the world's information. Perhaps their continued inability to do so will not after all mean that they are doomed to irrelevance.

## Conclusion

However the present role of libraries may be defined, and this is the issue that will occupy the first part of this book, it must be clear that as participants in the information 'business' they will be deeply affected by the changes that are taking place around them. They are among the best examples of 'information-based organisations' – selecting information, acquiring it, organizing it, storing it, making it available – at the present time. Does this signify a central role in the new dispensation? Or are they becoming anachronisms, the 21st century equivalent of the Zeppelin? Many writers have commented on these issues and many of these contributions will be examined later. Before those questions can be answered it is necessary to explore in greater detail what it is that libraries do, and why, and how, before turning to consider what roles they might usefully be able to play in the future.

# 2

# What is a library?
# The view from the sectors

Libraries form a vital part of the world's systems of education and information storage and retrieval. They make available – through books, films, recordings, and other media – knowledge that has been accumulated through the ages. People in all walks of life – including students, teachers, business executives, government officials, scholars, and scientists – use library resources in their work. Large numbers of people also turn to libraries to satisfy a desire for knowledge or to obtain material for some kind of leisure-time activity. In addition, many people enjoy book discussions, film shows, lectures, and other activities that are provided by their local library.

(*World Book Encyclopedia*, 1999)

## Introduction

The key concepts in the above description are *education*, *information storage and retrieval* and *the transmission of knowledge*, but it also makes clear that libraries provide a very wide variety of activities and services for people 'in all walks of life'. The aim of this chapter is to explore in some detail what it is that libraries are actually *for* – what purpose they serve in society – as perceived by practitioners and policy makers in the various sectors, and to begin to examine how external influences are forcing a re-thinking of these roles.

It is as well to begin consideration of libraries by going back to their origins – and that means going back a very long way. While no one knows who founded the first recognizable library, and speculation would in any case be futile, quite a lot is known about some of the most celebrated libraries in the ancient world. That at Nineveh, capital of Assyria, was founded in the seventh century BC and contained thousands of clay tablets. Even more famous is the library at Alexandria in Egypt, created by Ptolemy Soter some time around 300 BC and attached to the Temple of the Muses. With its unparalleled collection of papyrus rolls it contained the major part of the world's recorded knowledge. Here were collected in one place the writings of philosophers and scholars, scientists and poets, and here those with the time, authority, power and influence could come and consult humankind's memory. At a time when the term 'memory institution' is coming into use as a shorthand for libraries, museums, archives, art galleries and other similar organizations, it is worth remembering that Alexandria represented, all those centuries ago, the first real attempt to maintain the corporate memory of humankind from generation to generation in permanent, physical form.

The loss of the Alexandrian library resulted quite literally in the loss of much of human knowledge and it is a matter of speculation as to how world history might have unfolded had its treasures remained available – a lesson in the importance of preservation that should not be ignored today. Nor is it the only example of such loss. Recent excavations in South America show how the records of the remarkable Mayan, Inca and other civilizations were systematically destroyed by the European invaders of our medieval period. What knowledge and understanding we have lost as a result will never be known.

There were no great libraries in Europe in the early Middle Ages to rival those of Nineveh and Alexandria. What survived throughout the period from the destruction of the Roman Empire through to the 13th century were small – tiny by today's standards – collections of manuscripts in monasteries scattered across the continent, together with collections in private hands. These codices and scrolls represented only a fragment of the learning of ancient Greece and Rome, with a smattering of input from other civilizations, but what was there was guarded carefully. Thompson (1977) has pointed out that 'the common word for library in the early Middle Ages was *armarium*, the name for the bookchest where the books were kept; and the librarian of such a collection was known as the *armarius*'. Among his duties was that of ensuring that no one made copies without express permission, for the status of the library was linked in large part to the uniqueness of its collection.

This tradition of the library as the place where humankind's recorded memory is gathered together survives to the present day. It can most readily be seen in the great national libraries, which form the subject of the first of a series of sectoral descriptions below. In the following chapters, further consideration will be given to more theoretical concepts of the term 'library', including what is meant by 'collection'.

## The view from the sectors 1: National libraries

The development of national libraries has, not surprisingly, followed a variety of patterns, although a common route in Europe has been through royal collections: the Kungliga Biblioteket or Royal Library in Stockholm provides a typical example of this development. King Gustav Vasa is usually credited with starting the collections in the 1520s. His sons, Erik XIV, Johan III and Karl IX added to them and by 1587 a corridor lined with bookshelves, known as the 'Green Corridor' had been set up in a Palace attic. In 1661 legal deposit was enacted with all publishers in Sweden required to deposit two copies, one in the Royal Library and the other in the Royal Archives. The main reason for this appears to have been nothing to do with preservation or national bibliographic completeness but simply as a means of censoring, or at least checking up on, publishers and authors. Further additions to the Library came as a result of Swedish conquests abroad (the *Codex gigas* or *Devil's Bible*, perhaps the Library's greatest treasure, dating from the 13th century, was acquired from Prague in this way) and the confiscation of books owned by religious houses during the Reformation.

In similar vein, the British Museum Library's foundation collection, that of Sir Hans Sloane, was greatly enhanced when the royal collection was added in 1757 and then further enhanced with the collection of George III in 1823. Republics have taken a slightly different route, with the national library often developing as an adjunct of government, as with the Library of Congress in the USA, established in 1800 as a legislative library. The Australian National Library had similar antecedents, being separated from the Commonwealth Parliamentary Library in 1961.

The role of the modern national library was established during the 19th century, with the then Librarian of the British Museum, Antony Panizzi, providing leadership. His key achievements may still be seen as marking out the ground that a national library should occupy:

- He secured an annual block grant from the Treasury, thus establishing the principle that the national library should be funded on a permanent basis through general taxation.
- He enforced legal deposit, the system whereby the national library was entitled to a copy of every book published in the country.
- He employed a network of agents to purchase foreign works for the library, thus establishing that while the collection would not be comprehensive in such works, it was a function of the national library to provide access to a representative selection of non-indigenous works.
- He established the formal '91 rules' for the construction of the library catalogue.
- He fought for and established the principle of access for all who needed it.
- He established that the fundamental purpose of a national library was educational.
- He secured appropriate accommodation for the national library and ensured that this was of high status – the Round Reading Room in

Bloomsbury came to stand for the concept of a national library for many, leading eventually to a strong rearguard action by readers when the Library transferred to its new and modern building at St Pancras.

The functions of national libraries have been set out more formally by UNESCO, with one eye on developing countries, as:

- Essential functions
  - collect and conserve the national literature, aiming for complete coverage
  - produce a current national bibliography
  - operate a lending service
  - act as a national bibliographic information service
  - publish or support the publication of specialist bibliographies.
- Desirable functions
  - act as a centre for research and development in library and information work
  - provide education and training in library and information work
  - act as a planning centre for the nation's libraries.
- Possible functions
  - act as a centre for the exchange of material between libraries
  - supply specialized library services for government
  - act as a book museum.

Most national libraries still enjoy the benefits (and of course disadvantages) of legal deposit. In some cases, the privilege has been extended to newer media such as video (in Canada, for example – see Winston, 1997) but most countries are still trying to decide how to apply the requirement – if at all – to such material. A consultation paper issued by the UK Department of National Heritage in 1997 identified many of the issues, but there has been little movement on the key question of new media and in particular electronic objects. This is hardly surprising since such objects are often dynamic and transitory. While a few countries have extended their legal deposit legislation to electronic media (for example, the Netherlands with its Depository for Electronic Publications, described in Chapter 9) most are still struggling to come to terms with it. In the UK a Code of Practice has been agreed, but it lacks legal force and its efficacy has yet to be proved.

The question of preservation and conservation looms large on the national library agenda since a core responsibility is to ensure that the national bibliography is preserved for future generations. Clearly it will continue to be essential to conserve and preserve valuable objects from the past, although some may see this, as noted in Chapter 1, as a museum function inasmuch as it applies to print on paper.

The role of providing bibliographic access, in effect that of describing the contents of the national bibliography, is one that has become more difficult with increasing volumes of publication, globalization and the explosion of non-print media. It is hard to see that the justification for concentrating, in bibliographic terms, on paper-based products can be sustained even in the medium term. Further, it is by no means obvious, at a time when other agencies have taken on – albeit imperfectly – the task of describing electronic resources, that the national library is the only appropriate focus for this work. While the production of the national bibliography of 'traditional' materials may be a continuing and necessary role (at least that was the conclusion of a seminar reported by Cunningham (1997)), it is questionable whether that will be enough to justify the investment. Even the work of most national libraries of acting as 'honest broker' in the development of appropriate standards is under threat as the globalization of MARC, and standardization on USMARC for most purposes, continues on the one hand, while the standardization process for descriptions of non-print materials is pursued in other fora such as the Digital Object Identifier Foundation (see Chapter 8).

Because the volume of publication – even counting only the traditional media – continues to grow, national libraries continue to face the problem of how to cope with all the material they receive and select. For them the option of withdrawing material and discarding it is rarely open – they provide national back-up services and other libraries treat them as the libraries of last resort. As a result it is not surprising that the later decades of the 20th century saw a spate of building – the British Library finally opened its new premises at St Pancras, the Kongelige Bibliotek occupied its new building in Copenhagen, the National Diet Library's new building project started in Japan, and Die Deutsche Bibliothek opened in Frankfurt-am-Main. At the opening ceremony for the last of these, Helmut Kohl, then German Chancellor, said (1997):

> Libraries have always been a kind of memory for mankind. If the human race did not collect and organise knowledge it would forever lack history. For more than 3,000 years the great libraries have been the manifestation and a basic component of advanced civilizations . . . Libraries have always been the focal point of national identity as well. They provide a polyphonic sounding board for language. Here culture lives in the rhythm of the past and the beat of the present day. Here we can sense the melody of the future.

This brings us to an important conclusion from the perspective of the national library. In terms of function – leaving aside medium and content – the national library provides a cultural focal point that transcends the present and reaches into the past, in terms of the 'stuff' it secures, and into the future, in terms of transmitting human knowledge to future generations. It fulfils these roles by collecting a representative, although never comprehensive, set of records and by ensuring that they are organized and preserved so as to remain of use into the future. A national library that fails to build the representative collection or fails to secure its permanence has failed in its duty.

Looking at the role of national libraries from a global perspective, it is generally accepted that they cannot attempt comprehensiveness in their acquisitions and holdings of material from other countries. IFLA's Universal Availability of Publications (UAP) programme is founded on the principle that where a library requires a copy of an item published in another country it should be able to rely on the comprehensiveness of the collections there. One of the dangers of this approach, however, is that this encouragement of unique comprehensive collections risks catastrophic loss should there be a disaster in any participating country. There does not, however, appear to be any immediate solution to this danger, since it has proved impossible to organize long-term commitment to the acquisition and preservation of comprehensive, non-indigenous collections on a significant scale. As Line (1999) remarks, 'A possible solution is to organize "external" collecting of duplicates at an international level, by allocating to developed countries different regions or countries of the world. . . . Any such scheme would have to be voluntary and would almost certainly fade out after a few years.'

Of course, national libraries cannot shoulder all of even their national responsibilities on their own, and they are joined by major academic and other libraries in a cooperative endeavour that builds on specialisms that have developed over the centuries. The concept of a 'Distributed National Collection' has been put forward recently by the Research Support Libraries Programme (RSLP) as a way of formalizing relationships between such collections in the UK.

However, this highly laudable effort still leaves unanswered the question of how the role of national libraries, or national schemes of cooperation, should be continued in an era when the memory of mankind is no longer principally set down as print on paper. Collections of the types that are described above have always been principally concerned with printed books and printed journals. National libraries have struggled, with varying degrees of success, to capture, index, store and maintain other media – the NEWSPLAN Projects, originally funded by the British Library's then Research and Development Department, made a valiant effort to maintain collections of newspapers, but collections of images, of video, of audio and of other non-print media are much less comprehensive than those of print. Perhaps this did not matter too much when other agencies (such as the Hulton Getty Picture Library, especially when it was owned by the BBC) were contributing at least an attempt at representative collections. But what are we to do in the electronic era, when not only are the records of mankind's knowledge in non-print format, but many of them are dynamic and transitory? How should the role of the national library be redefined?

## The view from the sectors 2: Academic libraries

Academic libraries emerged with the modern university during the early Middle Ages, but were a somewhat neglected part of their parent institutions until at least the 18th century and in many cases much later. The medieval college or university library was small and grew very slowly. Cambridge University Library had only 122 volumes in 1424, but the number was starting to grow – by copying, by purchase, but most importantly by donations and gifts. Scholars would travel from library to library to consult rare and valuable manuscripts, as indeed they still do. This sense of the academic library's role as a centre for scholarly research has persisted to the present day – Lyman, for example, writes:

> Research libraries are homes for scholarly communities. . . . Since the turn of the twentieth century, research libraries have provided a sense of order for scholarly research – a center for teaching and research that is local and yet extends across time and even national boundaries. (Lyman, 1997)

Over 50 years ago Rider suggested a similar role, describing the research library as:

> A vast aggregation of all sorts of book and periodical and manuscript materials, assembled together, not for sustained, or for pleasurable, reading . . . but for 'research', that is, for the purposes of scholarly investigation. Research libraries are, primarily, the stored-up knowledge of the race, warehouses of fact and surmise.

Writing in 1964, Clapp observed that academic libraries do not rely solely on their own collections, even if in times past it tended to be the readers rather than the books that moved from place to place:

> . . . from earliest times two principles have controlled the growth of libraries – the principle of local self-sufficiency and the principle of sharing the resources. . . . [Their role is] to enable inquirers to identify library materials relevant to their inquiries and to supply them with copies of these materials for their use.

But he noted the impossibility of any academic library achieving self-suffi-ciency and suggested that the solution might lie in:

> the assignment of specific responsibility for certain conspicuous subjects to particu-lar libraries, each of which would be obliged to acquire comprehensively in the sub-ject, organize and publish its bibliography, and render a nationwide (or perhaps even international) backstopping lending or photocopy service in the subject.

Such ideas were taken up from time to time. For example, in the 1960s many British university libraries accepted limited responsibility for a particular range of subjects. In this way, each academic library would contribute to the library wealth of the nation. However, such schemes have fallen out of favour, largely for economic reasons. First, when budgets became tight each library needed to retain the flexibility to manage its acquisitions budgets as it saw fit, and sec-ondly the overriding concern of each library had to be to serve its parent insti-tution, reflecting its academic and in particular its research strengths.

An enduring metaphor for the academic library is that it is the 'heart of the university'. The exact origins of this phrase are unclear, although Grimes (1998) suggests that it was used first by the then President of Harvard University, Charles William Eliot, who was in that post from 1869 to 1909. The image was picked up in the UK and used in various reports, including the influential Parry Report of 1967 (University Grants Committee, 1967). However, as Grimes points out, the metaphor has been used loosely and with little evidence that it reflects institutional realities:

> The metaphor implies that the academic library is of unparalleled importance. Despite its persistence for more than one hundred years, there is a considerable dis-tance between the relationship it implies and institutional opinion and practice. Evidence of this difference is found in a number of areas. . . . Students and faculty alike fail to involve library resources and services in regular learning and instruction, turning to the library primarily as an undergraduate study hall or reserve book room. . . . National initiatives . . . fail to mention, much less to plan, improvement of library resources. . . . [There is] a disheartening decrease in academic library share of insti-tutional funding . . . they remain, for the most part, on the periphery of decision-making and innovative processes . . . librarians are often not involved in information policy development. . . . In all, the 'library is the heart of the university' metaphor leads librarians and academics to erroneous conclusions about the real relationships between the library and the university.

Many other commentaries on the academic library as the centre of scholarly activity neglect the fact that for most university researchers such notions simply do not reflect reality, if they ever did. It is true that scholars in the humanities need to access physical collections that contain original objects – manuscripts, incunabula and the like – but the same is certainly not true in the sciences, in engineering, in professional disciplines and in many of the social sciences. In fact the proportion of the scholarly population that relies on libraries for its raw material – in the sense outlined above – is actually quite small. Many scholars in these latter disciplines place a far higher priority on immediacy – on access to the very latest results – and they are developing their own mechanisms to achieve this.

First, e-print archives have mushroomed in popularity in recent years. The tradition of exchanging pre-prints has existed in many of the sciences for a long time – it can be regarded as the foundation of the scientific journal, since the original *Le Journal des savants* in France and the *Philosophical Transactions of the Royal Society* in the UK were created (in 1665) as a means of circulating 'letters' containing scientific results among the research community. More recently the pre-print has been used to counter the problems of long publication lead times in traditional print publications, and such usage is starting to expand not only in quantity but to embrace 'final' versions of papers including peer-reviewed contributions. The recent adoption of the Sante Fe Convention provides a standards-based framework for this expansion and more widespread adoption of these approaches (see Chapter 9).

These developments call into question the long-term future of the academic journal. To quote Ginsparg (1997), 'it is difficult to imagine how the current model of funding publishing companies through research libraries . . . can possibly persist in the long term'.

Secondly, a great deal of vital information is simply not published – it appears in what librarians would call the 'grey literature'. This includes reports and papers produced while projects are in progress and, perhaps most important of all, conversational transcripts. For example, most of the information exchange that takes place in major international research projects is now conducted by e-mail, either privately within the research team or using closed or open discussion lists. The mechanisms to facilitate, organize and maintain these media are virtually uninfluenced by and untouched by libraries. Even though many scholars still recognize the current importance of the traditional library and a few recognize that even when they do not visit the physical building, they still benefit greatly from its services – Appiah (1997), for example, remarks 'the library I never go to is already one of the most important places in my life' – in fact they are inventing their own equivalent of the 'library'.

However, important as even this issue is, there is a more important one still. The massification of higher education has led in recent years to much greater prominence being given to the academic library's role in supporting learning and teaching. It is worth reviewing the events of the last few decades to explore how this has come about.

In the UK, the 1963 Robbins Report (Committee on Higher Education, 1963) set the stage with its mould-breaking statement of principle: 'higher education opportunities should be available to all those who are qualified by ability and attainment to pursue them and who wish to do so'. Robbins recommended massive expansion: the beginning of the end of higher education for the elite and the start of mass higher education. As a result new universities were founded, colleges of advanced technology turned into universities, the Open University created and, before the end of the 1960s, polytechnics established as the second half of a binary higher education system. By the mid-1990s the system had been transformed: in 1963 there were only 120,000 students in UK higher education, by 1997 there were 1.6 million.

A similar expansion had occurred somewhat earlier in the USA, as Osburn (1997) has noted:

> The Industrial Revolution made it clear that knowledge and education presented an avenue to advancement for those not satisfied with the lot of the assembly line worker. Education became the doorway to options for one's future. The general public in America began to see higher education as useful – thus breaking with European tradition then – and, to varying degrees, this vision has significantly influenced colleges and universities ever since. . . . Unprecedented numbers of those who once would not reasonably have aspired to higher learning and to a place among the professions were attracted to, and accommodated by, the universities.

Back in the UK, the Follett Committee (Higher Education Funding Council for England, Scottish Higher Education Funding Council, Higher Education Funding Council for Wales and the Department of Education for Northern Ireland, 1993), set up to examine the impacts of this massive expansion on academic libraries and to recommend solutions, saw the future partly in terms of traditional services – for example recommending funding for expansion of buildings – and partly in terms of new services delivered through information and communications technologies (ICTs). It also set in train strategic thinking that has enabled libraries to take an institutional lead in some areas, for example in the development of broad, cross-organizational information strategies.

The UK higher education Electronic Libraries Programme (eLib), funded as a result of the Follett Report's IT-related recommendations, has been highly significant. A summative evaluation of Phases 1 and 2 or the three-phase programme (ESYS, 2000) remarked:

In 1993 it might have been possible to dismiss the impact of electronic information services on libraries as marginal. This was no longer the case by the end of 1998 by which time the impact on many areas, including the concept of universities themselves, could not be ignored.

eLib was structured to address what in 1993 were seen to be the key areas for academic library service development, a view that was largely vindicated by subsequent developments. The major strands of work were:

- electronic document and article delivery
- electronic journals
- on-demand publishing
- access to network resources
- training and awareness.

In Phase 3, attention was directed towards hybrid libraries, clumps and preservation of digital objects; these issues are discussed further in Chapters 5 and 9. Alongside this research and development, the establishment of national agreements enabling all members of UK higher education institutions to access a large range of major datasets, based on the all-important 'free at the point of use' principle, ushered in an era of real resource-sharing and cooperation. At the same time, evidence from statistical returns and other sources demonstrates a continuing high level of demand from students for traditional materials: user-satisfaction surveys continue to produce demands for 'more books'.

Looking at the broader context, a major review of higher education in the UK, the Dearing Review (The National Committee of Inquiry into Higher Education, 1997), had little short-term impact on libraries but considerable longer-term significance. The changes it recommended had been straws in the wind for some time, but some of the consequences can be seen to have been the following:

- A marked shift in the relationships between students and universities, arising partly because of the introduction of fees – already common almost everywhere else in the world – and partly because uncertainties in the job market have made students more aware of the need to obtain good qualifications. For libraries this change in relationship could be highly significant as students, seeing themselves as paying customers, demand services delivered to high standards and will not be put off with second best.
- Encouragement for institutions to explore the use of ICTs in learning and teaching more vigorously, including distance learning. The ways in which

such learning can be supported by libraries remain under-researched and underdeveloped.

- An insistence that teachers in higher education should be qualified to teach, which should include their having a clearer understanding of pedagogical issues and a commitment to excellence in delivering learning. This may well trickle through to academic library staff – if they are able to accept the challenge.
- Yet more emphasis on quality assurance of learning, teaching and research. For some years UK university libraries have been subject to external assessment as part of subject-based teaching quality-assurance processes and it is to be expected that this will continue. Importantly the context of such assessment is evidence of the contribution that the library makes to learning rather than an abstract assessment against, for example, library collection or service standards.

The major questions raised by these issues relate to the academic library's role in learning and teaching processes. For all the above reasons, at the start of the 21st century, academic libraries need to explore service developments to support a series of new scenarios. Briefly these can be characterized as:

- new publication and scholarly communication scenarios, such as e-print archives, which may bypass the library
- ever more intensive use of digital resources, but with less obvious (ie both more hidden and less crucial) roles for libraries in delivering these resources
- increasingly heterogeneous student populations, including many mature students who are demanding of library services in ways that students progressing direct from school have not been
- continuing high demand from students for traditional resources, ie books
- modes of study, including ICT-based and distance learning, with which libraries have had little involvement in the past
- ever-reducing levels of resourcing, particularly in staffing, leading to enormous pressures on individual staff and a severe challenge to management.

The role that academic libraries will play in the future is thus far from clear. They retain institutional expertise in information organization even if the recognition of this expertise is patchy. In the UK they have come through a decade of change in remarkably good shape, and university librarians have earned the respect of their institutional leaders, not least for their ability to accept and indeed lead change. Their legacy collections are important and recognized as such, again with programmes like the Research Support Libraries Programme (RSLP) providing national recognition and resources. The integration of their services into learning and teaching provides perhaps the greatest immediate challenge, alongside the possible loss of large numbers of researchers as direct users as alternative patterns of scholarly communication emerge.

## The view from the sectors 3: Public libraries

Public libraries have a proud heritage. In Britain the key event in the development of public library services was the 1849 report of the Select Committee on Public Libraries. The Committee took evidence from a wide range of interests, although it is notable that, as Murison (1971) has pointed out, many of the proponents of public libraries were concerned more with social control than with the development of individuals' potential or the enhancement of their leisure: 'Where witnesses [to the Select Committee] approved the need for the public library they almost unanimously showed themselves to be concerned with its effect as a counter-agent to evils rather than as a positive force for educational or recreational benefit.' Typical was James Buckingham, Member of Parliament for Sheffield, whose hope was that public libraries would 'draw off, by innocent pleasurable recreation and instruction, all who can be thus weaned from habits of drinking, and in whom those habits may not be so deeply rooted as to resist all attempts at this moral method of cure' (Murison, 1971). Public libraries, funded from local authority rates, opened in many towns and cities in the following half-century. The system developed slowly, although the 1919 establishment of county libraries was significant in raising standards and, of course, Andrew Carnegie was highly influential in providing funding for buildings – by the time of his death over half the library authorities in Britain had Carnegie libraries.

By the second half of the 20th century there was general agreement around the proposition that the public library fulfilled three interconnected roles: education, information and entertainment. It enabled its users to undertake informal learning as well as providing a place for study; it provided access to organized sources of information on all subjects; and it provided entertainment, primarily through lending fiction. Within these roles libraries developed all manner of specific services: children's libraries, business information services, music libraries, audio and video collections, even toy libraries and at least one example of a pet lending library. But as budgetary cuts started to bite, and the legacy of Carnegie's buildings started to show its age, it became apparent first that public libraries were struggling to define what this tripartite role really meant in an age of mass communication and mass formal education, and secondly that while the potential roles they could fulfil were almost numberless, there was little guidance on how they should prioritize their activities so as to be good at doing a limited range of things rather than doing everything poorly.

In recent years there has been a number of attempts to define the role of the public library more precisely. It is interesting that users themselves tend to take a conservative view and to see the public library in quite mechanistic terms. During the recent VITAL research project at CERLIM, public library users were asked to state their main reason for using the library. Interestingly, even in libraries with relatively well-developed IT facilities, the answers were overwhelmingly 'to borrow books'.

Policy-level studies have, of course, delved much more deeply into the role of the public library and the contribution it makes to society. For example, in 1993 the Comedia consultancy issued a report under the title *Borrowed time* which concluded that:

> Public libraries are currently making an impact in five main areas of public life:
>
> – EDUCATION Support for self-education and lifelong learning. . . . Responding to the impact of educational reform, providing space in libraries as homework centres.
> – SOCIAL POLICY Acting as an entry point into the wider culture for many of Britain's ethnic minority communities . . . playing a leading part in preserving local identities . . . supporting the emotional needs of particular disadvantaged groups in local communities – providing a quiet haven or refuge in the midst of the noisy city.
> – INFORMATION Providing more and more information services in a society in which individual rights and the need to know are at a premium. Yet unsure of its role in a society in which information is capital and an increasingly expensive commodity.
> – CULTURAL ENRICHMENT Providing a choice of books, recorded music, videos across a range of interests; acting as an entry point for children into literacy and "the book of life", story telling, after school activities, offering a home to art exhibitions.
> – ECONOMIC DEVELOPMENT Libraries play a role in developing local business information services and in a wider context, act as a focal point in the town centre mixed economy where retailing alone cannot sustain liveliness and vitality.

In 1995 UNESCO issued its *Public library manifesto* (IFLA, 1995) which stated that:

The public library, the local gateway to knowledge, provides a basic condition for lifelong learning, independent decision-making and cultural development of the individual and social groups.

The UK Audit Commission's 1997 report *Due for renewal* (Audit Commission, 1997) stated that:

(Public) libraries find themselves tackling needs in a number of separate areas:

- recreation and culture (for example, by lending books to people to read for pleasure)
- learning (for example, by making study materials available for reference and loan)
- social welfare (e.g. by taking materials to housebound people, or offering a safe and warm place where people can relax)
- economic development (e.g. by providing business information or by helping individuals with training and jobseeking).

Also in 1997 there was a response from government to a review of the public library service carried out by Aslib two years earlier. *Reading the future* (Department of National Heritage, 1997) saw ICTs as a means of restoring public libraries' importance in society, but offered little hard advice and even less in the way of resources. In any case, the government that had produced it was about to be defeated in a general election.

The new government received a much more influential source of advice with the publication in mid-1997 of *New Library: The people's network* by the Library and Information Commission, arguing 'for the transformation of libraries and what they do; it makes the case for re-equipping them and reskilling their staff so that they can continue to fulfil their widely valued role as intermediary, guide, interpreter and referral point – but now helping smooth the path to the technological future'. Its core recommendation was for the establishment of

a UK-wide information network made available through (public) libraries and implemented on the basis of a high-specification central core.

The network was to be known as 'the people's network', a clever piece of marketing since the new government was laying claim to be 'the people's' champion of virtually everything. The *New Library* report made five distinct claims for the new libraries:

- They would be agents to enable people of all ages to acquire new skills, use information creatively and 'improve the quality of their lives'.
- They would be integrated parts of the national educational system – and hence it was not long before even government ministers were referring to them as 'street-corner universities'.
- They would be truly inclusive, being 'open and accessible to all' and offering access to both print and online resources.
- They would be 'at the hub of the community', offering leisure and cultural opportunities and making available information about every aspect of life.
- They would provide access to official and government information so as to enable people to become more involved in the democratic process.

These are huge claims, but they stand in the tradition of the public library as an open, accessible, non-threatening resource that is closely linked into and a part of its local community. One aspect of public libraries that these definitions fail to bring out, however, is the way they differentiate their services among their client groups. One example is the mobile library or bookmobile, which enables a basic library service to be extended into rural areas and to people who would be unable or unwilling to travel to the main branch. Even more obviously, the children's library service offers opportunities for personal development through instilling a love of books and reading from an early age:

> Libraries, both in schools and in public libraries, contribute to children's leisure needs as well as to their intellectual, emotional, social and educational and language development. The public library fulfils a complementary social function through its programmes of storyhours and activities, providing a bright, welcoming, attractive and safe place for children to browse, to read, to study, to meet other children.
> (Elkin, 1998)

The same author later reported on a major study of children's use of libraries and pointed to the benefits they bestow (Elkin, 2000):

> *Quality of life*: 'Libraries are a good thing, and people will tell you that they are . . . [even if] you can't measure the effects. We have to accept that certain things are valuable.'
> *Citizenship*: 'We offer [children] the library membership card which belongs to them, the first thing they own for themselves. . . . Library membership creates a sense of belonging and citizenship at an early age.'
> *Social development*: 'A social space in a pretty desolate area. . . . The security to meet their friends on neutral, well-regulated territory.'

*Social inclusion*: 'Libraries can benefit children in fostering their socialization skills
. . . we won't tolerate any discrimination within our libraries.'
A *welcoming environment*: 'We're providing a context, which is non-threatening,
non-judgemental.'
*Educational*: (quoting Isaac Asimov) 'My real education, the superstructure, the
details, the true architecture, I got out of the public library.'
*Support for literacy*: 'Fostering recreational reading and . . . instilling the desire to
read.'
*Reading development*: 'The trick of reading, because it's fun, is what they learn from
libraries.'
*Support for parents*: 'Librarians not only read to children but model book-sharing for
parents'.

However, it is apparent that public libraries often lack a clear focus for their
activities and priorities. In recent years they have become enthusiasts for lifelong learning, but they are reluctant to give up other roles. Kinnell and Sturges
(1996) comment:

At the heart of the issues surrounding public libraries, from their inception up to the
present day, has been an imprecise formal definition of their role. Should they be a
medium of education and instruction, an information source, a cultural focus for
communities, or an addition to people's leisure pursuits through the lending of fiction? . . . There is so much that (public) libraries do and so much that they could do.

Perhaps the most useful conclusion is that public libraries continually try to
contextualize information usage – using 'information' in the wide sense to
include works of the imagination – within the concerns of their local communities, reinterpreting needs in terms of international, national, regional and
local priorities. In the past they have proved flexible in response to external
change; the key question may be whether they can change quickly enough to
remain relevant to the emerging information society.

## The view from the sectors 4: School libraries

Until fairly recently, even the best school libraries were fairly limited affairs,
with a very few exceptions. Mainwood, writing nearly 30 years ago with perhaps a touch of hyperbole commented:

Perhaps the most significant development in the post-war years in Britain has been
the extension of school library provision to pupils of all ranges of age and ability.
Where, hitherto, only the senior pupils pursuing academic courses in grammar

schools had access to reasonable library facilities in their schools – and even these facilities tended to range from large and comprehensive collections in well-endowed schools, to the woefully inadequate – we can now expect to find attractive and well produced books suitably displayed and accessible to children from the age when they first attend school, and providing for all types of interest and ability.

(Mainwood, 1972)

In the USA an event of particular importance was the issuing in 1961 of a policy statement by the chief officers of school districts, recognizing school libraries as 'intrinsic to the purposes of the school and . . . a basic service for which the board of education is responsible' (Council of Chief State School Officers, 1961). From this period there emerged a consensus on the importance of school libraries and a series of standards and guidelines were issued. By the early 1970s, Gaver (1972) was reporting:

The present situation, however, is quite different from the time a generation ago when only the exceptional school had a library with a qualified staff, an excellent collection of materials, and an effective program of services. Today, in American schools and communities, it is the generally accepted goal to provide both public library and school library service, although the achievement of that goal may not yet be universally recognized.

The reasons for this success were various – Mainwood (1972) lists them as:

the shift of emphasis from 'teaching' to 'learning', from class instruction to individual exploration, from the uniformity of sets of textbooks to the diversity of many different books of interest and information.

Much, however, remained to be done:

In the past, the school library has tended to be the special . . . concern of the English department . . . there is considerable need for the use of the resources of the library to form a normal part of the teaching of other subjects. Closely linked with this . . . is the whole range of possibilities which are being opened up by the current interest in educational technology, group teaching, curriculum development projects, and new teaching methods.

After another 20 years had elapsed it had become clear that this central, cross-curricular place was broadly recognized and indeed was being widened beyond the curriculum itself. In 1986 an official UK report proclaimed that the school library should be the 'foundation of the curriculum' (Library and Information

Services Council, 1986) and in the UK Library Association's 1992 *Guidelines for school libraries* (Kinnell, 1992) the purpose of school libraries is described as 'wide-ranging. . . . They have a central place in providing a range of information resources in support of the curriculum and of pupils' personal and social development.' Furthermore, 'school library resource centres have been recognized as part of the national information network.' More fundamentally still, 'the purpose of the school library is to facilitate teaching and learning . . . the emphasis on learning to learn, and learning to handle information, so evident in modern curricula, brings library and information services into the centre of the learning process.'

So, the modern view would be that the school library is:

> . . . not just a physical space in which various media are stored; it is a concept, a tangible expression of the school's ethos and values, its approaches to equality of opportunity, the moral and spiritual development of children and young people and its educational purposes. It has the potential to introduce young people to the world of literature and information and to enable them to develop skills which will enhance their lives as adults. (Tilke, 1998)

This concept takes the focus of the school library away from the bricks and mortar, and away from the information artefacts – books, video and audio tapes, learning packs and the like – to the issue of how information is used by children in the modern school. One study observed the following:

> A theme that emerged time and again was that information is gathered for a purpose, to solve some sort of information problem. Children's understanding of that purpose is often a function of teacher instruction and this influences their interpretation of the task and all facets of their information problem solving attitudes and actions. . . . Children need to develop an understanding of the information world that promotes choice among resources, builds flexibility in searching and encourages critical thinking about information and the overall information problem solving process. (Moore, 1998)

Moore gave a rather nice example of this issue. Some eight- and nine-year-old boys had been set the task of describing an invention: 'Evaluating information is difficult for children . . . there was a major conceptual problem for one of the boys. He could not imagine things working without electricity! It was impossible to see where one might insert batteries into a sundial or a water clock, and clockwork mechanisms were not shown in detail.' Recognizing an information need was an underdeveloped skill.

For school-age children an emphasis has therefore emerged on the need to develop broad information skills. But what is often forgotten is that information skills can only be built on the foundation of reading skills: that the child who not only *can* read but *enjoys* reading, the child who is a *voracious* reader, has an enormous head-start on others regardless of the medium in which information appears. McGonagle (1998) writes, 'For our children to take their place in today's world, being technically literate is not enough. They need to develop an enthusiasm for books, reading and acquiring information. Children need to learn to make fully informed decisions, so that they can influence their own destinies. The most effective way that this can be achieved is by having a central resource of books and other information material, so that all children and staff can have access to it – in other words, a school library.'

Royce (1998) goes further:

> Able users of information develop strategies for finding, choosing and using information. Their strategies are built on three skills areas: reading, information-handling, and technical. The skills are interdependent and often practiced simultaneously; their boundaries merge and overlap. . . . It all comes back to reading, and thus to the twin needs of getting readers hooked early in life, and that of providing plenty of practice, reading for information as well as reading for pleasure. You *can* survive in today's world, even if you can type with only one or two fingers. You *can* survive without ever using keyboard shortcuts or realising the full potential of your software. But even in a world of pictograms and icons, of sounds and pictures and Internet and intranets, you are going to find survival both difficult and expensive if your reading skills are poorly developed.

Yet although much is written about the embedding of the library – as often as not called the learning resource centre – in the curriculum, the perceptions of school pupils remain surprisingly traditional. Spreadbury and Spiller (1999) report that, in their survey of the users of school libraries:

> . . . nearly half of all pupils used the library 'to study', and 39% 'to borrow books'. Beyond these, there was a range of other activities, with in-house use of printed materials and use of the computers the most popular. . . . asked how they would describe the school library, by far the largest percentage responded to the prompt 'A quiet place where I can concentrate and do my work' – though there was much discussion of just how quiet a library should be. When asked what improvements they wanted in the library, 20% said 'more tables and desks'. . . . Asked what they did when they had trouble finding material, two thirds of the pupils replied 'ask the librarian' – many more than used the catalogue or browsed the shelves. . . . An encouraging finding was that staff help was found to be useful by 85% of pupils

'most or all of the time' – a really excellent response given the bluntness of children in responding to questions of this type.

The school library, then, even when re-named and clearly embedded within a 'whole school' paradigm, has retained its core emphasis on the provision of access to information resources, a role valued by pupils as well as teachers. It is notable that the library has become the location of choice in most schools for IT access, providing a shared resource that is highly valued. The development and exploitation of information content for schools has been patchy, although the National Grid for Learning will, if it is properly implemented, address this issue in what is in effect a large-scale, cooperative endeavour. Whether significant library expertise will be drawn into this development remains to be seen.

## The view from the sectors 5: Workplace libraries

Generalizing about workplace (or, as they used to be known, 'special') libraries is fraught with difficulties. The sector covered is immense – everything from information services in high technology industries through libraries serving the health service to advisory services in the voluntary sector. They differ enormously in scope and size – from what used to be called the one-man band (when translated into 'one-person band' the analogy somehow loses its edge) to multinational services employing hundreds. The terminology itself is difficult: 'special' has survived for many years when it really meant, if anything, 'specialized'; 'workplace' seems rather insulting to the other sectors (are they not also 'workplaces'?); while many object to the term 'library' on the basis that they operate an information service regardless of physical location and without physical objects such as books.

Again, it is useful to look at the way these services have developed over time. Although the origins of the workplace library can be traced back a very long way (perhaps the medieval alchemist poring over his secret tomes might form an appropriate genesis), it was only during the 20th century that a recognizable sector developed. The creation in the UK of Aslib (then an acronym for the *Association of Special Libraries and Information Bureaux*) in the 1920s drew on American experience, where a Special Libraries Association had been founded even earlier, and proved a seminal event. Hutton (1945), one of the founders, commented:

> We had all for long been interested in the improvement of provincial technical library resources and had been impressed by special library developments in the United States . . . we had prominently in mind two vital problems which faced industrial research associations . . . how to make as complete as possible a survey of

information on some special subject from world-wide sources, and how to bring the more important results of the survey to the attention of members of the organization.

From this comment it can be seen that special libraries concerned themselves not only with collecting information objects and organizing them, but saw part of their role as analysing the information, creating digests of key information and disseminating these to their clientele. These concerns have continued, but it is worth also reflecting on two trends that have greatly affected workplace libraries in recent years. From the health sector has come the demand for 'evidence-based practice'; from the commercial sector the emphasis is on 'knowledge management'. Both have significant implications for library services.

## Evidence-based practice

Evidence-based medicine is one of those concepts that, with hindsight, appears glaringly obvious – the idea that before embarking on a medical procedure or other course of treatment, a doctor should have weighed all the available evidence and, if challenged, should be able to demonstrate why one procedure was preferred to other possibilities. The issue has been brought into sharp focus by allegations of malpractice or ill-informed practice. The size of awards where liability is proved provides a particularly strong motivation for health professionals to take evidence-gathering seriously.

Evidence may be acquired from a number of sources, but the medical library clearly has an important role to play. It is interesting, for example, that one of the key services being rolled out by the UK's National electronic Library for Health (NeLH) is The Cochrane Library, part of an international collaboration to identify significant published information on health care, to arrange for its expert appraisal and to produce reviews and summaries that can be used by clinical practitioners. The need for services like Cochrane were demonstrated by observation of the difficulties encountered in the health field where:

- even expert searching of well-designed databases like Medline cannot guarantee to find all the relevant information
- it is not immediately clear how much reliance can be placed on many of the research studies reported, which may, for example, be based on small sample sizes
- there is difficulty in determining whether reported results are suffering from bias, since so much funding of medical research originates with pharmaceutical companies

- the practitioner is often faced with information overload and has no easy way to sift out the relevant from the irrelevant.

Each of these issues is familiar to librarians, but their identification in the health library context provides some useful pointers to how libraries' roles, at least in this sector, might possibly develop. For example, what health practitioners clearly need are:

- better and more reliable search tools
- expert evaluation of published work, going beyond standard peer review (which merely states an opinion that it is worth publishing)
- additional information on the source and background to any published report
- help to handle large volumes of data.

These issues are, of course, not confined to health practitioners even though they have become prominent in that context. The *British Medical Journal*'s definition of evidence-based medicine is surely capable of much wider application: 'the conscientious, explicit, and judicious use of current best evidence in making decisions' (British Medical Journal, 1996).

## Knowledge management

The development of knowledge management provides an interesting example of convergence between library and information services and broader business practices. An increasing number of businesses are based on the exploitation of knowledge – examples include management consultancies where work on one contract needs to draw on experience gained in earlier, similar work and many dot.com companies where knowledge of customer preferences and previous transactions provides the key to future sales. So McKinsey and Co have roles defined as 'Knowledge Interrogators' while Anderson Consulting has 'Knowledge Integrators'. Hewlett-Packard has a programme called 'KnowledgeLinks' that involves a group of staff in collecting knowledge from the various divisions of the company and interpreting it for other divisions to use.

The essence of knowledge management lies in the capture and exploitation of learning, expertise and understanding as well as information. Thus a company that has learned from the experience of advising a client in, say, bringing an e-commerce company to market can gain competitive edge if it can exploit the knowledge gained to the full in the next similar contract. The knowledge that is captured and used consists not just of formal reports, but best practice digests, 'war stories' (including those of battles that were lost) and interpreted statistical data. Subjects may include such matters as the impact of outsourcing, how production times were speeded up, improved error handling and customer relations. It is interesting that the focus during the 1980s on expert systems – software that would solve problems using the distilled experience of human experts – has given way to this new emphasis.

An issue of great importance is that knowledge management is not primarily about building IT-based knowledge systems, although many companies are benefiting from systems that permit online access to the corporate knowledge resources. However, the following comment from a Japanese perspective is pertinent (Takeuchi, 1998):

> Many American companies equate 'knowledge creation' with setting up computer databases. Professor Nonaka [Takeuchi's co-author of *The Knowledge-Creating Company*] argues that much of a company's knowledge bank has nothing to do with data, but is based on informal 'on the job' knowledge – everything from the name of a customer's secretary to the best way to deal with a truculent supplier. Many of these tidbits are stored in the brains of middle managers – exactly the people who re-engineering has replaced with computers.

An important insight from this viewpoint is that knowledge is, in essence, socially located, being invested in individuals and in groups. Because much of knowledge is tacit it is difficult to capture, store and transfer. In this view, knowledge management may be better thought of as the process of engineering conditions under which knowledge transfer and utilization happen. It could be argued, for example, that the library that creates attractive social spaces in which users chat and exchange ideas is engaging in knowledge management.

Oxbrow and Abell (1998) emphasize this idea when they argue that knowledge management is not simply a matter of identifying and codifying knowledge but just as much concerned with its effective use: 'The ultimate corporate resource has become information – the ultimate competitive advantage is the ability to use it – the sum of the two is knowledge management . . . the essence of KM is connection. The connection of people with people – enabling people to share and build on what they know, to collect information of value and make it easily and appropriately available, to ensure that people understand the value and potential of what they know.' The insight of Malhotra (1999) that knowledge management is also about 'obsoleting what you know before others obsolete it' also provides a useful warning about the volatility and rate of obsolescence of knowledge!

These analyses lead naturally to the idea of the 'intelligent enterprise' that is able to exploit knowledge both to deal with current challenges and to be effective in achieving its future strategy. Knowledge is seen as the underpinning resource that enables organizations to act intelligently, and this in turn leads to a view that at the heart of the successful organization is the ability to build relationships. These are not just supplier–customer, contractual arrangements: the view suggests that the organization should regard itself as part of a wider social system, paying due regard to the needs, views, knowledge and intelligence of all its stakeholders – customers, suppliers, employees, members of the local community, local and national government, voluntary organizations and others.

Of course, managing knowledge and enabling intelligence at the organizational level are not without their pitfalls. Many employees are reluctant to reveal or share their knowledge – after all it may represent their real value to the company. Much knowledge may be too specialized, when the issue is how to draw general conclusions from it. Knowledge may be used as a weapon instead of an asset. There are few rewards for being a good knowledge manager and thus helping others to improved performance. And, as noted above, knowledge management easily becomes subverted into IT systems development.

Abram (1998) draws some interesting and perhaps controversial conclusions about the implications of knowledge management for workplace libraries:

> . . . special librarians made a potentially disastrous error, those many years ago when we decided to position ourselves in the 'information business'. Information businesses are marked by their ability to create information, and disseminate it widely – often for a profit. Generally, special librarians do not, as part of our core mandate, create information. While we do create information about information (metadata), I believe this is a higher level calling in the knowledge continuum. . . .The plain fact is that knowledge, per se, *cannot* be managed. In fact, capturing knowledge in any form other than into a human being's brain, reduces it to mere information, or worse, data. Only the knowledge environment can be managed.

He suggests a four-fold strategy. First focusing effort on where libraries can add value by transforming their resources, whether traditional information or knowledge based, by organizing them for users. Secondly, placing emphasis on the idea of the learning organization (discussed in more detail in Chapter 6). Thirdly, providing guidance and navigation tools that enable people to put knowledge to work. Finally, taking a broad view of 'transformational librarianship' that sees the key resource as the people who adopt technology and other tools and use them to enable improved knowledge creation and management.

While it is difficult to extract generic lessons from across the whole workplace sector, the examples described above suggest that the most dynamic services are those that have succeeded in embedding the 'library' – often under a different name – in the core strategic concerns of the organization. In the best examples, libraries have recognized the implications of an information-based economy and taken their place at the heart of the enterprise. But it must also be admitted that others have failed to secure this position, and new information and knowledge structures have emerged that have sidelined the library or made it irrelevant.

## Conclusion

At this stage of the information revolution, libraries across most sectors appear to be in remarkably good heart. Each sector can contribute strengths and demonstrate signs of the regard in which it is held – whether it is the new build- ings that so many national libraries have achieved, the continuing collection strengths and cooperative endeavours of research libraries, the leadership of public libraries or the innovative practices and paradigms characterizing work- place libraries. In mapping the library of the future each sector offers intriguing and useful insights into ways forward.

What is more difficult to gauge is what is happening beneath the surface of these 'fanfare' stories. Yes, national libraries have impressive new buildings, but are they providing national information policy leadership suitable for an e- world? Are academic libraries as a whole positioning themselves to operate within new models of scholarly communication and to integrate resources in learning? Are school libraries becoming IT access centres providing glitzy access to impoverished resources? Are the bulk of workplace libraries simply disappearing and information or knowledge handling, as it enters mainstream business practice, proving that such entities are no longer appropriate? Are the majority of public libraries, the branches in every suburb and village, really engaged in the 'new library' process? These are the great unknowns.

# 3

# What is a library?
# Cross-sectoral models

Nobody will say what precisely libraries are supposed to be doing.

(Hawgood and Morley, 1969)

## Introduction

In this chapter attention turns from the issues raised by consideration of libraries in their various sectoral settings to more general approaches that have validity across all sectors. Theoretical models of this type are intended to be simplified representations of reality that, because they do not describe particular cases, allow general conclusions to be drawn and principles elucidated. They can be used to shed light on purposes, functions and structures, to identify meaningful interactions between sub-systems and the broader environment and to enable the whole to be seen as greater than the sum of its parts. They also help in the identification and exploration of commonalities between practical implications, which on the surface may seem very different. In short, to quote Underwood (1996), 'a model . . . stands in place of reality in order that we can think, negotiate, play or experiment'.

When thinking of libraries people have many different images in front of them. By stepping back from individual cases and examining the context in which library services are provided, and the trends that are likely to affect them in the future, it is possible to arrive at some conclusions about how libraries' roles are likely to develop and to start to answer the central questions posed in Chapter 1 – do libraries have a central role to play, or are they in fact simply anachronisms?

Three models are identified here, drawing on the descriptions of sectoral roles, purposes and functions from Chapter 2. These are: the library as collection; the library as provider of access; and the library as organizer of resource sharing. The chapter then concludes with some comments from outside the library arena that shed further light on these models.

## Alexandria: the enduring collection

The library as a collection of books provides perhaps the most enduring model of the library and the one that is probably most common in the popular mind – represented by the image of lofty rooms lined with bookshelves on which books are carefully arranged in long rows. Its essence is the physical collection in its own, dedicated building. The great library of Alexandria, described briefly in Chapter 2, is the archetype. The collection of such a library, whether it consists of clay tablets, papyrus scrolls, wooden blocks, parchment codices, bound paper, microform or even digital media, is representative of the recorded knowledge of humankind – as George Dawson is reported to have said at the opening of the Birmingham Free Library in 1866, 'a great library contains the diary of the human race' (Taylor, 1993). Its ideal lies in its comprehensiveness – if possible it would possess a copy of everything ever published, although realism acknowledges that this is impossible, which turns out to be, in many ways, a benefit. Selection is, in essence, a form of quality assurance that is added to the existing information chain processes from peer review to publishing houses' market research.

Yet comprehensiveness of collection persists as a target even when the scope is limited. For example, as described in Chapter 2, a national library pursues the Alexandrian model, usually limiting its 'comprehensive collection' to its own nation's output, using legal deposit as a mechanism to acquire a copy of each item in the national bibliography. The public library pursues comprehensiveness of its local history collection. The academic library pursues the model in relation to its parent university's areas of research excellence. In each sector there is still an unconscious equivalence drawn between size of collection and excellence of the library, a point that will be examined in more detail in Chapter 6. The Conspectus methodology, originating in the USA in 1979 but now much more widely used, enables collection strength to be described in terms of both comprehensiveness and currency. Behind this ideal lies the concept of the research library, sometimes described as the scholar's laboratory, allowing researchers to explore a large collection of material brought together in one place. This perspective also draws attention to the function of libraries of selecting, describing and organizing their collections. They are not merely warehouses of books heaped anyhow on their shelves, but each item that is judged suitable for addition to the collection is carefully described and placed where it can with certainty be retrieved. Organization is thus of the essence of the library as collection. Greenberg (1998) notes, 'the modern research library is a marvel of the human genius for organization, structure, and order, as well as for creating the tools through which that order can be understood and navigated'.

The importance of description in the development of library collections can hardly be over-emphasized and, as already noted, it was one of Panizzi's seminal contributions to the field. Long before his day, Callimachus created a catalogue of the holdings of the great library at Alexandria known as the *Pinakes* – a name now used for a subject gateway access website run by Heriot-Watt University in Scotland. The library catalogue was developed to fulfil a number of functions:

- It forms a record of ownership of each item in the collection, and as such has to identify each copy uniquely.
- It enables the collection to be searched by a variety of descriptors (eg author, title, subject) to check whether a known item is present. In passing, it is worth noting that users' criteria do not always seem to have had much influence on the choice of descriptors, witness the lack of title catalogues in the pre-automation era.
- It may enable comparison between seemingly similar items, as, for example, when it differentiates between editions or when pagination differs within the same apparent edition.
- It is constructed to collocate works that are intellectually similar or equivalent, for example by enforcing the use of standard forms of headings.
- It simplifies the description of items by selecting elements that will aid unique identification – so, for example, it will always include title but rarely the colour of the binding (even though, again, some library users prefer the latter description!).

The world would be greatly impoverished were it to lose collection-based libraries modelled on that at Alexandria – the general condemnation of the destruction of the national library in Sarajevo is testament to this. They have been and remain responsible for preserving some of the greatest artefacts of civilization, and it is idle to pretend that new technologies could make this function redundant – scholars will always want to be able to examine the original, not merely its electronic surrogate. Yet the model has its limitations. Its emphasis on acquisition and preservation can make actual use a secondary consideration, and the scholar's laboratory is certainly shifting its focus towards electronic networks. Perhaps more seriously, the model has yet to demonstrate that it is capable of adjusting itself to the era of electronic publication – as noted in Chapter 2, most national libraries have no more than dabbled in the field – and already a vast part of the electronic memory has been lost. Finally, while the embodiment of the Alexandrian model in the national library context may (just) be sustainable, it can no longer provide the basis for university and research libraries. Even the University of California has had to conclude that 'the building of . . . comprehensive research collections . . . cannot be sustained' (Ober, 1999). So, while the building, organization and maintenance of a large collection remains a function of some libraries, it is no longer adequate as a generic model for the library of the future. The concept of the collection, and more specifically of the organization of knowledge that it represents, does however make an enduring contribution to understanding some part of the future role, for if there were no collections in the world, there could be no libraries and far less access. Furthermore, the experience of selecting items for addition to collections has provided libraries with unparalleled expertise in the art of quality assurance, while ensuring that individual items are retrievable has generated a high level of skill in the science of information description. These professional assets should not be neglected.

Before leaving the 'collection' model it is worth adding an observation that in practice nearly all of these libraries organize their resources as 'collections' rather than as 'a collection', and this was particularly marked during the latter half of the 20th century. Books generally form the core of the collection, closely followed by journals – described and housed separately, and often listed in a quite separate catalogue. There may also be collections of images – perhaps with slides, prints and other forms collected separately – secondary publications such as printed abstracts and indexes, report series and so on. Sub-collections may be provided for particular users, as with undergraduate libraries and short-loan collections in academic libraries. In addition many libraries perform an explicit and separate archival function with special collections of different types, each divided into its own sub-collections by form or other criterion. It is interesting and of considerable significance that, while libraries have developed the description of books into a fine art, in general they have left the description of journal articles to other agencies, limiting themselves to the description of journal titles – rarely of sufficient granularity for the user.

## The access model

The idea that the library's *primary* role is to provide access to books, journals and other sources of information is relatively modern, although access as *part* of the role is of course ancient in origin. After all, there was never much point in developing comprehensive collections unless someone at some time was going to use them. In medieval times, access was carefully regulated – chained libraries bear witness to some of the problems it presented. But arrangements were always made for those with sufficient reason and warrant to gain access.

The move of access to centre-stage can be seen in a number of different developments in different sectors, and more recently in the massive shifts taking place in the environments in which libraries operate. Early entrants to the access approach can be found among public and subscription libraries, where, by the early 20th century, members were allowed to browse freely among the shelves. Academic libraries followed, mainly in the second half of the 20th century, with closed access giving way to open collections.

A number of trends accelerated the move towards access as the central tenet of librarianship, not the least being the influence which Ranganathan's ideas had on a generation of librarians. Ranganathan's 'Laws of Library Science' (Ranganathan, 1931) represent an early 20th-century attempt to express the role of the library and significantly turn away from collections *per se* and even from organization as a primary objective:

- Books are for use.
- Every reader his book.
- Every book its reader.
- Save the time of the reader.
- A library is a growing organism.

While some of these statements have dated – the last in particular must be questionable (unless it is taken to refer to the world wide web!) – it is interesting to note that the emphasis in these 'Laws' is very much on the library user rather than the collection itself and very much about access. The great 'access v holdings' debates which occupied professional librarians for much of the 1970s and 1980s served a useful purpose, but the issue no longer engenders much controversy.

## The resource-sharing model

It was the expansion of publishing and of higher education in the 1960s and 1970s, when coupled with the mid-1970s oil crisis, that brought home to academic librarians too the impossibility of any semblance of comprehensiveness. Not only were budgets insufficient to keep up with increasing quantities of ever more expensive books and journals, but there was little hope that buildings would be expanded to create the space needed to house such collections. Clearly something had to give.

The defining moment for academic libraries in the UK was the publication of the Atkinson Report (University Grants Committee, 1976). In 1975 the University Grants Committee (UGC) had set up the Working Party on Capital Provision for University Libraries with a brief to consider how best to cope with the situation where demands for enhancements to library space and for new library buildings simply could not be met. The Working Party reiterated that 'the library is the core of a university', but went on to propose the idea of 'a "self-renewing" library in which new accessions would be relieved by the withdrawal of obsolete or unconsulted material to other stores'. University librarians did not let go of the collections model lightly, however, as this comment from Norman Higham, then University Librarian at Bristol, indicates:

> If the library is full, and the space limit of those who set the rules (the UGC in Britain) . . . has been reached, it is one book out for every book in, new books for old. . . . Not only the reserve store, but the library itself would be a transit camp between acquisition and obsolescence. Consumer durables may have a predictable obsolescence but books do not, and we should find ourselves discarding books which we wanted to keep.                                                    (Higham, 1980)

Today the dynamic model is widely accepted and very few librarians, even in the academic sector, would argue that it did not lie at the heart of their concerns. Interestingly, the argument can be taken somewhat further and examined as part of the debate not just about libraries but about new businesses emerging within networked information spaces. Branin (1998) suggests that it may be helpful to think of the 'provision centre' as a core concept:

> The old models for global provision will not work in the new environment of the twenty-first century. The highly distributed provision and voluntary resource sharing system of interlibrary loan is breaking down under the growing traffic, high costs, and inefficiencies of a system that was designed for marginal, specialized, and complementary services. Today, access rather than ownership of information is becoming a more central activity of research libraries, and provision centers are springing up to fill this need. Provision centers are libraries or commercial organizations that have strong collections, effective bibliographic access to those collections, rapid delivery services, and a business goal of making money through marketing, guaranteed turn around times, and competitive pricing.

A common solution has been to share information on one another's collections. The union catalogue has a long history, and remains as a common means of making the contents of collections known widely. Many regional consortia – such as the Regional Library Systems in the UK, set up in the 1930s, or statewide systems in the USA – have the union catalogue as their core resource. Member libraries contribute copies of their bibliographic records (and hopefully remember to inform the consortium when an item is withdrawn) so that all may benefit from the broader collection strength. Of course the catalogue itself is of little use without some kind of access arrangement, whether through formal interlibrary loan, an agreement to allow reciprocal access for members of the constituent libraries or some other arrangement. The problem remains of checking availability – it is more difficult to attach holdings and status data to union catalogues than to those of individual libraries which can integrate their circulation systems far more easily. As a result delays can occur while a location with an available copy is found.

The union catalogue remains an important focus for resource sharing, and there is an ongoing debate (referred to in greater detail in Chapter 9) as to the place of the union catalogue in networked environments where each library's own catalogue is available online. Although it is possible to search each catalogue individually, and to automate the process, there must be a cut-off point where the number of catalogues to be searched makes that approach uneconomic. It is notable that the union catalogue approach is in effect the basis on which virtually every Internet search engine is built – they take in bibliographic data, usually in the form of keywords, from web resources and combine them into a single, searchable database.

A union catalogue, or even access to another library's catalogue, is by no means essential for interlibrary lending, which is probably the best example of the resource-sharing model. For most libraries, of course, interlibrary borrowing – and still more interlibrary lending – forms a very small part of their operations if counted by volume of transactions. It does, however, form a vital service for users, since it in effect places the local library at the centre of a regional, national and international network of resources. The library may then be seen as not so much concerned with developing its collections, or with acquiring items on the basis of an assessment of likely access requirements and then later discarding them, but as a node in the international recorded memory, the local library's own resources being, for these purposes, irrelevant. The legal environment of most countries recognizes this situation by making provision for library and individual 'fair dealing' privileges within its copyright legislation.

In most countries there are some regional or national arrangements which, having evolved over time, offer particularly well-developed interlending service support. The UK has perhaps the most centralized of these services, with the British Library's Document Supply Centre being used as a matter of automatic choice for interlending requests by many libraries. Indeed there are some that do not even bother to spend their own staff's time on checking requests, preferring to let the BLDSC staff do it for them on the basis that this is more economic. In the USA the existence of the OCLC database provides a major resource for interlending, although requests are referred to the participating libraries rather than to a centralized national resource.

It is worth adding, when considering this model, that commercial document delivery or individual article supply companies fit well with the resource-sharing approach. Non-library players, like the Uncover service (now part of ingenta), have entered the market as an alternative to library supply. Although their charges are generally higher than library-to-library prices, and they tend still to address niche markets (although the niches are getting bigger), they are in effect members of resource-sharing networks. Viewed in this light they make a valuable contribution to the concept of the library as a shared resource.

One final point about the resource-sharing model is worth making, relating to the *internal* sharing of resources in an organization. The essence of a library can be seen in its role as neutral umpire between resource demands in an institution, ensuring fair distribution. For example, the whole point of lending books for a fixed period of time, rather than giving them away to the first-comer, is to ensure that the resource – in this case the opportunity to read the book – is shared out between users. Fairness is expressed in having the same loan period for all – there is incidentally an interesting issue in academic institutions regarding the differential loan periods offered to students and academic staff, which may be interpreted as an indication of what the institution (or at least the librarian) regards as equitable. This role can also be seen in extending opportunities to individuals that would otherwise be unavailable. So, for example, very few individuals would be able to justify purchasing an expensive encyclopaedia for themselves, but they can justify their share of the cost when they are but one of thousands of users gaining access through the resource-sharing arrangement that is the library – especially when it is raised indirectly through taxation or a general membership fee. In this view, libraries are in practice cooperatives.

## Standing outside, looking in

While the three complementary models described above are derived largely by observing and analysing how libraries operate today, another useful way to think about possible future libraries is to look at other sectors and observe how they are reacting to trends and redesigning services to maintain and increase their market share. Bookshops have already been mentioned, but consider this comment from a trade 'insider':

> Bookselling ain't how it used to be. On the eve of the new millennium it seems that 'lifestyle' shopping is here to stay. What this actually means is something of a mystery, but if it involves drinking coffee and buying books, I'm all for it. An increasing number of booksellers across the country seem to be embracing this combination with enthusiasm. The movers and shakers of book retailing are already crediting cafés in bookshops with increasing footfall, staving off Internet competition and creating 'destinations'. All this and a decent cup of coffee too. How can it fail?
>
> (Sanderson, 1999)

Another commentary from the same trade sector predicts a rather more revolutionary upheaval for the academic bookseller at least, affecting the whole supply chain:

> The academic book market looks to be on the verge of . . . a transformation. It has characteristics that set it apart from the supply chain associated with high street bookselling, and a series of factors is in the process of converging to produce a marketplace that has dramatic implications for both academic publishers and booksellers . . . tomorrow's 'Martini' generation – any time, any place, anywhere – of demanding, consumerist students, whether on campus or distance learners, will certainly expect their course materials to be customised and fragmented just for them; to be interactive and media-rich; to be updated and supplemented online; and to be delivered overnight to their doors or directly to their PCs.          (Taylor, 2000)

Many other sectors could be considered. Wilson (1998) suggests that the academic library model may be understood by analogy with the 'case officer' role in the insurance industry, where the case officer acts on behalf of the client to bring together all the processes needed to complete the 'case' – in his example the issue of an insurance policy. In an academic library the case officer would need to bring together for the end-user the four key processes that Wilson identifies: 'acquisition of physical materials; processing of physical materials and sources of networked electronic information; diffusion of information (e.g. lending); and an information enquiry service'. This analysis helps to define how staff and end-users might interact in the mixed-mode environment of the future, with professional library staff taking on a very active role. It also illustrates the convergence that has taken place between former concepts of the academic library and those of the information service in other sectors.

## Conclusion

The dominant view through most of history has been that libraries were places where written, including eventually printed, materials were held together both for security and to create a collection organized for use. The enforcement of legal deposit by Panizzi in the 19th century can be seen as the clear outcome of such a view – the collection was paramount and steps had to be taken to secure its development and representativeness. Alongside the collection, its organization became of ever increasing importance, and the outcome of this view can be seen in the work of pioneers of library cataloguing and classification such as Melvil Dewey and Charles Cutter.

Alongside the concepts of the collection, the organization of access to knowledge and the needs of the user as an individual, a view developed – expressed most clearly by the early public library pioneers – that the library was a social institution that played a role in the organization of society. While some saw this as social control, others took a more liberal and progressive view, seeing in the public library a means to spread literacy and a love of learning.

More recently, Sack has suggested that 'instead of the traditional "Ptolemaic" view of the library world with the library at the centre and users at the periphery we now have a "Copernican" view with the user at the centre and a variety of services and people surrounding and supporting the user' (Steele, 1995). This echoes a comment made ten years earlier by Surridge (1984) when he remarked of the emergence of community librarianship that it represented 'a move from the subject materials orientation of yesteryear, to the orientation to users and their needs'.

What is notable from each of the sectors is the very clear focus on user needs that has emerged during the second half of the 20th century. Collections remain important, and there is an almost non-stop debate on the role of ICTs, yet each sector has focused itself on its users – the public, students, researchers, pupils, employees. The conclusions of a 1991 study of academic library mission statements could almost certainly be broadened to the other sectors: 'the most frequently cited purpose of the . . . library is "to serve the needs of the users" or "to provide services to the library's users" ' (Brophy, 1991). Although often unstated, the needs that are being referred to are those related to information, knowledge, understanding and learning so that in their different ways the sectors have refocused on purposes of information use. What remains unanswered is the question as to whether the library is the best way to meet those needs.

# 4

# What is a library?
# The profession's view

The library as a *total* system, and the *social context* within which it operates, must first be analysed, and in the light of the analysis an appropriately designed system developed. (McClellan, 1973)

## Introduction

Given that librarianship and information science form a well-established profession, it is useful to explore the views of professionals – who after all have been trained to provide library services, have experience of doing so and are, presumably, at the forefront of developments in their profession – on the role that libraries play. Taking this approach, this chapter examines six arenas in which the role of the library, or that of the library/information science professional, is exposed. These are:

- various published statements and a list of the professional issues with which the UK Library Association is concerned
- the Institute of Information Scientists' *Criteria for information science* which define the knowledge that is needed to be recognized as an information scientist, again from a British perspective
- the above two bodies' statements in consultation documents issued as part of the process of negotiating a merger between them during 1999
- the draft 'benchmark statement' for academic librarianship and information management courses, issued by the UK Quality Assurance Agency in January 2000
- the American Library Association's published *Key action areas* and *Library Bill of Rights.*
- the American Society for Information Science's statements on its purpose and structure.

Before turning to these statements and position papers, however, it is interesting to observe the profession's first faltering attempts to define its underlying philosophy. In 1887, Melvil Dewey, then professor in the School of Library Economy (SLE) as well as library director at Columbia University, launched the first formal 'library school' class. Wiegan (1999) records its underlying character:

> The job . . . was to acquaint SLE students with how best to function as librarians – how to run the institution and what expertise was necessary to select its information resources and exploit them most efficiently for the benefit of the public. They were also expected to inculcate the library 'spirit', an attitude about library use and access to collections that distinguished Dewey's from previous generations of librarians who were more concerned with security and preservation. . . . They firmly believed that by providing the masses with access to quality literature and information resources they would benefit society and make America a better place to live for all.

## The Library Association's view of the profession

The first purpose of the Library Association (LA) is, according to the preamble to its Royal Charter, 'to represent and act as the professional body for persons working in or interested in library and information services' (Library Association, 2000b). Its mission is more a declaration of principle than a purposive statement but it does focus on the needs of library users within a societal context:

> The Library Association affirms that libraries are fundamental to the maintenance of a thriving democracy, the health service, the voluntary sector, culture, civilisation and economy.
>
> The Library Association is therefore committed to allowing its members to achieve and maintain the highest professional standard, and encouraging and supporting them in the delivery and promotion of high quality library and information services responsive to the needs of users.        (Library Association, 2000c)

To understand what the LA regards as the core of these 'library and information services' of which it speaks, it is necessary, however, to dig somewhat deeper. The list of professional issues which had recently secured its attention included, in early 2000, the following (Library Association, 2000a):

• unification between the LA and the Institute of Information Scientists (discussed in more detail below)

- access to information, including impending Freedom of Information legislation
- archives, including issues raised by electronic documents
- copyright
- equal opportunities and the implementation of the 1995 Disability Discrimination Act
- funding of libraries
- ICT futures
- knowledge management
- legal deposit
- lifelong learning and libraries
- the strategic review of the British Library
- public libraries, including their role in social inclusion, charging for services and internet filtering
- the sale of rare books by libraries
- regionalism and its impact on libraries
- the research agenda in the field
- school libraries, including funding issues and the impact of various homework initiatives
- theft of books from libraries and resulting security issues.

Considerable care has to be exercised in treating this list as entirely indicative of the LA's overall concerns, since it is noticeable that very many of the 'professional issues' listed are actually generated as responses to government discussion documents, green papers and white papers, so that the list is reactive rather than proactive. Some balance may be achieved by highlighting a comment from the LA's annual report in its centenary year (Library Association, 1998):

> Libraries are fundamental to a thriving democracy, culture and economy.  . . . Libraries – of all kinds – can play a key and creative role in delivering the current government's stated objectives; notably those in the areas of education, literacy, developing ICT skills, social inclusion, lifelong learning and a buoyant economy.

It is interesting that the LA does not, in these key statements, say much about *how* its ambitions for libraries are to be achieved – rather the discussion is very much about the social and political agenda that it addresses and *what* it believes libraries can contribute to national well-being. It does not, for example, define what a library *is*.

# The Institute of Information Scientists' *Criteria*

The *Criteria for information science* (Institute of Information Scientists, 1998) have been in use for some considerable time, both as a statement of the knowledge and skills that are required before anyone can be admitted as a corporate (ie professional) member of the IIS and as a baseline against which courses of study in universities can be evaluated. They are presented in four sections: the 'core area' of information science, information management, information technology and ancillary skills. The following is a summary of the contents of each section:

1   *Information science*: includes the characteristics of information and information flows, information providers and users, information sources, information storage and retrieval, the analysis of information and the theory of information science.
2   *Information management*: incorporates planning, communications, management information and control systems, human resource management, financial management, promotion of information services, economics and marketing, and political, ethical, social and legal factors.
3   *Information technology*: refers to hardware and software systems, telecommunications, applications of IT, and the IT environment – including ergonomics, health and safety and data protection.
4   *Ancillary skills*: includes research skills, linguistics and foreign language skills.

Although this list is perhaps showing its age (it was agreed in the 1980s with some revision in 1998), it provides a useful view of a profession with a core to which it can lay special, if not exclusive, claim surrounded by knowledge, skills, techniques and procedures that are shared with, and in some cases borrowed from, other disciplines. Indeed, it has to be acknowledged that even the core is shared to some extent with others – the concept of 'information' itself is used in many fields although some, like cybernetics, would lay claim to a special meaning. This does not invalidate claims for the discipline of information science, however, but could be taken simply to indicate its multidisciplinary focus. Summers et al (1999) argue that it should be regarded as, in Popperian terms, a 'pseudo-science': it 'is dependent on human activities such as writing articles, having information needs, creating search strategies, and making relevance judgements (and) shows itself to have a mixture of science-like and nonscience-like characteristics . . . it shows characteristics in common with other disciplines that are concerned with human behaviour'. The same authors remark that the emphasis of information science, for long focused on practical applications, is shifting towards more theoretical approaches while at the same time its boundaries with disciplines like management science (presumably another pseudo-science) and computer science (about which there might be more argument) will become more fuzzy. In contrast to the view of librarianship that emerges from the LA's statements, this suggests a basic focus on the content (or 'stuff' as it is often referred to now), rather than on users and society.

## Negotiating merger: What does the profession stand for?

During the consultation process in which the LA and IIS discussed possible merger during 1999, a document was issued that saw the future of the profession in the following terms (IIS and LA, 1999). First it provided a vision statement to locate a new, merged organization in the information society:

> Access to information, ideas and works of imagination is an essential characteristic of thriving democracies, cultures and economies. . . . We believe that the information profession needs a new organisation for the new Millennium . . . [that will] position us at the heart of the information revolution.

Then it provided a draft mission statement:

- To set, maintain, monitor and promote standards of excellence in the creation, management, exploitation and sharing of information and knowledge resources.
- To support the principle of equality of access to information, ideas and works of the imagination which it affirms is fundamental to a thriving economy, democracy, culture and civilisation.
- To enable its members to achieve and maintain the highest professional standards in all aspects of delivering an information service, both for the professional, and the public good.

It is interesting that these statements demonstrate a willingness to draw together the different emphases of the two bodies, on content and on users, in an attempt to capture the high ground with a much broader framework, at the 'heart of the information revolution'.

## Benchmarking librarianship

Following work by a distinguished group of library and information management academics during 1999, a 'benchmark statement' was published by the UK Quality Assurance Agency, the body charged with assessing quality standards in all subjects in all UK universities (Quality Assurance Agency for Higher Education, 2000). A similar statement has been prepared for every subject that is taught in these institutions. These statements cover both the specific subject knowledge and skills that it is expected graduates will have acquired and their generic, transferable skills – among them generic skills related to knowledge acquisition and understanding, the ability to learn and to work autonomously, management skills, communication skills and competence in the use of ICTs.

The more specific knowledge and skills expected of graduates of librarianship and information management were based upon the following definition of the discipline:

> Librarianship and Information Management encompasses the study of information, from its generation to its exploitation, so as to enable the recording, accumulation, storage, organisation, retrieval and transmission of information, ideas and works of imagination.

The core areas of the discipline were then defined in the following terms:

1  The processes and techniques whereby information is created, captured, analysed, evaluated, moderated and managed in a variety of media and formats in the service of defined user populations
2  The application of techniques for planning, implementing, evaluating, analysing and developing library, archive and information products, services and systems within the context of organisational culture, objectives and client base, professional statutory and ethical frameworks, and national and international legislation and regulations
3  The broad concepts and theories of information systems and information and communication technologies insofar as they apply to the principles and practices of information management
4  The dynamics of information flow in society, in and between nations, governments, organisations and individuals.

Following this, the benchmark statement went on to describe the more specific subject knowledge and skills required, such as regulatory frameworks, information evaluation and information retrieval. Again, it is the twin emphases on information content, and the techniques for exploiting it, and on users, including societal and organizational dimensions, that is striking.

## The American Library Association's *Key action areas* and Library *Bill of Rights*

The American Library Association (ALA) publishes a number of documents that define its interests and concerns. Central to these statements is ALA's *Library Bill of Rights* which states:

The American Library Association affirms that all libraries are forums for information and ideas, and that the following basic policies should guide their services.

I   Books and other library resources should be provided for the interest, information, and enlightenment of all people of the community the library serves. Materials should not be excluded because of the origin, background, or views of those contributing to their creation.

II   Libraries should provide materials and information presenting all points of view on current and historical issues. Materials should not be proscribed or removed because of partisan or doctrinal disapproval.

III   Libraries should challenge censorship in the fulfilment of their responsibility to provide information and enlightenment.

IV   Libraries should cooperate with all persons and groups concerned with resisting abridgment of free expression and free access to ideas.

V   A person's right to use a library should not be denied or abridged because of origin, age, background, or views.

VI   Libraries which make exhibit spaces and meeting rooms available to the public they serve should make such facilities available on an equitable basis, regardless of the beliefs or affiliations of individuals or groups requesting their use.

(American Library Association, 1996)

The interpretation of this document occupies considerable space on the ALA website and there is a separate office (and website) concerned with intellectual freedom. The interpretation of the document also reveals a great deal about what the ALA regards as its priorities at the present time (American Library Association, 2000d). There is a general emphasis on the library as a *collection*, for example in an interpretation entitled *Diversity in collection development* (American Library Association, 2000b), which states:

Librarians have a professional responsibility to be inclusive, not exclusive, in collection development and in the provision of interlibrary loan. Access to all materials legally obtainable should be assured to the user, and policies should not unjustly exclude materials even if they are offensive to the librarian or the user.

Another example, a document on 'evaluating libraries' (American Library Association, 2000c), talks in terms of the continuous review of the library collection and warns that this process 'is not to be used as a convenient means to remove materials presumed to be controversial or disapproved of by segments of the community. Such abuse of the evaluation function violates the principles of intellectual freedom and is in opposition to the Preamble and Articles 1 and 2 of the Library Bill of Rights.'

The ALA has, of course, also been involved in the issue of access to world-wide electronic information and has been particularly concerned with issues arising from Internet filtering. In the USA, the First Amendment to the Constitution guarantees freedom of expression and this has been upheld in the courts as requiring libraries that provide Internet access to do so without filtering (at least on some workstations provided for adult use). The celebrated (or infamous) *Loudon County* library case, in which a US district judge ruled that the installation of *X-Stop* filtering software on public library Internet terminals 'offends the guarantee of free speech in the First Amendment' (McCullagh, 1998), was a *cause célèbre* for the ALA. It is worth noting here that these issues, although they have received wide international attention, apply only to the USA with its constitutional guarantee of freedom of expression – in Britain, for example, there is no such provision and the position of libraries is very different (see Brophy, Craven and Fisher, 1999).

*Key action areas* include:

- diversity
- education and continuous learning
- equity of access
- intellectual freedom
- 21st century literacy.

while its expressed areas of interest and activity (American Library Association, 2000a) include:

- advocacy for libraries
- censorship
- copyright and intellectual property
- diversity
- education and accreditation
- employment
- equity of access
- ethics
- fundraising
- intellectual freedom and censorship
- international relations
- legislation
- literacy
- preservation of library materials
- public awareness
- public education

- research
- standards and guidelines
- technology.

An organization the size of the ALA has manifold interests, of course, and this list of areas of interest reflects its diversity and the heterogeneity of the membership. Nevertheless it is interesting to note the very clear emphasis on social issues – the library is seen as having a major impact on the major societal issues of our time, such as social inclusion and equity. Even where technology is emphasized, it tends to be the social impacts – as in the case of filtering – which are given greatest prominence.

## The American Society for Information Science

The American Society for Information Science (ASIS) describes itself as: 'The society for information professionals leading the search for new and better theories, techniques, and technologies to improve access to information' and has a series of special interest groups that demonstrate the scope of its concerns. They include:

- automated language processing
- classification research
- history and foundations of information science
- human–computer interaction
- knowledge management
- medical informatics
- technology, information and society
- visualization, images and sound.

As with the IIS in the UK, the emphasis here is on information as content, on techniques for its acquisition and manipulation, and on applications of those techniques. It is not that users are neglected, but that the focus is primarily on information itself.

In 1999–2000, ASIS started to examine its underlying focus, encouraged by its president, Eugene Garfield (Garfield, 2000):

> Ever since I joined the American Documentation Institute (ADI) in the 50s, the predecessor of ASIS, our Society has been challenged by new technological and other crises. In the early days, we regularly agonized over the definition of documentation but eventually, we recognized that the term information science better described our aspirations. . . . Later, we faced the challenge of newer infor-

mation technologies. The 1970 Annual Meeting theme, *The Information Conscious Society*, recognized that information science and technology are in a constant inter-related state of change. In the late 1960s and 70s, ASIS members were leaders in the 'online' revolution and helped society adapt to this new technology. . . . In the 1990s, the Internet is yet another major technological development that has already had a great impact on information science and raises once again the need to redefine our-selves. This is an opportune time for a major strategic assessment of the society and the environment that is impacting it.

Picking up that theme, ASIS devoted its Mid-Year Conference 2000 to discussion of 'information architectures', described by Peek (2000) as 'part of an overall campaign to reinvent itself'. Although there was little agreement on what this concept means, Peek noted that 'the growth of increasingly large and more complex Web sites, intranets, knowledge management systems, and digital libraries has left many of their creators looking for better ways to define their jobs and their functions' – and maybe 'information architect' will fit the bill.

What this and other current discussions in ASIS appear to point towards is an attempt to find a focus within the ICT-dominated, rapidly expanding Internet technology community. Garfield favours a change in name from ASIS to the American Society of Information Science and Technology (ASIST) as a means of attracting such people into the professional community and thus building a stronger professional body. It is interesting to note this rather differ-ent approach to the challenge of positioning oneself at the 'heart of the infor-mation revolution'.

## Conclusion

The tensions between librarianship and information science that surfaced in the 1950s, and found expression in the UK in the formation of the Institute of Information Scientists, are still apparent in the public statements of purpose which the professional bodies issue, even if there is less animosity between them and a much greater willingness to work together. Information science organizations emphasize techniques, the *how* of information provision and use. Library associations tend to take a loftier view, looking much more at *impacts* and viewing the profession in its broader social environment. But while there are these apparent differences, on closer examination they can be seen to be two sides of the same coin. The commonality across the whole profession rests in its concern with what the benchmarking group refer to as 'information, from its generation to its exploitation . . . [enabling] the recording, accum-ulation, storage, organisation, retrieval and transmission of information, ideas and works of imagination'. Differences are mainly about priorities and about how alliances should be formed.

# 5

# What is a library?
# Digital and hybrid libraries

The cost of data storage is coming down rapidly . . . so for the money we can store more data. But all that we will then have is cheaper garbage.          (Shank, 1983)

## Introduction

Any study of libraries and librarianship at the present time will almost inevitably be dominated by concerns with the impacts of technology in general and ICTs in particular. In the preceding chapters it is clear that whether the view taken is sectoral, theoretical or professional, ICTs have become of supreme importance to the library and information management profession. In later chapters the technological underpinning of future libraries will be examined in some detail, but first it is useful to examine some of the approaches being taken to designing new types of library on technological foundations. While terminology is unsettled – with digital library, electronic library and virtual library vying for prominence – the first of these is preferred here because it appears to encompass the widest scope. In a final section of this chapter, the concept of the *hybrid library*, a kind of half-way house between the traditional and the digital, is examined.

Perspectives of digital library developers and commentators tend to be driven by their backgrounds in librarianship, information science, computer science, systems development, education or other disciplines. The discussion focuses most often on the technology, but also encompasses the development of new economic models, legal frameworks, user perspectives and social impacts. A small selection of the more theoretical approaches are discussed here in order to shed light both on the concept itself and on what it has to contribute to the development and shaping of future libraries. A lengthier discussion of digital library research can be found in Brophy (1999), while a survey by Chowdhury and Chowdhury (1999) and an analysis of underlying concepts by Bawden and Rowlands (1999a, 1999b) and Rowlands and Bawden (1999) have also appeared recently.

## Knowledge mediators

A study by Owen and Wiercx of NBBI in the Netherlands, undertaken as a supporting study within the European Commission's Telematics for Libraries Programme, developed what were called 'knowledge models for networked library services': 'libraries, as a component of the information chain, act as a link between knowledge sources and users' (Owen and Wiercx, 1996). The authors suggested that they can therefore best be understood as *knowledge mediators*: 'the process whereby libraries provide users with insight into the existing body of knowledge and assist users in acquiring resources referring to or containing such knowledge'.

In the context of networked information sources, libraries will no longer be 'restricted to the catalogue' but will make use of a wider range of tools in fulfilling this function. Three fundamental functions of the digital library were defined in this work:

- Making available various types of knowledge resources
- Providing resource discovery mechanisms which allow users to identify relevant or requested resources and their locations
- Providing mechanisms for delivery of specific resources to the user; delivery includes both obtaining a resource when it is not already available in the library, and passing it on to the user in a suitable way.

The process of acquiring information, or *resource discovery* in the authors' terminology, was shown in this model to involve three processes: *resource location* through which the user discovers the existence of an item and a location for it; *resource provision*, involving the provision or acquisition of the resource to the library; and, *resource delivery* which involves such processes as on-site consultation, photocopying and downloading. The resource discovery system itself contains document descriptions, pointers to locations, searching or browsing mechanisms and, sometimes, abstracts or full text. Owen and Wiercx pointed out that the choice of resource discovery mechanism restricts the set of resources that the user can access – most obviously, the library catalogue usually restricts the set to those publications held by that library.

Owen and Wiercx developed their model further by examining parallels with traditional library functions (such as user support) and then developed a series of 'application models' to assist libraries to incorporate networked resources alongside traditional services. One of the main issues for libraries that they identified was the management of user expectations, which they recognized as being raised by the ease with which networked resources could be accessed directly: 'This creates an unfavourable situation for both sides: the user has to cope without the support and quality mechanisms of the modern networked library, and the library loses part of its user base' – this echoes earlier theoretical work by Buckland which is considered in the next chapter. Other issues include staff awareness and skills, and the availability of adequate financial resources needed to migrate to networked services.

## Moving to distributed environments for library services

The eLib *Moving to Distributed Environments for Library Services* or MODELS study has developed a 'MODELS Information Architecture' (MIA) as a way of describing systems that unify access to service providers through an intermediary while providing flexibility of data presentation to the user – and where the 'user' may in fact be software that processes, analyses and possibly re-uses results in some way on behalf of the human end-user(s). The MIA has been described as both 'a conceptual, heuristic tool for the library community' and 'a tool to assist developers as they think about future systems work' (Dempsey, Russell and Murray, 1999).

In brief, the MIA characterizes libraries as 'brokers' that both hide the complexities and differences of underlying resource discovery services from their users and facilitate data flows so as to enable processes to be automated. The broker is a *trading place*, 'where service requests and service providers come together'. A generalized description of such services includes the provision of:

- user access, including the presentation of an 'information landscape' and support for user profiles
- an applications framework consisting of software and data needed to manage the services, passing data between functions
- distributed service interfaces, which determine and control how requests are presented to underlying services
- access control, including the authentication of users and commercial transactions such as payments.

New or revised underlying services are handled by the applications framework and distributed service interfaces without requiring changes to the user access layer, since the service must operate in an environment of rapidly changing target services. Thus adding a new service should be cost-effective (and the library both scalable and sustainable) since it does not require a new user interface to be built.

The applications framework can be defined in terms of four key functions (similar to Owen and Wiercx's analysis described above): resource discovery, location, request and delivery. These require descriptions of the underlying services, including collection descriptions and interface descriptions (ie what information is available and the protocols needed to access it), and profiles of users that enable the system to determine access rights, preferences and so on. The MIA provides an underlying theoretical framework for the UK's Distributed National Electronic Resource (DNER) – described in Chapter 9 – and is of enormous significance for both digital and hybrid library developments.

## The architecture of the digital library

A series of papers produced as part of the US Computer Science Technical Reports Project, associated with the Library of Congress's National Digital Library Program (NDLP), and its precursor programme, American Memory, have suggested a basic architecture for digital library services (Kahn and Wilenski, 1995, W Y Arms, 1995; C R Arms, 1996; W Y Arms, Blanchi and Overly, 1997 – see also **http://memory.loc.gov/ammem/ftpfiles.html**). In essence the digital library is seen as constituted from digital objects – as described briefly in Chapter 1 – 'handles' or unique object identifiers, and repositories. The architecture has been implemented in developing the digitization of the Library of Congress's historic collections.

The handle system is central to the implementation of the concept in real-life systems, and has developed over recent years into an internationally significant service to the networked information community as a whole. Its essence lies in the development of persistent identifiers for digital objects that are independent of the current location or other 'state' of the resource, but can be resolved into a location by a resolution service. These issues are examined more extensively in Chapter 8 below. The handle system has been developed by the Corporation for National Research Initiatives (CNRI), which is also the publisher of the influential *D-Lib Magazine*, a monthly publication on digital library research and development.

An interesting aspect of this work is the way in which different types of object are placed in explicit categories, such as web pages or digitized audio, and are then subject to specific category rules. Arms, Blanchi and Overly (1997) describe this approach as follows: 'the rules describe the digital objects that are used to represent material in the library, how each is represented, how they are grouped as a set of digital objects, the internal structure of each digital object, the associated metadata, and the conventions for naming the digital objects'. With the categorization and rules in place, a query system – whether a user interface or another intermediary system – can determine how to access, store and display any object, including correctly interpreting its relationship to other objects. It is explicit that the digital object delivered to the user is conceptually not the same as the stored object but may be delivered by processing. Arms (1995) suggests that eight principles should inform the development of digital libraries:

1  The technical framework exists within a legal and social framework
2  Understanding of digital library concepts is hampered by terminology
3  The underlying architecture should be separate from the content stored in the library
4  Names and identifiers are the basic building block for the digital library
5  Digital library objects are more than collections of bits
6  The digital library object that is used is different from the stored object
7  Repositories must look after the information they hold
8  Users want intellectual works, not digital objects.

## Reference architectures

Related to the National Digital Library Project described above, work at Cornell University has explored issues related to the development of distributed digital libraries. The Cornell Reference Architecture for Distributed Digital Libraries (CRADDL) defines a number of core services of the digital library (Lagoze and Fielding, 1998). These include:

- a *repository service*, where digital objects can be deposited and stored, and to which the digital library provides access
- a *naming service*, which ensures that each digital object has a globally unique name and that this can be resolved into at least one physical location
- an *index service*, which enables sets of digital objects to be described and queries to be resolved into result sets containing unique names
- a *collection service*, which performs selection against defined criteria, tailored and specialized catalogues or other resource discovery aids, and administrative processes.

Not surprisingly, as the teams have worked together closely, there are many similarities between this and the approaches described above, but there are additional emphases that are important to the development of more generic models.

CRADDL emphasizes that without effective *naming* conventions and systems effective retrieval is impossible: in the CRADDL model this element consists of the application of Uniform Resource Names (URNs) to digital objects, coupled with the provision of a *naming service* that links the URN to physical locations – implemented using the handle system described in the last section, ie CNRI's *Handle System®* (**http://wwwhandle.net**). It thus takes on the traditional library's catalogue-as-finding-tool role, but within a distributed environment. Again it is important to note that the architecture separates *naming* from *location*, which tend to be concatenated in the traditional library catalogue.

CRADDL's definition of *index services* provides the mechanism to enable users to perform structured queries and receive result sets: essentially they are collections of metadata defined according to a criterion that may relate to a physical or virtual 'repository'.

CRADDL also defines the *collection* as 'a set of criteria for selecting resources from the broader information space'. This is a very important approach because it removes the concept of 'collection' from that of 'physical location' (whether physical artefacts or electronic entities on a particular server) back to the idea of the creation of collections by selection from the universe of information objects available. In the CRADDL model the collection need have no existence beyond the criteria for its selection: items may be selected for the collection dynamically from a wide range of sources as they are needed. Furthermore, the 'collection' may, through a carefully crafted set of criteria, grow or shrink with the development of its subject. Lagoze and Fielding suggest that this provides three key advantages: location and administrative independence, dynamic information object membership and extensibility.

## The control zone

Observing that one of the key features of the traditional library is the careful selection of stock to add to the collection, Atkinson (1996) argues that 'it is time . . . for the academic community to begin work on the creation and management of a single, virtual, distributed, international digital library, a library that has [conceptual, virtual] boundaries, that defines its service operationally on the basis of the opposition between what is inside and outside those boundaries, and that bases that service on the traditional social ethic that has motivated all library operations in modern times'. He argues that the role of the library is to control a systematically selected sub-set of published information, and then to ensure that 'such a subset remains stable and accessible over time'. To achieve this he defines five characteristics of such a 'control zone':

• *Core definition* – materials selected by the library on the basis of the value of their content and against which material outside the core may be evaluated.

- *Particularization* – a combination of the *level* of a work and its *significance*, as attested by its being accepted by specialists and scholars in the field – in essence a form of peer review.
- *Maintenance* – the library accepts responsibility for maintenance of the integrity of all objects admitted to the zone, both in terms of physical integrity and authentication – they remain as they were when originally 'acquired'.
- *Certification* – moving an information object into the control zone becomes the equivalent of publishing it, so university presses and university libraries are amalgamated in the digital environment.
- *Standardization and coordination* – the use of agreed protocols and standards.

This analysis is interesting in addressing one of the major issues of the digital environment, namely how the long-term authority and preservation of digital objects is to be achieved. It suggests that merging publisher and library functions, and undertaking an explicit 'maintenance' function, should be seen as important digital library functions. Furthermore it offers a possible framework for distinguishing 'useful' digital content from the dross of which users so often complain by offering what is in effect a 'kitemark' for each individual information object.

## Conceptual frameworks

Most of the above studies consider the digital library from a technological perspective. In a series of recent reports (Bawden and Rowlands, 1999a; Bawden and Rowlands, 1999b; Rowlands and Bawden, 1999) a conceptual framework is put forward based on Yates's work-oriented perspective (Yates, 1989) and a model adapted from the work of Reid (1999). An important and useful aspect of this model is its explicit identification of three 'domains' within which understanding of digital libraries can be developed:

- the *social domain*, which considers human factors including such issues as information skills and literacy, social impacts on the information transfer chain and information law and policy
- the *informational domain*, including knowledge organization and discovery (including such issues as description) and implications from a documentary perspective for the information transfer chain; a particular emphasis within this domain is on the role of metadata
- the *systems domain*, including human–computer interaction, software agents and systems architectures; issues within this domain that Bawden and Rowlands isolate as of special significance are scalability and interoper-

ability – again these are considered in greater detail in Chapter 8, where sustainability and personalization are added as key issues.

This work includes an attempt to place the concept of the digital library in the broader context of 'library' development, using a diagram with analogue–digital and localized-distributed axes. The authors are led to suggest the use of the term 'complex library', based on work by Crawford (1999), which they prefer to 'hybrid library' which they feel suggests 'an awkward transitional phase'. Given the widespread use of the latter terminology, however, there may be some doubt as to whether their preferred term will catch on.

## Summary of digital library concepts

There are very many approaches to modelling the digital library, but a number of common features emerge from the research and development that has taken place in recent years. These are:

- recognition that in the real world the information of interest to digital library users is to be found in a range of heterogeneous databases and collections, physically distributed but connected by electronic networks and containing objects of many different types
- distributed ownership and rights, including complex intellectual property rights
- a need to provide organization, provenance and authority for items and collections
- a wide range of users with a variety of client systems operating within a broad selection of environments and pursuing many different purposes
- a business need to control access to resources although the models, and especially the economic models, are far from clear
- a role, variously defined, for a broker or other intermediary which connects the users to the resources of interest to them
- a range of standards and protocols, for describing resources, for encoding them and for delivering them, including for searching and retrieval; many existing systems cannot interoperate effectively and there is thus a pressing need to agree open standards.

## The hybrid library

A pragmatic view of the future of libraries would suggest that it is likely that most libraries will for the foreseeable future – which after all is not all that long – base their services on a mix of physical objects (books, paper-based journals, videotapes and the like) and electronic 'stuff' (web pages, remote data services, CD-ROMs etc). For this reason, approaches that stress the management and delivery of 'hybrid library' services would appear to be the most useful. Crawford (1999), who argues somewhat controversially that 'the glory days of the all-digital brigade seem to be in the past', refers to 'ever-shifting complex combinations of digital and analog collections' which, as noted above, he terms 'complex libraries'.

The most widely used definition of the hybrid library is that provided by Rusbridge (1998):

> The hybrid library was designed to bring a range of technologies from different sources together in the context of a working library, and also to begin to explore integrated systems and services in both the electronic and print environments. The hybrid library should integrate access to all . . . kinds of resources . . . using different technologies from the digital library world, and across different media.

Brophy and Fisher (1998) comment:

> It follows that most users will continue to be offered a mix of formats via a mix of delivery systems. The challenge for library managers is to create integrated services which provide a 'seamless' service to the user. The user should be able to access services through consistent interfaces which provide compatible features (so that, for example, the user does not have to adjust her search strategy and syntax each time she wishes to use a different source). The hybrid library should not, however, be homogeneous: it should be able to adjust its services to the needs and rights of each user – for example by 'remembering' previous search strategies, by storing details of the user groups to which the individual belongs and by 'knowing' the user's willingness to pay for premium services.

Work on hybrid libraries has also embraced the wider resources available, including the need to bring together descriptions of items in collections situated either in geographical proximity or with common subject strengths. The Electronic Libraries Programme's 'clump' projects were designed to explore this territory (Brack, 1999):

> The clump projects are based on the need to aid discovery of, and increase access to, the vast scholarly bibliographic resources available to the Higher Education community, as proposed in the Anderson Report [Higher Education Funding Council for England, 1995b], which examined library provision for researchers in UK higher education. In the current financial climate it is impossible for individual institutions to acquire adequate research collections within their libraries, and although union

catalogues have been available as central resources for many years, they have not necessarily taken advantage of network technology. Since the beginning of 1998 the clumps have been investigating the use of such technology in opening up access to these bibliographic resources.

A 'clump' is a term that was coined by the 3rd MODELS (Moving to Distributed Environments for Library Services) Workshop [see **http://www.ukoln.ac.uk/services/elib/projects/models/**] and is used to describe an aggregation of library catalogues. The clump may be 'physical' – in traditional terminology a union catalogue, such as COPAC (the CURL OPAC) or the BLCMP union catalogue – or it may be 'virtual', being created at the time of searching.

The hybrid library concept is important precisely because it stresses that in the real world both traditional and digital resources can and must be managed together. The UK parliamentary investigation of public libraries, which reported in May 2000, put it this way (House of Commons, 2000):

> There is a continuing tendency in some analyses of trends in library services to stress the competition between the book and new technology. This is a false antithesis. Their development must be complementary not competitive. We are convinced that the book will survive for the foreseeable future. It will be supplemented, not superseded. The challenge for the library sector is to ensure that the development of information technology in libraries broadens library services and does not take place at the expense of the book.

## Conclusion

There are a considerable number of concepts being explored in digital and hybrid library research and development. In essence, though, the focus is on distributed and local collections of information objects – in the hybrid library including analogue as well as digital objects – and on ways of identifying objects of interest to a user and arranging for the user to access them. Although the concentration has tended to be on the objects themselves, on their description and on their organization, many of the research teams have pointed to the wider social contexts and the need to understand the human as well as the technological domain. This broadening of perspective, although not yet greatly in evidence, will undoubtedly become more prominent in the future.

In the meantime it is useful to note the close parallels between the digital library models and the key characteristics of modern libraries that emerged from earlier discussions of traditional library approaches. The twin concern with information and with its use is common to all these models, while the modelling of processes such as resource discovery, resource location and resource delivery formalizes operational concerns that have concerned the designers of library services from earliest times.

Learning Resources
Centre

# 6

# What is a good library?

Librarianship is a curious profession in which we select materials we don't know will be wanted, which we can only imperfectly assess, against criteria which cannot be precisely defined, for people we've usually never met and if anything important happens as a result we shall probably never know, often because the user doesn't realize it himself.

(Charlton *quoted in* Revill, 1985)

## Introduction

A useful way to explore the essence of libraries is to examine how researchers and practitioners view 'goodness' in the library context. What is it that makes a 'good' library? The question was formalized some decades ago, most notably in a seminal paper by Orr (1973) entitled *Measuring the goodness of library services*. He suggested that in fact two questions need to be asked: 'How good is this library?' and 'How much good does this library do?'; today we might be more likely to label these as the *effectiveness/efficiency/economy* and *impact* questions. The first is in essence concerned with measuring and assessing the performance of the library against some agreed criteria, as when the number of books issued per head of population is compared with the national average. The second, much harder to measure, is whether the library made a difference, for example to the student studying for a degree.

During the last third of the 20th century, a great deal of work was done on library performance, much of it based on systems views of the library, and this approach informs the first part of this chapter. During the late 1980s and 1990s, the emphasis shifted somewhat towards the application of quality management concepts to libraries, and this is considered later in this chapter.

## The library as a system

The term 'system' can become a catch-all, and is particularly dangerous in an ICT-intensive world where it is too often assumed to have technological meaning – Smith (1980) referred to it as 'a piece of status-raising jargon'. But it has a long history in management and organizational theory, and is helpful in defining libraries, because, as earlier chapters have indicated, they are concerned with *processes* in their particular context of information and its use.

The essence of the systems approach lies in the view of the library as an organization operating within an external environment and interacting with that environment in terms of inputs and outputs. The organization itself is concerned with processing inputs to create outputs. At its narrowest, the systems approach can lead to a rather blinkered view of the library – although outputs (such as book issues) have outcomes (such as well-read students) that may not be seen to be the concern of the librarian. This is, of course, a dangerous state of affairs, since users can find other ways to satisfy their reading needs – or not bother! The simple closed system model is clearly inappropriate.

Libraries are better thought of as open systems, where the influence of the system on the environment and the environment's influence on the system are explicitly considered. At one level this is a question of survival – Childers and Van House (1989) have commented, in terms of inputs: 'To survive, the organization must acquire resources, which are controlled by various external groups. Therefore the effective organization is one that responds to the demands of its environment according to its dependence upon the various components of the environment for resources.'

The simplest view of a system is thus:

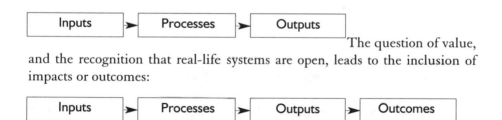

The question of value, and the recognition that real-life systems are open, leads to the inclusion of impacts or outcomes:

Management of the system assumes that outputs and outcomes generate feedback which is used to control inputs and processes:

The question of goodness can then be related not only to the efficiency and effectiveness of the *processes*, and not only to actual outputs and outcomes, but also to the adaptability and responsiveness of the library to its environment. This model underpins many of the studies of library performance and library quality that have been published in the past 30 years.

## Library performance

Among the studies of traditional library performance, those in the academic
sector by Van House, Weil and McClure (1990) and in the public library sector
by King Research (1990) are particularly useful. The International
Organization for Standardization (ISO) has published a standard set of performance indicators for libraries, ISO 11620 (International Organization for
Standardization, 1998). A 1995 academic library sector report, prepared for the
UK higher education funding councils, provides a helpful model (Higher
Education Funding Council for England, 1995a) suggesting that library per-
formance should be assessed by reference to five areas:

- integration: the level of integration between the mission, aims and objectives of the institution and those of the library
  – strategic cohesiveness
  – resourcing mechanisms
  – planning processes
  – service-user liaison
  – assessment and audit mechanisms
- user satisfaction
  – overall user satisfaction
  – document delivery services
  – information services
  – study facilities
  – information skills programme
- delivery: are stated objectives being met and is the volume of outputs high?
  – meeting service standards
  – meeting development targets
  – documents delivered per full-time equivalent (fte) user
  – enquiries answered per fte
  – information skills instruction per fte
  – library study hours per fte
  – volumes in stock per fte
- efficiency: outputs related to resource input
  – items processed per library staff fte
  – total library expenditure per item processed
  – documents delivered per library staff fte
  – total library expenditure per document delivered
  – total library expenditure per study hours per annum
  – volumes in stock per library staff fte
  – total library expenditure per volume in stock

- economy: cost per unit
  - total library expenditure per fte
  - library staff expenditure and operating costs per fte
  - space per fte
  - fte per number of libraries
  - acquisition costs per fte
  - fte per professional library staff
  - fte per seat.

While many of these indicators are concerned with internal management and are not particularly relevant to the present discussion, it is highly significant to note that, for example under 'user satisfaction', the four services that are regarded as significant are document delivery, information services, study facilities and information skills programmes. This gives us some insight into the working groups' thinking about libraries – these four services are clearly regarded as in some way 'core'. The first set of indicators is also of considerable significance, since it lays emphasis on impacts and in particular on how well the library is integrated with its parent organization. Clearly, this integration – in systems terms the effectiveness of feedback mechanisms between the organization and its environment – is seen as particularly important.

Turning to the public library sector, the UK's Department for Culture, Media and Sport (DCMS) published draft public library standards in June 2000 that explicitly focus on 'both library users and potential users, and their needs for service' (Department for Culture, Media and Sport, 2000 – original emphasis). The headings used for the 23 proposed performance indicators are:

- location of libraries and access to them (3 indicators)
- opening hours (2 indicators)
- application of the new information and communication technologies (2 indicators)
- issuing and reserving books (2 indicators)
- use of the library service (3 indicators)
- user satisfaction with library services and staffing (6 indicators)
- books and materials (5 indicators)
- local application (no specified indicators but 'all authorities should build on the national standards with local schemes to measure sub-authority-wide service levels').

It is interesting that so many of these indicators are based on traditional library operations and so few on ICT-based services – in fact of the two ICT-related indicators, one refers to access to an online catalogue while the other sets a standard of 0.7 workstations per thousand population, including OPACs.

The question of how the performance of digital and hybrid library services can be measured is being explored in parallel research projects in Europe and the USA. The former work is currently centred on the EC-funded EQUINOX project (**http://equinox.dcu.ie** – see also Clarke, 1999) which is based on earlier studies reported in Brophy and Wynne (1997) and Wynne and Brophy (1998). The latter study is focused on a project entitled 'Developing statistics and performance measures for the networked environment' (**http://www.albany.edu/~imlsstat** – see, for example, Bertot, McClure and Ryan, 1999, as well as the key precursor report in McClure and Lopata, 1996).This work sheds some interesting light on the underlying models of the 'library' that are being addressed. Issues which have been identified include the following:

- It is very difficult to find a satisfactory definition for 'document' in the electronic environment, where an object may be dynamic and may be made up of many smaller information objects, as when an article refers to images which are held as separate files.
- The boundaries of the 'library' are very fuzzy, so that it is difficult to know what is a 'library' service. For example, use of a link from the library web pages while using a PC in the physical library would seem to qualify as a 'library service', but it is unclear whether account should be taken of exactly the same action performed by a library user when at home.
- The number of items delivered may be irrelevant to performance, since users can download many items in the process of browsing through them and discarding most. The traditional information retrieval measures of precision and recall have limited application in such environments.
- Readily available statistics are often worse than useless. For example, website 'hits' can be counted in so many different ways and hits are generated by so many different applications that interpretation is almost impossible. All that can be said with certainty is that zero hits is a bad thing!
- The response times experienced by users, frequently viewed as a key user satisfaction issue, are often outside the library's control as delays may be caused by downstream bottlenecks. Extracting true *library* performance data in this area is thus very difficult.
- The convergence of library and computing services, common in the UK and not unknown elsewhere, makes the organizational model behind traditional library performance indicators inappropriate.

To date work on alternative performance indicators has looked mainly at how existing indicators can be adapted to meet the new paradigm. However, current work which is seeking to extend the EQUINOX project is examining a new range of indicators based on the library models that are discussed later in this volume.

## Demand for library services

A key issue for libraries, whether traditional, hybrid or digital, is how to generate appropriate levels of demand for services. However, libraries are rather peculiar, along with some other public sector services, in that their immediate customers do not pay directly for their services. Brophy and Coulling (1996) put it this way:

> In most settings, the customers pay for goods they receive; in academic institutions and public libraries . . . this is not the case, and care must be taken not to make assumptions that providing the funders with the service they demand will satisfy the actual users and the other stakeholders.

Equally, of course, providing the end-users with the services they want may not satisfy the funders!

Buckland (1988) has written extensively on these issues, particularly on the 'double feedback loop', which separates the responses of library managers and those of users to unsatisfied demand. If demand for a particular library service – perhaps for a particular book – is higher than the service can immediately satisfy, then the librarian may take action to increase the service, perhaps by buying extra copies or by reducing the loan period (in academic libraries usually by placing items in a short loan collection) so that existing copies circulate more rapidly. Quite independently, the user, when faced with the book's unavailability, may reduce demand on the library's service by a variety of strategies, such as going to another library, buying a copy, borrowing one from a friend or tutor, or simply giving up. (Incidentally, real-life examples of each of these strategies were discovered by Goodall and Brophy (1997) in their study of franchised course students.) The librarian's actions may stimulate additional, or at least reveal pent-up, demand; the users' actions may reduce demand on the library. However, as Buckland points out:

> . . . since library services are normally free, the library's income does not depend directly on the level of demand. Reduced demand, therefore, does not weaken the library as it would a business, where a drop in demand would reduce sales and, therefore, income. Quite the reverse, a reduced demand for a free service reduces the

pressure, leaving the existing resources more adequate to cope with the remaining demand. (Similarly, serving increased demand may not be as rewarding as it would be for a commercial business.)

It is interesting to apply this logic to electronic services and this will be considered at greater length later. However, it may be noted here that while a single electronic copy should, bandwidth and other technical factors permitting, be able to serve virtually unlimited demand, other factors start to come into play that tend to uphold the double feedback loop mechanism. For example, the decisive factor may become which of several possible services the user finds it easiest to access – an issue examined in detail later in this chapter when quality attributes are examined.

In addition to elucidating various aspects of the systems model applied to libraries, Buckland suggested six 'barriers' that have to be negotiated if someone is to access and use an information object successfully:

1   *identification*: 'strictly speaking, this is usually at least a two-stage process: deciding where to look ("channel selection") as well as identifying a specific book, record, or other source'
2   *availability*, defined as the process of delivering the object to the user
3   *price to the user*, including the cost to the user of 'time, effort and discomfort as well as money'
4   *cost to the provider*, which again includes direct costs but may also involve decisions on, for example, whether providing access contravenes values – such as 'social values in the case of indecent or irreligious materials'
5   *cognitive access*, which requires the user to have the cognitive ability to understand and use the resource
6   *acceptability*, which covers such issues as credibility (which might be judged by reference to source or author) and cognitive conflict (where an information object's content conflicts with the user's beliefs).

A particular issue in this analysis would be to determine where the boundaries of the library's responsibilities stop – for example, how much responsibility does the library take for helping users develop their cognitive abilities?

## Quality management

A considerable amount of work has been carried out in examining the application of quality management to libraries (see, for example, Milner, Kinnell and Usherwood, 1994; Brophy and Coulling, 1996; Brockman et al, 1997; Brophy et al, 1997a). At the heart of this work is the recognition that, as services, the primary motivation for libraries should be to meet the needs of their users as well as is possible. Quality management is based on precisely such a premise, its foundations being laid on definitions of quality which stress that the 'goodness' of a product or service can only be measured in terms of the extent to which it meets the customer or user's requirements – in formal terms quality is defined as 'fitness for purpose' or 'conformance to requirements'.

Total Quality Management (TQM) stresses a customer focus and continuous improvement as core values. Brophy and Coulling (1996) list ten intertwined facets of TQM which need to be developed simultaneously:

- developing a clear purpose for the organization
- providing vision, commitment and leadership
- encouraging teamwork and involvement by all staff
- ensuring that the design of all products and services is customer-oriented
- having clear, systematic, unambiguous and universally applied processes
- investing in continuous training and development of all staff
- monitoring performance continuously and acting on the results
- benchmarking achievements against the best in the sector
- developing cooperative rather than confrontational relationships with suppliers
- careful control of resources and awareness of costs.

Recently, there has been a noticeable movement towards redefining TQM in terms of 'business excellence' and the 'learning organization'. The latter concept is based on the idea that organizations need to go beyond the training of individuals, to become a 'learning entity'. The organization itself should be capable of learning, of adapting and changing in response to internal and external stimuli, through facilitating the learning of individuals, teams, sections, departments, and ultimately the whole enterprise. Of course organizations themselves cannot think or feel, so what is being suggested is the organization of individual learning in a systematic way that enables the total contribution to be brought to bear on all activities in a planned, yet dynamic fashion. The link to knowledge management, described in Chapter 2, is clear.

## Library quality

An approach taken in a number of research projects at the Centre for Research in Library and Information Management (CERLIM) has been to relate the understandings of service organizations in general that have arisen from a quality management perspective to libraries. The importance of this approach lies first in its very clear focus on customer perspectives – quality is defined in terms of customer purposes and expectations – and secondly in its emphasis on continuous improvement. It is thus concerned with change, but change that is motivated by a closeness to user needs and wants.

Quality management generally builds on systems models and thus, in library terms, fits closely with the systems approach described above. However, its further relevance for present purposes – ie for helping to improve understanding of what libraries are for and what role they might play in the future – lies in the definitions of quality itself. While the broader quality management approach has been described by Brophy and Coulling (1996), this tighter focus draws on work initially undertaken by Garvin (1988) in the USA. In essence, it identifies a series of quality attributes: Garvin's initial eight have been modified and expanded to ten attributes in their application to libraries (Brophy, 1998a, 1998b). The aim is to increase understanding of what makes a library service attractive to users and potential users alike. In the following account the initial description of each attribute is followed by two examples. In the left-hand column these are taken from the automobile industry, an area with long experience of quality management approaches and with a need to cope with intense competition and rapid change. The right-hand column is related to library services.

## Performance

These are the primary operating attributes of the product or service – what every customer would expect the product to have without having to ask. Their presence has little effect on customer satisfaction, but their absence leads immediately to complaints and dissatisfaction.

| Automobile | Libraries |
|---|---|
| • Seats<br>• Gear change<br>• Heater<br>• Interior light | • Catalogue of stock<br>• Logically organized stock<br>• Study space<br>• Knowledgeable staff |

The exact definition of these core performance attributes depends, of course, on the individual library and the mission it is trying to accomplish.

## Features

These are the secondary operating attributes, which add to a product or service in the customer's eyes and make the whole service more attractive but which are not essential to it.

| Automobile | Libraries |
|---|---|
| • CD player<br>• Air conditioning<br>• Side airbags<br>• Automatic windscreen wipers | • Link to document delivery from the online catalogue, so that clicking on the item results in it being delivered to the user's home or place of work<br>• Personal notification of new acquisitions<br>• Coffee shop |

It is not always easy to distinguish 'performance' characteristics from 'features', especially as what is essential to one customer may be an optional extra to another. Furthermore, over time 'features' tend to become 'performance' attributes – it is likely that document delivery will take this path, becoming an essential adjunct to library services. Nevertheless there is a valid distinction to be made. One way to check this distinction is to ask, 'Can this aspect of service produce "customer delight"?'. Generally, performance attributes are taken for granted – it is only when they are not there that customers notice, and then complain. Features, on the other hand, are usually not noticed when they are absent since the customer did not expect them. When they are provided, customers are surprised at this 'extra' benefit and express delight with the service.

## Conformance

The question here is whether the product or service meets the agreed standard. These are both national or international standards (for example technical standards) and locally determined service standards. The standards themselves, however they are devised, must of course relate to customer requirements.

It is of course important not just to have stated service targets but to determine whether they are being met consistently.

| Automobile | Libraries |
|---|---|
| • National 'type' standards<br>• Performance in crash tests | • Anglo-American Cataloguing Rules, edition 2<br>• MARC (which version?)<br>• Service standards<br>  – Average acquisition time<br>  – Average ILL delivery time |

## Reliability

Customers place high value on being able to rely on a product or service. For products this usually means that they perform as expected (or better). For services the idea of reliability translates best into 'correct service'.

| Automobile | Libraries |
|---|---|
| • No breakdowns | • Are correct answers given to queries?<br>• Are links on the library's website working correctly? |

Reliability also includes service availability – at one time this was a common problem with computer systems but usually now only occurs if a library subscribes to very limited concurrent access so that a user cannot get on to a database until someone else logs off.

## Durability

Garvin defines 'durability' as 'the amount of use the product will provide before it deteriorates to the point where replacement or discard is preferable to repair'. For library services, especially those which are IT based, the question is likely to revolve around longevity of the solution adopted. To some extent this is dependent on technological progress, which may be difficult to predict, but views can be formed on whether a service is within the mainstream of development effort or adopting a more risky approach.

| Automobile | Libraries |
|---|---|
| • How prone to rust?<br>• Mechanical durability | • Technology has likely development path<br>• Existing user base is large and growing |

## Currency

For most users of libraries, the currency of information, ie how up to date the information provided is when the user retrieves it, is a more pressing issue than durability.

| Automobile | Libraries |
|---|---|
| • Is it the latest model?<br>• Does it have the most up-to-date features? | • Latest editions of books<br>• Latest issues of journals<br>• Today's newspapers available when the library opens<br>• Current CD-ROM mounted |

## Serviceability

When things go wrong, how easy will it be to put them right? How quickly can they be repaired? How much inconvenience will be caused to the customer, and how much cost incurred? This last will include not just the direct cost, but the inconvenience and consequential losses the customer faces.

| Automobile | Libraries |
|---|---|
| • Ease of obtaining spares<br>• Network of garages<br>• Complaints procedures<br>• Comprehensive warranty | • Corrections of errors in document supply<br>• Courtesy of staff<br>• Receptivity to complaints and suggestions |

In general, libraries and information services have not had to give a great deal of attention to these issues in the past, but they are becoming of major importance, especially where an online information service is being provided on a commercial basis. A particular issue for libraries will be the ability to deliver the 'right' information object in response to poorly formulated queries, something that is occupying the attention of all the leading Internet search engines.

## Aesthetics

While this is a highly subjective area, it can be of prime importance to a customer.

| Automobile | Libraries |
|---|---|
| • Design (exterior and interior) <br> • Finishes <br> • 'Lifestyle' statements | • Building design, including finishes <br> • Web home page design |

A modern, light, airy building, which is well designed and well laid out, can give an impression of quality that can override the actual experience of using the service. Relatively poor service in an aesthetically pleasing environment may be preferred to an average service in a building that is drab and uninviting. First impressions are often the basis for user selection of services, and may have little to do with actual functionality.

## Perceived quality

This is one of the most interesting attributes, because it recognizes that all customers make their judgments on incomplete information. They do not carry out detailed surveys of 'hit rates', or examine the performance of rival information retrieval systems, or check the percentage of interlibrary loan requests completed within two weeks. They do not read the service's mission statement or service standards and they do their best to bypass the instructions pages on the website. However they will quickly come to a judgment about the service based on their preconceptions as users and on the reputation of the service among their colleagues and acquaintances.

| Automobile | Libraries |
|---|---|
| • Japanese cars are reliable <br> • German cars are well built <br> • British cars fall apart | • The library is great – the staff are really helpful and nothing's too much trouble <br> • The library is a waste of time – they never have the books you want and the staff always give the impression that you're interrupting them when you ask for help |

## Accessibility

The question posed here is, 'Can *this* user make use of *this* service?' Most services and products are designed for the 'standard' customer – a tall person may hit their heads on the hanging signs while small users may be unable to lift books off a top shelf. More seriously a high proportion of library users have a disability of some kind and need special consideration if they are to access library services in the electronic era: for example, 2% of the UK population – over a million individuals – have some form of visual impairment.

| Automobile | Libraries |
|---|---|
| • Seat adjustment<br>• Conversion for disabled users available | • Some of the OPACs have the mouse situated where left-handed users can use it<br>• Large screen PCs<br>• Audio-based browsers for web access<br>• Braille option instead of print<br>• Text telephone for deaf people |

A multicoloured, dynamic, multimedia website may look wonderful to many users but will be a barrier to those who are visually impaired.

The ten attributes outlined above provide some insights into what is meant by 'quality' in a library context. They reinforce the strong user-orientation of much work in this field but provide additional analysis that helps to demonstrate the issues likely to be of particular importance to libraries in the future.

## Conclusion

Attempts to answer the question 'What is a good library?', whether from systems or quality management viewpoints, demonstrate a twin concern with quantitative measures of (mainly) outputs and with user perceptions. As yet there have been few attempts to answer Orr's second question, 'How much good does this library do?'. Although user satisfaction and quality attributes analyses start to address the issue, it remains the great unknown of library services. While it is reasonable to infer that users would not continue to use services from which they gained no benefit, the complexity of interactions, particularly in the learning processes that so many libraries claim as their core area of concern, makes the isolation of library contributions difficult.

Nevertheless, it is a matter for concern that libraries as a whole are not able to provide evidence of the value and impact that they claim.

Despite this limitation, the evaluation of library services reinforces the conclusions of earlier chapters that the essence of the library is to be found at the nexus of information and use, of information provider and information user, and that the successful library is the one that manages services to maximize the benefits to stakeholders, of which the end-user is the most important. Meeting the information needs of users remains at the core of library services, whatever else they may do.

# Part II
## Future libraries

# 7

# The core functions of a library

The library of the future will be less a place where information is kept than a portal through which students and faculty will access the vast information resources of the world. . . . The library of the future will be about access and knowledge-management, not about ownership.                                                     (Hawkins, 1998)

## Introduction

The examples, models and approaches described in earlier chapters reveal a wide range of perspectives on the concept of the 'library'. Some of these views are driven by technology, some by the library's environment (for instance, the demands of its parent body) while some take a broad managerial, systems or societal perspective. Yet despite the differences within and between sectors, technological approaches and organizational environments, a clear commonality of purpose is revealed. It can be expressed succinctly as a common mission:

*To enable users to gain access to and use the information that they need*

The mission is focused first on users and is driven by their needs. It involves ensuring that users are able to access all the information of possible relevance to them, akin to the traditional information retrieval idea of 'recall' – being able to retrieve as much as possible that is relevant despite the heterogeneity of sources and descriptions. The library also enhances that access by limiting and controlling it in ways beneficial to the user – rather like precision, producing a selected but highly relevant set of results, removing the dross and avoiding over-loading the user. But it is also important to stress that *use* is behind the access and retrieval processes – it moves the issues into the realm of outcomes and impacts, which earlier chapters suggested were valid and indeed vital issues for librarians to involve themselves in.

The basic mission is expanded in the following commentary (Brophy, 2000):

. . . 'enable' may involve delivery to the user, or training in information skills or sim-ply organisation of sources in a way that users find helpful. 'Users' may sometimes be seen as passive, sometimes active and all kinds of terminology may be used to reflect sometimes quite subtle differences of approach – customer, client, patron, and so on. 'Gain access' may again be an active or passive process, may rely on 'pull' ("Come and get it") or 'push' ("Here's what you want") approaches, or more likely on a mix of the two, and certainly includes ensuring that the necessary skills and infrastructure are in place to enable use to take place. 'Information' may include works of the imagination, ideas, concepts, even persuasive literature. 'Need' will be expressed in many ways, and will be interpreted and modified as it is turned into requests for information objects. . . . In all of the processes involved in achieving this mission, the issues of quality, encapsulating factors such as timeliness, relevance, aesthetics, reliability and so on, are important.

This common mission is represented in all types of libraries in all the different sectors, whether they are traditional or digital or hybrid services. The aim of this chapter is to attempt to provide a generic model that is adequate to form the basis of further discussion of what the process of achieving such a mission will entail in the future.

## The library as expert intermediary

Virtually all of the descriptions of libraries that are available stress in one way or another that the library 'intermediates' between the user and the information resources that are potentially available, in order to help the user make sense of, and gain access to, information sources. The term 'intermediates' is not used here to suggest that the library forces itself between the user and the information so that barriers are set up, but in the sense that the library puts useful processes and procedures in place without which the user would be unable – or able only with great difficulty – to access and use the information. In other words, the library adds value to the process of finding and using information – by making otherwise unknown or inaccessible sources available, by saving the user's time, and so on. At its simplest this function is as shown in Figure 7.1.

**Fig. 7.1** *The library as inter-mediary*

The terminology for the 'intermediary' role is at present rather confused. Among the alternative terms in use, each of which has something to offer, are:

- *Agent*, stressing that the library acts on behalf of the user, going out and finding relevant information, repackaging it and presenting it. The analogy is with an 'estate agent' ('realtor' in US terminology) who has detailed knowledge of the market and attempts to fit the would-be purchaser's requirements to the available housing. The problems with this term are first that it is in common use for software that searches the web on behalf of users and secondly that in the analogy (and in reality) it is not always clear whose interests the 'agent' serves.
- *Guide*, with emphasis on helping the user to find useful ways through the information maze and on information access and use as a learning process. This term also echoes a mantra that has become common in education, the move of the teacher from being a 'sage on the stage' to a 'guide on the side'. The idea is that users are perfectly capable of pursuing information (and learning), provided they are given appropriate help and guidance at appropriate times. However, it seems to neglect the role of organizing both information and systems.
- *Mediator*, which carries with it the idea that libraries protect users from the vastness of unstructured resources by interpreting their needs and selectively limiting the materials provided. Again, however, it does not carry with it the role of organizing the content and systems.
- *Broker*, which places stress on the use of expertise to work on behalf of a user in order to acquire a product. The analogy is with a stockbroker who offers investment advice and is able to acquire shares or other investment products on behalf of the client. For many sectors, however, the term has a rather commercial edge; it also suffers from much the same narrowness as 'guide'.
- *Gateway*, which suggests that the library acts as an entrance to information resources. The problem with this terminology is first that libraries do a lot more than simply provide a door that users can pass through and secondly that the term is now used widely for a specific type of networked information service (as in 'subject gateway'). The term, in its more specific sense, is discussed further in Chapter 9, along with the associated term *portal*.

For the purposes of this chapter the term 'intermediary' is retained, although its limitations are recognized.

## Disintermediation

One of the paradoxes of the identification of the intermediary role as core to libraries is that it occurs against a backdrop of 'disintermediation' – which sounds like its exact opposite. This term is used for the process whereby users are encouraged to interact directly with services. So, for example, buying a book from Amazon does not consist of telephoning a human salesperson and negotiating to find the correct title, followed by reading out credit card data, waiting while address details are noted down and so on. Instead the customer interacts directly with the system. Similarly, in libraries, the introduction of self-service issue – to take one example – is a process of disintermediation since it removes the need for staff to intermediate between the issue system and the user. The economic advantages of this process are obvious, but it can also bring benefits to the customers, for example by reducing the need for queuing or by enabling them to be presented with choices and additional services that would be difficult to offer individually in person. Equally, many customers prefer the personal control that direct interaction with a system gives them. Were the phrase not so clumsy, it would be tempting to describe libraries as 'disintermediated intermediaries'!

It is possible to view disintermediation in a different light if the boundaries between 'users' and 'staff' are allowed to become fuzzy. Brophy and Coulling (1996) put it like this:

> Customers are participants in the service, because they can alter the product being delivered and the way in which it is delivered in response to the situation as it develops. . . . Information technology . . . enables services to move from customer–employee relationships to customer-service direct interaction. It is helpful when analysing these customer–service interactions to think of the customer as being (in part) an (unpaid) employee. People deliver services to themselves. This has enormous implications for improving quality provided that the sense of participation and ability to influence design and delivery that would be taken for granted by other employees is nurtured.

The removal of direct interaction between library staff and users is an ongoing trend, although there are some issues associated with it that deserve deeper analysis. For example, the EC-funded SELF (the provision of self-service facilities for library users) project (Brophy et al, 1997b) found that 'interviews and surveys showed that users would greatly value the extension of self-service facilities. . . . [However] concern was expressed . . . that the human contact aspect should not be lost entirely'. This latter finding provides some evidence that users do in fact value a measure of direct intermediation.

Taking this factor into account, it seems appropriate to continue to use the term 'intermediary' to describe the role of the library of the future but with awareness of its limitations. In particular *some* services are directly intermediated but others are organized on behalf of the customer with the library staying in the background, ensuring service availability and that everything runs smoothly – indeed it can be argued that in these cases the intermediary is most successful when the user hardly knows of its existence.

## Library users

This brings into focus another terminological issue, concerned with what have so far been called the 'users'. Again there are many alternatives, this time including:

- *Customers*, which stresses that users interact with libraries in order to 'purchase' (albeit indirectly) a service and that they have choices – more and more they have opportunities to take their custom elsewhere. The term is also a reminder of the *service* context of libraries with its obvious links to quality management's emphasis on customers, to 'customer care' and so on.
- *Clients*, emphasizing that the relationship is one between a user and a professional adviser and that the latter owes some kind of duty to the user. Just as a lawyer must act in the interests of his client, so the library user-as-client concept puts emphasis on the librarian working for the user regardless of the employer's interests. So, for example, librarians owe a duty of confidentiality to their users that overrides their employment duties.
- *Patrons*, a term that arrived in the UK with American library management systems but has little common currency among the users themselves. In British English it carries a meaning of a 'sponsor' or 'supporter' of a service, rather than a user – the Queen is the patron of various charities!
- *Readers*, which suggests that the primary purpose of the library is to provide both materials to be read and a place in which to read them.
- *Members*, which carries a sense of ownership but is perhaps less appropriate in some sectors, especially where the service has a more commercial edge, than others.

There is no agreement on the most appropriate term, for there is value in each of the alternatives, yet each offers only a partial view of a complex, changing relationship between each individual and the library. As Pinfield and Hampson (1999) remark:

Libraries carry out a large number of different activities, each of which implies a slightly different relationship with users. It might be said that there are a range of possible relationships. At one end of the range 'transaction-based' activities, such as lending and enquiries, might be described as a 'customer service' relationship with users. At the other end, activities such as providing information skills teaching alongside academics or the selection of major new electronic packages might be described as a 'partnership' relationship.

Interestingly, a survey at the University of Central Lancashire Library in 1992 revealed that staff and students themselves preferred to be known as 'users' (Brophy, 1993). This book retains that term but does so in full recognition of its limitations and ambiguities.

## User populations

Each library serves a defined group of users. For the public library these may be the members of the local population (defined either by place of residence or by place of work or both) who have registered as users. For the academic library the group may be the students and staff of the institution. For a commercial organization it may be the employees. One of the library's first tasks is to establish clearly the criteria by which membership eligibility will be judged. In effect the library selects, or acknowledges the existence of, a sub-group from the 'universe' of possible or potential users. For example, a university may define its user group as those registered as staff or students of the institution, but may equally determine that members of the public resident in the locality will be eligible for limited services. The universe of possible users is then the total of the members of the institution and the population of the locality. The user population is the sub-group registered with the library. In a few cases, for example, where the user population is defined as all those in the user universe – as for instance in a commercial firm where all members of staff are automatically 'members' of the library but no one else is permitted to use it – then the user universe and user population are co-terminous. Usually, however, it is useful to differentiate between the two because the library needs to gather specific information about those registered to use its services, not least if those services include the use of third-party systems with limited access rights, but needs to market services to the wider group.

The user population, once defined, may of course be subdivided by reference to other criteria – as when undergraduates and academic staff are treated as distinct groups for an academic library's membership purposes or a public library differentiates between adults and children.

## Information populations

Just as there is a universe of potential users there is also an 'information universe'. This may be thought of as the sum total of recorded information that exists in the world (or maybe beyond if satellite data and data streamed from Mars probes and the like are counted!) and that is potentially available. For many years librarians have drawn attention to the rapid explosion of published information and to the difficulties this poses for libraries and information services attempting to provide ordered access to the world's information for their users. The advent of digital information, together with the development of world-wide information and communications networks, has brought a new order of magnitude to this problem. While in the past the library's role may have been defined in terms of the collection that it brought together, and that would largely satisfy its clientele, the modern library, as we have seen, is more likely to act as an access interface to the global wealth of information, the 'information universe'. It includes the books held by the world's libraries, all current and past journal issues, newspapers, databases of various types, the resources of the world wide web, report literature, ephemera such as handbills, patents, recorded visual images whether still or video, audio, realia such as artistic and museum objects, representations in virtual reality, and so on.

It should be noted that the information universe also includes proprietary sources that may be restricted to a particular set of users, an example being the laboratory records of a pharmaceutical company, which while 'recorded information' and thus part of the information universe are not 'published' in any real sense.

While libraries can act as the interface to this wealth of information, one of their most important tasks is to create order out of potential chaos. They do this by selecting and describing information sources that they will offer to their users. Today libraries select both physical materials to hold in their own stock and virtual materials that they do not own but to which they can provide access and about which they can offer some guarantee (or at least opinion) on quality and availability. The term 'information population' is a convenient way to describe the sources selected by a particular library from the universe of possible sources. In the past the term 'collection' would have been used, and some would still use it, but of course much material is not now 'collected' in any real sense – instead access agreements are negotiated. It is worth noting that libraries have always had the capability to go beyond their initial 'information population', by buying additional items, or requesting interlibrary loans to supplement their own collections. However, the speed with which electronic resources can be provided from remote services means that the library's information population must increasingly be treated as dynamic – it is therefore less and less appropriate to call it a 'collection'. Chodorow and Lyman (1998) suggest that 'collection development will increasingly shift toward what might be called continuous live action'. The management of this dynamic resource is considered further in Chapter 9.

One of the tasks of the library is to make sense of this universe for its users, partly by mapping and codifying it (including borrowing from the codification of others) and partly by selecting from it those parts that are likely to be of interest and are known, or likely, to be accessible. It is easy to forget that in the library's traditional role, book selection was often regarded as one of *the* professional tasks (see, for example, Fonfa, 1998).

It cannot be emphasized too strongly that this process of selection is in essence concerned with the provision of quality assurance. The library admits to its information population only those objects that it is satisfied meet a series of quality criteria – remembering that quality is essentially concerned with the 'fit' between a product and its users' requirements. In the traditional library it is possible for libraries to use important cues – such as publisher reputation – and to outsource some of the intellectual work, for example by relying on purchase recommendations, reading lists and the like. In the digital environment cues are far less obvious and reliable, although outsourcing may be achievable by cooperative activities like national subject gateways.

Because information sources may be available conditionally (eg only to certain groups of users, or only on payment of a fee, or only if copyright conditions are met) the library may choose to subdivide the accessible information population depending on the user (increasingly generating this dynamically so that who you are controls what you see), or may attach conditions to what can be viewed. The version of the information population that the individual user sees might be termed a 'conditional information population', which changes and evolves continuously. The actual information population displayed to an individual is then equivalent to the 'information landscape' defined by the MODELS Information Architecture, as described in Chapter 5.

The simple intermediary model thus becomes that shown in Figure 7.2.

**Fig. 7.2**  *User and information populations*

# Intelligence

The basis of the services the library provides lies in its 'intelligence' about both the user population and the information population. Traditionally, the former requirement has been met by collecting registration data, while the latter has been represented by the library catalogue and associated status data. Registration data would typically include the user's name, address and telephone number while the catalogue would be augmented by location information, such as shelf-mark, and status data, such as whether or not the item is on loan, being rebound or available on the shelves.

In an electronic or hybrid environment, this is insufficient. Ideally, the library needs to have a detailed 'profile' of each member of the user population. This profile might include:

- individual identification data: name, address, telephone and fax numbers, e-mail address, and so on
- preferences data: level (especially in education), subjects of interest, languages, form (including accessibility requirements such as Braille output), geographical locations for hard copy delivery (eg home and office, but with selection criteria identified)
- past history of information access, which may be analysed to predict future interests
- sub-group memberships (linked to a general profile for each sub-group to define borrowing rights, for example)
- credit data, including limits and credit addresses
- public key for cryptographic requirements
- blocks: either withdrawal of general privileges or PICS levels (see Chapter 8), the latter perhaps defining access to 'adult' sources for children.

When held in a digitized directory, such intelligence provides the basis for automatic authentication and authorization of users and thus for seamless access to a wide variety of potential sources.

Intelligence about the information population also needs to be enhanced beyond what was contained in traditional catalogue records. For example, part of this intelligence relates to terms and conditions. One source may charge by items delivered (the classic interlibrary loan model) while another may allow unlimited usage but only by a particular sub-group of users. Yet another may impose restrictions on the purpose for which it can be used. The adequate description of the information population is achieved in a number of ways:

- through the way in which the library as a whole and its services are described – perhaps via a web home page but also in printed guides and signs

- by describing collections of material to which the user may have access
- through the way in which objects or descriptions of objects are arranged (whether in the traditional library, with its books on shelves, or on a web page)
- by providing details at a higher level of granularity – at the level of the book or similar object through the catalogue or at the individual paper through, say, an indexing or abstracting service
- possibly, especially with digital objects, at an even higher level of granularity, such as the individual files that make up a multimedia package.

The library must ensure the reliability of the descriptions it uses. Clearly it is preferable if descriptions are machine-readable, whether the objects themselves are analogue or digital.

The essence of an intermediary role is to use the intelligence to create links selectively between the customer and service provider: in a library context, between the user and the information sources. High-quality user and information intelligence will, other things being equal, distinguish the excellent service from the rest. Figure 7.3 illustrates this model.

It is pertinent to add here that user and information intelligence is necessary not just at the micro level, of putting a particular user in touch with a particular piece of information, but also at the macro level where decisions have to be made about the service mix to be offered. For example, managers have to decide whether it would be more efficient to subscribe to an electronic journal, paying per use, or to the paper version, paying once for unlimited use for ever. This is not just a matter of trying to estimate likely numbers of uses, but is also concerned with the nature of likely use – for example, will users be seeking specific papers, or will they wish to browse? Added to this, the life-cycle costs of different formats need to be considered, especially where traditional formats impose space and staffing costs. As a result of these decisions, the service mix further down the line – when demands are received from users – will be determined. The decision making itself is crucially dependent on the quality of intelligence about both users and information sources.

| User universe | User population | - - - - - - - - - - -<br>◄ Library ► | Information population | Information universe |
|---|---|---|---|---|
| | User intelligence | | Information intelligence | |

**Fig. 7.3**  *The role of user and information 'intelligence'*

## The user interface

Having determined *who* is to be served and *what* they are to be offered, the library needs to provide the processes that enable each user to gain access to his or her required information and then to make use of it. The user needs an interface through which interaction can take place, a real or virtual place where they can interact with the service.

The user interface in a traditional library consists of a welcoming physical building and, within it, places and staff where service demands can be made – ranging from the card catalogue, through shelf guides to enquiry points and an issue desk. Although not always thought of in terms of an 'interface', this is in fact a helpful way to characterize front-of-house library services: they are the places where users interact with the service. As the library moves more towards electronic services so the interfaces start to be delivered electronically. The first may be the library's web home page, initially doing no more than describe services, but increasingly these interfaces will offer a high degree of sophistication. They will enable users to formulate complex search strategies, provide advice and feedback and be constructed to reflect the individual user's preferences and interests. The whole user interface will thus become a complex but managed array of access services.

## The source interface

A source interface (a concept best articulated in the MIA model referred to in Chapter 5) that controls and facilitates access to the information population is also required. The source interface is typified in the traditional library by its acquisitions and interlibrary loan departments, with their systems for acquiring objects from remote suppliers and, hopefully, ability to turn to new suppliers without major restructuring of those processes. In the electronic or hybrid library, where it is necessary to provide access to literally thousands of underlying services, the source interface must be capable of 'translating' user queries into the correct syntax and protocols that will enable data to be retrieved from the target service. The source interface must then negotiate with and present data to the user interface just as the traditional library processes books and journals before making them available on the shelves – the MIA describes this as a separate 'applications framework'. The model is depicted in Figure 7.4.

The separation of user and source interfaces is an important insight from models of the digital library and itself derives from the client–server approach needed to operate effectively in a networked environment. It is worth repeating here the principle that when these interfaces are properly designed it should be possible to add new resources to the information population without making changes to the user interface – an essential requirement for effective intermedi-

| User universe | User population | User interface | Source interface | Information population | Information universe |
|---|---|---|---|---|---|
| | User intelligence | | | Source metadata | |

**Fig. 7.4**   *Library model with user and source interfaces*

ation in a world where there are hundreds of thousands if not millions of remote resource banks. In effect the ease of adding a book to the stock of a traditional library should be mirrored in the ease with which a new electronic resource can be offered.

With these interfaces in place the library can then enable users to interact with the information resources of their choice. The actions supported are related to the classic 'search and retrieve' functions of information retrieval systems, although it is helpful to expand them beyond these two terms in order to understand fully the library's role in the overall process.

## Information access and use

A number of different models of information access and use processes are available. Kuhlthau (1991), for example, employs a problem-solving approach that also forms the basis of current work by Wilson (1999) at the University of Sheffield. Although the process of using a library as an information discovery and retrieval system is not identical to that of using an online information retrieval system, these models can help to inform the specific services that libraries need to offer within the general framework described above. In this section, typical navigation through the user and source interfaces to obtain required information is employed in order to elucidate the more detailed library processes required. It is recognized that these processes are not always linear and that there is considerable iteration as users go back to refine their queries in the light of the progress of their search. Figure 7.5 is a simplified illustration of the processes that may need to be undertaken to enable users to complete an information access and use transaction.

The processes, which apply within both traditional and electronic environments, are described in greater detail below:

## Formulate query

Users, possibly with the assistance of library staff, formulate queries to represent the information (or whatever) that they require. This representation

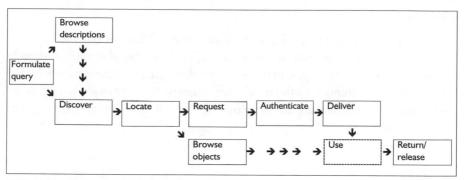

**Fig. 7.5**    *Information access and use processes*

of their requirements could be in the form of terms that describe a sub-ject, an author, a 'book like the one I had last week', or in many other ways. The library has a role in helping users express their requirements in ways that can be used within the subsequent retrieval system, whether it is human, electronic, or both. In Chapter 2 the importance of using standard catalogu-ing rules was noted, and this issue will be further explored in Chapter 8. It is important to note here that users will almost certainly need considerable help to express their requirements in 'standard' terminology that can be mapped on to the descriptions used by the underlying services. One of the most common causes of user failure is the query being formulated in a way that the target ser-vice cannot interpret or interprets incorrectly – which is not, of course, to blame the user!

## Browse descriptions

At this stage the system responds to the query by offering descriptions of infor-mation objects that *may* meet the requirement, and the user examines them. Classically this would be by browsing through a section of the card or other printed catalogue, but the OPAC, together with a wide variety of online indexes and other tools, provides much more sophisticated ways of using these sources. Typically, browsing of descriptions is by author, by subject and/or by level to identify a range of items that may be of interest. Much access to the world wide web involves browsing among lists of records of possibly relevant items, before narrowing down the search. The user may not need to go beyond this stage if, for example, descriptions include abstracts or if the query was to establish whether a particular author had written a particular book.

## Discover

This is the process of identifying a particular item as being of potential interest and finding sufficient data about it to enable it to be identified uniquely. Closely linked to browsing, it may also occur through an alerting service bringing items to the attention of the user. With 'known-item' searches, where a user is following up a specific bibliographic reference, it may replace browsing of descriptions.

## Locate

This comprises finding where an item, previously selected, is held. In the traditional library this could be a special collection or a particular bay of shelving. It will sometimes be revealed within the process of discovery – as where the classification number given in the catalogue record also serves as the shelf-mark, although the user may still have to locate the correct floor of the library and track down the correct bay of shelving. However, an item discovered in a bibliography may not have location information associated with it and therefore an additional step will be needed to find an accessible place where a copy is held. In an electronic environment this may involve identifying a remote supplier. Very often the library will take on the responsibility of finding the location, as with traditional interlibrary loan services where the user would not be expected to determine the location of a supplying library.

## Browse objects

In a traditional library, once a location had been identified it is possible to browse through shelves of books or through the issues of a journal, not necessarily to find one in particular, but perhaps to look for ideas. There is some equivalence in browsing through items selected by a web search engine, although in general electronic services are not particularly supportive of this function. Line (2000) remarks, 'Browsing electronic sources has its own merits, but it is a different process from browsing print; it may prove impossible to offer a good electronic surrogate for book browsing.' Where users are able to browse objects, they can of course immediately use them.

## Request

Where objects that have been discovered are not immediately available to the user a request for them has to be initiated. For instance, in a traditional library with closed-access collections a form may have to be completed to request staff to retrieve the item from the stacks. With electronic services, where delivery of a resource depends increasingly on software systems 'negotiating' to enable users to be given access, it is a core process. As noted above, with some types of resource such as web pages, the request process may effectively deliver the item to the user.

## Authenticate

The library needs to know that users are who they say they are and that they are authorized to access the material requested. It then needs to ensure that the appropriate 'business process' is put in place to deal with the transaction. Is the user a member with a right to interlibrary loan requests, for example? In the electronic environment, this might include asking whether the user has the means to pay (credit) to use the system, and then setting up a transaction with appropriate non-repudiation features. The stage at which authentication and authorization are carried out is dependent on a number of factors. Ideally, in the electronic environment, it occurs when the user logs into the system so that the permissions can be carried through until the end of the session. However, there is also a parallel with traditional services where it is desirable to offer free and open access to many resources without requiring users to identify themselves – this can be fundamental to retaining the open, non-threatening environment on which public libraries in particular pride themselves. In these cases the authentication and authorization may be delayed until the user first generates a request for a restricted item – 'restricted' in this sense meaning that it is not open to all users without question. Authentication and authorization are considered further in Chapter 10.

## Deliver

This comprises the actual process of delivering the requested item to the user. With a book this might involve the completion of a lending transaction; equally it could involve delivering an electronic document as an e-mail attachment in a form in which it can be displayed at the user's workstation. A complication in the electronic environment – which incidentally also applies to exploring descriptions – is that if multiple sources are queried on behalf of the user, there may be all kinds of incompatibilities and duplication between the objects returned. Delivery must therefore interpose some processing in such environments if users are not to be presented with a mass of unstructured data.

## Use

If the above processes form the core of the library's functions as it attempts to create the connection between each user and his or her ideal information objects, use of those objects provides the whole justification for the existence of libraries and indeed of information objects themselves. Use will be considered in more detail later, but it is worth noting that, for the user, 'use' leads on through processes of extracting and analysing information to personal storage and indexing of personal files and links – the creation of personal hybrid libraries with all the processes that they imply.

## Return or release

In the traditional library the transaction is not complete until the user returns the book, and the staff reshelve it. In many cases there is no real equivalent in the electronic library because each user is provided with their own copy of the information object. However, in some instances a licence restriction (eg on numbers of concurrent users) means that the end of the process occurs only when the individual user releases his connection, thus enabling it to be assigned to someone else.

## Advice and training

An area that pervades all the services libraries offer, although it is not always apparent in theoretical models, is that of providing advisory, enquiry and training services. Although these were mentioned above in the context of query formulation, they are clearly much broader, ranging from literacy classes, through children's reading hours to formal training in the use of advanced information retrieval systems. This area of activity will be considered further in Chapter 10, but is mentioned here for completeness.

## Management

All of these processes must be managed both strategically and operationally to achieve effective and efficient services, and to ensure that service delivery remains within the legal environment of copyright, negotiated and contractual rights and obligations, and so on. A library is a great deal more than simply an agglomeration of disparate services and its management is a complex matter. As Cowley (1985) remarked, echoing much of the discussion in Chapter 6:

> The main aim of the library manager is to create and maintain a high quality service matched to the needs of the users. To achieve this he or she is given formal

authority to make decisions affecting the allocation of resources. . . . The manager is concerned with the creation of policies and procedures designed to make the best use of resources in relation to stated objectives. It is also necessary to assess the impact of changes in the interaction of managerial and resource variables in order to determine the continuing viability of the library's aims and objectives. Regular monitoring of performance and resource distribution helps to identify the changes needed to maintain the library's momentum.

Managing libraries in hybrid environments is likely to be extremely complex, especially as both users and information sources may be far more dynamic than in the past.

## Conclusion

This Chapter has explored the common features that libraries display, in terms that should be sustainable in the future for both traditional and electronic services. Figure 7.6 depicts this generic model as a whole, shaded areas indicating the scope of functions and processes that have to be managed.

It is important to reiterate, however, that each library is fundamentally affected by the environment within which it operates. Thus while the model demonstrates commonality of processes and functions, it does not imply commonality of mission, emphasis, content or style. The library that is supporting a learning environment will therefore look very different from the library of an industrial corporation, but beneath the surface of those differences similar processes will be at work. It is these similarities that enable the concept of the 'library' to be retained meaningfully within traditional, hybrid and electronic contexts and across all sectors.

| User universe | User population / User intelligence | Advice and training | | | Information population / Source intelligence | Information universe |
|---|---|---|---|---|---|---|
| | | User interface | *Information Access and use* | Source interface | | |

**Fig. 7.6**   *Generic library model*

*Note*: This chapter is based on Brophy, P (2000) Towards a generic model of information and library services in the Information Age, *Journal of Documentation*, **56** (2), 161–84.

# 8

# Enabling technologies

*In a world that is forever changing, the only certainty is change.* Therefore, strategies for building 21st century libraries and librarians must focus on the ability of librarians and libraries to not just adapt to change, but to prepare for it, facilitate it, and shape it.
(Tennant, 1998)

## Introduction

Libraries have been using information and communications technologies for many years. They were early adopters of administrative systems – by the start of the 1970s many libraries were using computer-based (then referred to as 'mechanized') systems for catalogue record creation. At first these systems produced printed catalogue cards or slips for manual filing; later libraries used microform as the output medium, enabling multiple copies of the catalogue to be distributed for the first time and new sequences, such as title catalogues, to be introduced. Alongside catalogue automation came a move into the use of computer-based issue systems, usually doing little more than associating a book number with a borrower number in a flat file.

By the 1980s these early, first-generation approaches were giving way to semi-integrated systems that enabled the functions to 'talk to' one another. Thus the circulation system was able to look up bibliographic data in the catalogue and use it to generate, for example, overdue or recall notices. By the early 1990s such systems had been expanded to include most library functions – cataloguing, circulation, acquisitions, serials, financial control, and so on. Notably, interlibrary loans systems were usually still separate.

Alongside these developments libraries started to adopt computer-based information services. Initially these were remote database services, often accessed from a local dumb terminal, and charged on a connect-time and item-retrieved basis. This economic model forced libraries to restrict severely the access they provided to such services, and the common approach was for a mediated search by a subject librarian or other expert, perhaps with the end-user sitting alongside. There was even a trend at one point towards software that enabled searches to be formulated off-line so as to minimize connect time. A few services allowed for local operation by delivering files of data on (usually floppy) disk, but not surprisingly these tended to be severely limited in scope and content.

The picture changed dramatically as a result of four developments:

- The introduction of high-bandwidth wide-area networks. In the USA this was based on the Internet (originally designed for research use) while in the UK the Joint Academic Network (JANET) provided high-speed links between all universities.
- A change of economic model towards annual subscriptions which enabled unlimited access. In the UK academic sector this was accompanied by an explicit policy that all centrally funded services must be delivered 'free at the point of use'.
- The development of a wide range of data services delivered on CD-ROM, which overcame the severe file-size limitations of floppy disks and could be mounted locally. Quite quickly, libraries pioneered the use of networked CD-ROM 'jukeboxes' and stacks to enable users to access more than one CD-ROM at a time at their workstations and for multiple accesses to each.
- The availability of networked workstations (PCs or Apple Macs) which enabled end-users to gain direct access to the data services provided, both those available across the wide-area networks and those networked locally.

By the mid-1990s, however, it was clear that a further massive change would be needed in the technology that underpinned library operations. Library management systems needed to shift from the 'integrated' second-generation systems towards relational database models that handled all operations seamlessly. Ways needed to be found to integrate CD-ROM and other local services, such as the Campus-Wide Information Systems (CWIS) of academic institutions or the Community Information Systems (CIS) of public libraries, into a truly integrated service. And libraries would have to find ways to provide and manage access to the vast information resources of the networked world. The world wide web, starting to impinge on library operations by the mid-1990s and the dominant front-end to their services by the end of the decade, epitomized the new environment. Clearly, old technological approaches would not suffice, but neither would an evolutionary approach that simply relied on a series of small changes to existing practice.

New libraries require a new approach to their technological infrastructure. That is the subject of this chapter.

## General issues

Just as the design of traditional libraries depends on the application of some reasonably well understood general principles, the development of hybrid and digital libraries needs to take account of a number of general issues. The key ones for the purpose of the present discussion are scalability, sustainability, interoperability and personalization; these are described below.

## Scalability

This refers to the ability of solutions to be implemented widely across a whole service or across a sector, such as the whole of higher education, or perhaps across all library and information services. Very many 'projects' that work well with small numbers of users fail to 'scale', either because the software cannot support larger numbers or because the operational and managerial overheads are too high. For example, a project that relied on users having a particular type of hardware (say a particular sound card) could not be scaled across higher education, though it might just scale across one institution – until the users demanded access from home. More frequently it is the sheer effort required to support a service that prevents it scaling. Experience shows that failure to scale is one of the most frequent reasons for failure to turn electronic library experiments into viable services.

## Sustainability

Sustainability is the ability of a service to be supported over the long term. Will it be possible for the project first to be maintained as a service and secondly to 'grow' with the needs of the users? The first point emphasizes that, although extra effort may be required to set up the service, it will then need to operate with minimal overheads and minimal support as one of a portfolio of services offered by the library. Services must be able to cope with all possible forms of 'stress' – handling failures gracefully (so that the whole system does not crash each time an error occurs), operating in a wide variety of environments and with a source of ready maintenance advice when problems occur. The second recognizes that the environment and the supporting technologies will develop and change over time, so that the new service needs to be maintained and to grow alongside it. An example of a sustainability problem would be software that was designed exclusively for Windows 3.1 and had to be entirely rewritten to run under Windows 2000 or NT.

The concepts of scalability and sustainability are linked. So, for example, a careful analysis of both the existing technological base of higher education and its likely development, if considered early in the design of a project, can go a long way to ensure that it is both scalable and sustainable.

## Interoperability

Of perhaps even greater importance than scalability and sustainability is the whole question of interoperability – the ability of services to work together effectively and efficiently, so that software can be used to interrogate one service and integrate the results with those from another, and so that the user receives a seamless service. In the UK the Interoperability Focus at UKOLN has been established to assist services to address this issue (see **http://www.ukoln.ac.uk/ interop-focus/about/**) and has suggested that it might best be viewed from six separate viewpoints (see Miller, 2000):

- *Technical interoperability* is concerned with the standards needed to enable systems to interact and information to be stored, transported and communicated between and across them.
- *Semantic interoperability* is concerned with bringing standardization to the ways in which terms are used to describe objects or concepts. For example, the use of a thesaurus may assist interoperability at this level. A particular issue is that while terminology may be used consistently *within* a subject domain, it is frequently used differently *between* domains. Systems, such as gateways and portals, that try to provide 'seamless' access to disparate resources often encounter semantic interoperability problems.
- *Political/human interoperability* relates to the exercise of control over resources, such as decisions on whether to make them available, and as to the ability of staff to handle complex systems that each pose different problems if the end product is to be brought together as an integrated service.
- *Inter-community interoperability* is concerned to facilitate sharing of information objects and collections across communities, such as libraries, museums, art galleries and other 'memory institutions'.
- *Legal interoperability*, particularly where legislation differs between countries, for example in the areas of data protection and freedom of information.
- *International interoperability* includes issues such as language and culture.

*Accessible interoperability* is related to the use of standard 'display' features that are designed to meet the needs of individual users, ie ensuring that each object presented to the user is consistent in its accessibility requirements and does not require the user to switch between different applications. For example, a user who is blind and who has installed voice-output software should not have to switch applications to 'read' different objects. This has been suggested as an additional interoperability issue by Brophy and Craven (1999) in their work on access to electronic services by visually impaired people, but is broader than a disability access issue, since accessibility affects everyone and is vital in encouraging participation by individuals and groups currently suffering exclusion from full participation in access to networked services.

## Personalization

Personalization refers to the need to deliver to each individual user a set of options and services that are tailored to their particular needs and interests. It is becoming less and less acceptable to offer a 'one size fits all' solution, and with competition for the attention of customers – in information service provision as much as anywhere else – the ability to construct personal front-ends to software will be crucial. The issue of personalization and its implications is considered further in Chapter 10.

## Library systems

As noted above, libraries have been using computer-based systems for many years. Until recently, however, these systems were limited largely to 'housekeeping' operations – acquisitions, cataloguing, lending, and so on. This is slowly changing as networked information becomes more important, although to date most of the commercially available systems are functionally little different from those of a decade ago, albeit with a greater degree of integration between modules.

A major challenge for systems suppliers is to develop from this operational management base into systems that provide access to the much broader world of networked information, in which the library's 'information population' is far wider than the resources that it acquires for its own 'stock'. While management of the local collection will remain important, it should not form a conceptual 'centre of the universe' for the library's IT systems.

## Client–server approaches

Nearly all library systems now operate on client–server principles. In essence this means that the 'client' (for example, the user PC) runs software that enables it to undertake processing of data, display etc, and it accesses the 'server' where a database is held and queries are processed. In fact the amount of processing done at the client and server ends varies enormously. However, the importance of this approach in the networked environment is that a client built in accordance with agreed standards should be able to 'converse' with any servers that are also compliant. Since servers can also act as clients, thus chaining a retrieval process, this provides the basic mechanism under which a user can gain access to a very wide range of applications and datasets. The client–server approach underpins the world wide web since the client browser processes the data it receives to generate its display, simply making requests to remote servers for pages etc as and when required. It is important, of course that the client and server use and understand the same protocols, hence the importance of HTTP to define how messages and commands are to be structured, as well as standards relating to the various lower layers.

## Middleware

It may be helpful in future to think of library systems as providing the essential 'middleware' that links together the user with the information. This reinforces the model described in Chapter 4 and suggests that a rather different design paradigm needs to be adopted. Instead of supporting a library-defined linear process based on operational functions (acquisition–cataloguing–lending–return) the software needs to link together the user with an information object and dynamically resolve the acquisition (or electronic equivalent), lending (again or electronic equivalent) and other processes, including user authentication. It is the search and retrieve and associated business processes, rather than the cataloguing, function that becomes central.

## The user interface

As the emphasis shifts more and more towards end-user access to electronic systems, whether to retrieve information objects themselves or merely to access the metadata that describes physical objects, the interface provided for the user becomes ever more crucial.

A number of writers (eg Winograd, 1997), coming from the human–computer interaction (HCI) research perspective, have suggested that the key research area for computer science has shifted away from hardware, from communications networking and from software development towards the user interface, the place where the end-user interacts with the applications. Dempsey (1999) suggests that we should see such places (that term is itself significant) as ' living and working places. We can see a progressive shift in perception from a computer, to a workspace, to an environment. . . . Viable digital information spaces will depend on the ability to allow the user richer interactional abilities.' The term information landscape, coined by Dempsey and colleagues at UKOLN, emphasizes the idea that resources will need to be presented to each user or group of users in a tailored fashion and interfaces will have to be designed accordingly.

Interface design is of course a highly specialist subject with an extensive literature of its own, but some general principles can be stated. Because many libraries are currently developing their own front-end web pages, it is important that these principles are widely known and adhered to. In essence user interfaces should:

- be simple, avoiding unessential complexity and in particular using the minimum of graphics and images so as to maintain fast download times
- be consistent, so that the user can predict where to find information on each page, how it will be laid out, what terminology will be used, how controls will be used, and so on
- adhere to all appropriate standards
- provide flexibility of input; for example, it is interesting that online bookshops can routinely deal with authors expressed in either 'forename, surname' or 'surname, forename' format, while many library OPACs are confused by the former
- provide flexibility of output, so that the user can select display, print and other options
- support intuitive navigation, so that the obvious next step is the correct one; this can only be designed in by observing how users actually interact with the system
- provide shortcuts for experienced users and help facilities suitable for both novices and experts
- be accessible to all, and in particular adhere to internationally recognized accessibility standards such as the Web Accessibility Initiative (WAI) guidelines.

The interface software of choice is now the web browser, with Netscape Communicator and Internet Explorer being dominant. It follows that many, but by no means all, of the issues about interface design are concerned with the design of web pages. However, this should not lead to designers making assumptions about the browser being used, and based on these assumptions exercising undue control. There is a vast range of guidelines and books on web page design available, although the *HTML Writers Guild* (**http://www.hwg.org/**) is a particularly useful resource and source of advice.

# Information objects

The concept of an 'information object' was introduced in Chapter 1, where it was used to describe any object, including physical books and journals, electronic documents and multimedia, that might form part of a library collection. The term is a useful one, but it is helpful to try to define it more precisely, especially as these broadly defined information objects will, presumably, be the raw materials with which libraries will continue to deal. This section will, in the main, be concerned with digital information objects, because that is where the most challenging issues lie, but it is worth stressing that analogue objects, including traditional books, will almost certainly remain a key part of nearly all libraries' collections and services. Indeed, it is useful to recall that an effect of concentrating on individual 'objects' can be to lose sight of and even destroy the purpose of the work in question. Most books, for example, are much more than collections of individual chapters. The organization of objects at this micro level is all-important to their coherence and meaning. A book cannot simply be deconstructed into discrete chunks, each handled independently, in the way that individual journal papers can. The level of granularity at which digital objects are treated is discussed later, but similar arguments apply to analogue media.

It is also worth noting that the digitization of analogue objects opens up the possibility of enrichment by providing deep context. For example, historical documents may be indexed by place and date, and tools provided to enable researchers to cluster such objects in novel ways. A digitized resource may thus be much more than the simple equivalent of the original object.

Libraries have had the problem of defining information objects, albeit writ small, in the past when they have created or acquired 'items' where the physical manifestation of an item does not coincide with the smallest unit of useful information. An example would be a bound volume of a journal, or even a single issue, where the useful 'item' from the user's point of view is usually the individual article while the 'item' for the library (as represented in its catalogue and physically manifested on its shelves) is the volume or issue. The same argument could be applied to an edited collection of essays or to a database of bibliographic or other records. A complexity is that the library's 'item' may evolve over time into a different manifestation, as when the individual journal issues are bound into a volume – the library then ceases to regard the issues as items and treats the bound volume as the basic unit, even though the users' interests have not changed.

In the electronic information field the situation has become even more complex. A web page provides a good example: it may consist of a series of frames, each of which may contain text, images, sound files or other embedded 'objects'. What in these circumstances should be regarded as the basic 'information object'? This is a particularly difficult question because the same image, or piece of text, could well be regarded as an information object in its own right in one circumstance, but as an embedded (and in effect inseparable) part of an intellectual and indeed physical construct (the whole web page for example) in another. Web pages also display another problematic property for libraries and users, in that they do not persist. Unlike physical books and journals, and some electronic formats like CD-ROM, there is no guarantee that a web page that exists today will still exist, anywhere in the world, tomorrow. Furthermore, even if the page does survive its location may have changed, rendering it inaccessible.

A further area of complexity lies in the existence of varied forms or editions of information objects. Libraries are used to handling new editions of books, but the complexity of the digital world goes far beyond this. For example, a web page is increasingly likely to be created dynamically when it is requested, with no two occurrences – even if delivered to the same user in response to an identical request – being identical. Even where the content is identical, a document may be packaged in different ways; so, for example, documents available for downloading from the web may be offered in .pdf or .html versions. Should the librarian treat these as different information objects? If so, how should the relationship between them be expressed?

In order to make some sense of this situation, it is useful to have some working definitions. As yet these cannot allow for every possible eventuality, but consensus is emerging around ways to handle, describe and locate information objects.

Many of the difficulties arise because the systems that have been developed in the print-on-paper world no longer apply in the electronic, and still less in the hybrid information universe. Paskin (1999) suggests that in place of the printed object we now need to think in terms of three

spaces in which 'the same' article appears:

- Information space = the work as intangible entity (ideas)
- Cyberspace = digital manifestation (electronic, made of bits)
- 'Paper space' = physical manifestation (cellulose and ink, made of atoms).

The logical approach is clearly to have a unique identifier for the first of these instances and then in some way to reference the digital and paper manifestations of it from that basic definition ('paper' being used here to represent any non-digital formats). A number of approaches are being explored to achieve this, and these will be described briefly below.

First, however, it is important to note that this does not solve the question of the level of granularity at which a 'work' should be recognized – is the basic unit, for example, the book, the chapter, the illustration, the sentence or what? A practical suggestion is that we define a 'document like object' (DLO) (Caplan, 1995), which is, in essence, a common-sense approach to the basic useful unit – so it might be, say, a journal article, a web page or a video presentation. Paskin (1997) suggests that it may also be useful to define a lower level of object, the 'component of a document' that may become especially useful as multimedia packages become more commonly used, as well as the higher level 'cluster of documents' that is represented by, for example, a database or journal volume. Although not entirely satisfactory, this categorization allows useful discussion and the development of systems capable of handling information objects. It is also pertinent to add that much discussion of this area refers not just to 'information objects' but rather to 'digital objects', on the basis that once digitized all objects are, at least in principle, capable of being handled in the same way. However, noting that it is difficult to conceive of a digital object that did not have the potential to convey information and that the term 'information object' is inclusive of non-digital resources, that remains the preferred term for this discussion.

Libraries have used 'document identifiers' for many years. For example, the International Standard Book Number (ISBN) and International Standard Serial Number (ISSN) are used to identify a specific edition of a particular book and a specific journal title uniquely. These are examples of what are sometimes called 'intelligent' or 'compound' identifiers, because the numbers themselves contain meaning. Provided the structure is known, and there is access to a table of values, the publisher can be deduced from the number itself without recourse to the actual item. By contrast, a 'simple' identifier is just a number – the accessions number used by many libraries in the past was an example, since it was simply assigned in sequence and nothing could be deduced from it by itself. The use of identifiers to convey meaning is discussed in the next section.

ISBNs and ISSNs are also good examples of identification systems that are of limited usefulness because of the particular stakeholder view they embody. For example, they are usually of little interest to the user, since it is impossible to resolve the request for 'a copy of *The Pilgrim's Progress*' (or whatever) by a single ISBN. The only library users who are likely to find them helpful are scholars who need a particular edition, but even then the varied practice among publishers with regard to reprints and versions makes this usage hazardous. Use of separate ISBNs for hard-cover and paperback editions is undoubtedly useful to publishers and booksellers, but much less so to other stakeholders. What is needed is an identifier system that has much broader applicability.

Some of the approaches to a resolution of these problems currently being pursued are described below.

## Uniform Resource Names (URNs) and Persistent Uniform Resource Locators (PURLs)

These are designed to resolve the problem with web Uniform Resource Locators (URLs) which describe the *location* of an object and which do not persist if that location changes, for example when a resource moves from one server to another. Although pointers can be created from the old location to the new, in practice this happens rather infrequently. In essence the URN or PURL would stay with the document forever, and the local web administrator, or a more general resolution service, would maintain the location information. A client request for a document using a PURL or URN would in effect query the resolution service which would supply the location. The generic term *Uniform Resource Identifier* (URI) is used to include URLs, PURLs and URNs.

### Digital Object Identifier

The Digital Object Identifier (DOI) system, which is compatible with the URN system but more advanced, assigns a number to each document which uniquely identifies it and a 'handle', which is a mechanism for resolving the identifier into a location. The use of handles was outlined in the description of the NDLP in Chapter 5. It is intended that the DOI system should be generic (ie not limited to one medium and document type, like URNs) and that in the future it should support multiple document locations to enable the user to select the most convenient copy (for example where there are multiple mirror sites). It is also being designed to support look-up from a bibliographic citation to the DOI, to cater for the very frequent occasions when the user does not know the DOI in advance. It will also be possible to attach some metadata (see below) to the DOI itself. The International DOI Foundation, based in Geneva, is responsible for the standard, for approving naming conventions across different sectors and for appointing resolution (location) agencies.

### Others

More specific unique identifier systems include:

• the Serial Item and Contribution Identifier (SICI), used to identify both serial titles and individual documents regardless of the medium (paper, electronic, etc)

- the Book Item and Component Identifier (BICI); in essence a book version of SICI, enabling parts of books (eg chapters) to be uniquely identified
- the International Standard Work Code (ISWC) used to identify musical compositions.

There are many other approaches which are being tried, particularly in specialist fields. Libraries will need to be in a position to handle unique identifiers in a variety of domains for the foreseeable future.

## Document formats

Even if the problem of identifying objects uniquely were to be resolved, libraries would still be faced with handling, and enabling their users to handle, a vast array of different document formats. Leaving aside non-digital media (paper, film, magnetic tape and so on) the range of electronic formats remains huge. It includes:

- *American Standard Code for Information Interchange* (ASCII) character strings, containing virtually no structural information
- a variety of word-processor formats such as *Word* and *WordPerfect*; *rich text format* (RTF) can be used as a common transfer format
- *bitmaps* of various types, which are a bit by bit image representation and are sometimes used to store text as an image; this was at one time a popular way of securing text against widespread copying as it is difficult to extract parts of the image
- various e-mail formats, such as *Simple Mail Transfer Protocol* (SMTP) and *Multi-purpose Internet Mail Extensions* (MIME), which can be used for alerting services, delivering documents as attachments and the like
- *Standard Generalized Mark-up Language* (SGML), of which HTML is an application; some journals have used a full(ish) version of SGML; for any application of SGML there needs to be a *Document Type Definition* (DTD) which defines the rules for marking up and thus interpreting the document; an instance of an SGML document then consists of a 'declaration' to define the processing environment, the DTD name and the data itself
- *Hypertext Mark-up Language* (HTML) used for hypertext, including web pages, and the most commonly used DTD of SGML; *Dynamic HTML* (DHTML) is used to enable interaction and greater control over presentation of web pages

- *eXtensible Mark-up Language* (XML), which is a simplified subset of SGML that provides support for user-defined tags and attributes (unlike HTML where these are defined in the HTML standard); XML is of enormous importance for libraries and is described in greater detail below
- *TeX*, used especially in the scientific, engineering and mathematical fields because of its extensive facilities for representing mathematical formulae; *LaTeX* is a widely used implementation of TeX
- *Postscript*, a method of defining the look of the page representation or 'page description language' – it defines the printed page rather than a display
- *Portable Document Format* (PDF), a proprietary format from Adobe which nevertheless has a huge and growing application base, especially for downloading documents from the web; it is in effect an enhanced PostScript format, providing embedded fonts, hypertext links, index and search facilities and a number of other features
- a variety of still image formats, including the *Graphics Interchange Format* (GIF), *Joint Photographic Experts Group* (JPEG), *Tagged Image File Format* (TIFF) and so on
- audio formats, including *RealAudio*, *Digital Audio based Information SYstem* (DAISY), *Audio Interchange File Format* (AIFF), Sun's AU, and Microsoft's WAV
- video formats, including *Motion Pictures Expert Group* (MPEG), *Audio Video Interleaved* (AVI) from Microsoft and *QuickTime* from Apple
- multimedia formats including the *Synchronized Multimedia Integration Language* (SMIL) and Macromedia's *ShockWave*.

Examples of the application of many of these standards to information objects have been provided by Wusteman (1998), who also points to the growing importance of interactive documents using 'mobile' programming languages like *Java*.

It is difficult to be sure of the impacts of this proliferation of document standards on libraries. Mainstream formats are almost always supported by standard client software, such as the mainstream web browsers (if not directly then by means of plug-ins) so that few problems should be experienced. However, there are serious issues for the library's role as a preservation agent and this is discussed further in Chapter 9.

## XML

XML has been developed largely in response to the acknowledged shortcomings of HTML, which is concerned primarily with the *appearance* or *presentation* of a web page on a screen rather than with what the *content* actually is.

HTML was never designed for the kind of complex task that has now become routine on the web, for example where a company wants to upload orders from customers or interact in real time with a remote site. The data is simply not tagged in a way that is meaningful to another computer – for instance, there are no universally recognized tags for the content of a personal record. Because HTML tags have to be approved by an international committee, the process of adding a new one is time-consuming and laborious, and in any case it is highly unlikely that a specialist tag – say for an application specific to libraries dealing with incunabula – would be approved. One deleterious result of this is that because the only way to communicate such information is to embed it within the web page, when just one element changes the whole page has to be re-transmitted, which has severe bandwidth implications and explains at least part of the slowness of the web. For example, when trying to book a flight or train ticket, if an error is detected in the page sent by the user to the server, the whole page has to be sent back with an indication of an error inserted. This can, of course, go on for a considerable time, to everyone's frustration.

XML, which is within the SGML family, is designed to provide the shell or framework within which anyone can create a specialized mark-up language of their own, so that any community can create its own tags. There are no predefined tags, as there are in HTML. There are, however, a few simple rules that have to be obeyed, such as tags always coming in pairs so that they surround the data to which they refer, and use of the basic tree structure so that every element is in a known relationship to others. In order to define a new XML 'language' it is necessary to agree three aspects: the tags themselves and their meaning, how they are allowed to be nested within each other and how they are to be processed. The first two of these are contained in the language's Document Type Definition (DTD), as with any SGML application. The processing of XML-encoded data, for example for display purposes, can then be carried out by reference to stylesheets, defined in a new standard called eXtensible Stylesheet Language (XSL). Further XML standards are emerging, such as XLink for defining links between documents and XQL for querying XML documents. The concept of namespaces is also important as a means of sharing the meaning of tags (eg to define what 'name' means across a range of application environments that may wish to share processable data). The fundamental point, however, is that because XML tags are meaningful in terms of data content, XML documents are ideally suited to machine processing.

There are many reasons for the importance of this new approach to libraries, since it allows information objects to be analysed and manipulated and permits much more sophisticated handling of metadata objects. A particular example of the advantages to users would be the ability of client software to interpret data and output it more appropriately for a blind or visually impaired user. Current

HTML causes problems because the display tags, such as '<H1> ... </H1>', are of little use to non-visual displays. XML should therefore assist in making information and other services much more inclusive than in the past.

## Metadata

Metadata – 'data about data' – consists of descriptions of information 'objects' (whether books, web pages, audio tapes or whatever). It may more formally be defined in the following way:

> Metadata is data associated with objects which relieves their potential users of having to have full advance knowledge of their existence or characteristics.
> (Dempsey and Heery, 1997)

Metadata serves a number of purposes: it aids resource discovery (ie establishing the existence of an information object that may fulfil a user's needs), it assists the user to evaluate the object, without necessarily having to access the object itself, it enables the user to check the object's availability (to that user), it describes the terms under which the object may be used, it enables a location for the object to be determined, and it serves many other purposes. In the traditional academic library card catalogue the use of metadata might be typified by a search in the classified catalogue to discover a book title of potential interest. Information on author, language, publisher and date of publication might be used to form a preliminary view of its likely value; a note might indicate that it is in a restricted collection not normally available to undergraduates, while a shelf-mark would provide its exact location; a loan category indicator would inform the user of the permitted length of loan.

Apart from the user's interests, metadata also provides the owners of the objects with a means of asserting their rights. It may state ownership, IPR rights, terms for use and so on. It may also assist those responsible for managing collections of objects – including librarians – by describing features such as frequency of use or condition, as when circulation staff add a note to an item record.

Libraries have thus long created metadata in the form of catalogue entries and have generally bought in further metadata, especially in relation to journal papers, in the form of published indexing and abstracting services. However, many other parties are involved in the production and utilization of metadata: publishers, abstract and indexing service providers, archives, Internet search engine companies, document supply services, booksellers, subscription agents, governments and many more. All of these stakeholders have their own approach to metadata and most have developed their own standards, usually based on their particular view of the information chain. For example, libraries have developed metadata based largely on the description of book titles, publishers and wholesalers have developed metadata suited to electronic trading including pricing, and governments have encouraged the development of content labelling, for example to enable screening of 'unsuitable' content.

In the networked information environment metadata has become more and more important, since it holds the key not only to providing individuals with descriptions for them to browse but more importantly to the use of software to locate relevant information, to negotiate terms for its supply, to request it and to receive it. At present metadata of web pages is particularly problematic: it often does not exist, and where it does exist it may not provide the data required (for example, it is very difficult to determine the author of a web resource without additional indexing).

It is important to note that metadata standards need to encompass two distinct issues: the *structural format* of a metadata record (which fields are valid, their syntax, and so on) and the *content*. Both issues have received considerable attention from librarians, with the development of thesauri, cataloguing rules, various subject heading lists, etc, and some of the most important examples of these are considered next.

## MARC

The MARC (MAchine Readable Cataloguing) standard has been in use for well over a quarter of a century, and nearly all large libraries now make use of it, often buying in records from the national library or other supplier. It is by far the longest established computer-readable metadata standard, but on the negative side it is not particularly well suited to describing electronic documents. MARC was designed for the *exchange* of bibliographic and other related information in machine-readable form, although it is often regarded as an internal format also. A further complication is that MARC is really a family of formats based on ISO 2709 (International Organization for Standardization, 1996): USMARC, UKMARC and UNIMARC are all variants, although USMARC is becoming dominant.

MARC uses a structure of tagged fields and sub-fields for each element of the record. Although its use for electronic information objects is not well established, the 856 tag is available for object identifiers such as Uniform Resource Locators (URLs).

It is worth noting that the Z39.50 'search and retrieve' standard (see below) was developed as a means of searching remote MARC databases, although it can be used more generically. To date, most experience with Z39.50 is with MARC datasets. The question for libraries is not so much whether MARC will persist – it is not under serious threat – but how it can be handled alongside other approaches, especially those designed for digital objects. Its structure and schema, although well suited to the bibliographic requirements of libraries, are too complex for it to be applied widely outside that arena.

## The Anglo-American Cataloguing Rules

Probably the best-developed set of rules for describing library-type materials, the Anglo-American Cataloguing Rules (second edition, known as AACR2), based on the concepts established in the International Standard Bibliographic Description (ISBD), are used by most libraries. The rules are particularly important in providing a neutral, standard way of describing names, titles and other elements of a bibliographic record. Maxwell (1989) provides a handbook to describe their use.

The importance of AACR2 is that, while it was never designed for a digital or even hybrid environment, it represents the main, coherent body of work that has established how variants, for example in names, should be handled so as to ensure that all records referring to the same entity use the same form – an obvious example being to bring all works by William Shakespeare together under the same main entry heading so that all can be retrieved when that name, or a variant of it that is referenced to the main heading, is used in a query. AACR2 also defines the order of bibliographic elements and the separators to be used between fields.

Again, the issue is the extent to which AACR2 can be promulgated for digital object description and how it can be used alongside other approaches. There is also a body of opinion that suggests that in very large information spaces complex analysis of natural language queries and relationships is capable of producing at least as successful a retrieval rate as controlled language.

## Other approaches to cataloguing

The examples above concentrate on what might be described as the standard or classic library approaches to cataloguing. They are focused on the description of the printed book as the primary information object, and adapted more or less satisfactorily to other media. But other traditions have developed their own approaches. Greenstein (1999), for example, reports that the UK Arts and Humanities Data Service (AHDS) uses at least five separate major approaches:

- The Archaeology Data Service (ADS) uses a scheme based on the National Geospatial Data Framework.

- The History Data Service (HDS) uses the Data Documentation Initiative's Codebook.
- The Oxford Text Archive (OTA) follows the Text Encoding Initiative (TEI) approach to encoding electronic texts and as a result uses the TEI header for encoding metadata.
- The Performing Arts Data Service (PADS) and the Visual Arts Data Service (VADS) use proprietary formats, the former reflecting the lack of standards within its domain, the latter the proliferation of standards in its field.

In the museums sector the Spectrum standard, developed by the Museum Documentation Association, is widely used in the UK, although there are many proprietary approaches in use. The Consortium for Computer Interchange of Museum Information (CIMI) is active in the development of standards, and has actively supported the use of Dublin Core (see below). Similarly, the archives community has exploited the Encoded Archival Description (EAD) standard.

The importance of these approaches for the library of the future, of course, lies in the nature of digital objects themselves. In networked environments what is retrieved and presented to the user may be a digital representation of a library object such as a book, an archival object such as a manuscript or a museum object such as a glass vase. Each could relate to an enquiry on, let us say, Roman Britain. Each could, assuming the use of appropriate object standards, be displayed to the user. But could they all be found in a single search?

## Resource Description Framework

A generic approach to description syntax, called the Resource Description Framework (RDF), is now under development by the World Wide Web Consortium (W3C) to provide a framework that can be used within any application area in the networked information environment – including for such requirements as e-commerce, digital signatures and content rating systems (World Wide Web Consortium, 2000). The aim is to develop a robust framework within which metadata that can be processed by software is created to common standards.

RDF, which uses XML syntax, is based on a mathematical model that enables metadata statements to be grouped together as 'triples', consisting of a subject (the object being described, eg a particular web page), a property-type (a property of that resource, eg an author) and a value (of that property, eg John Smith). However, triples can also be arranged in complex structures, for example by replacing the value by another triple.

Dublin Core and PICS (see below) are in effect standard schemas within RDF.

## Dublin Core

The Dublin Core (**http://purl.org/metadata/dublin_core/**), so-called because the first meeting of the working group which designed it was held in Dublin, Ohio, was developed to improve resource discovery on the world wide web. Unlike MARC it was deliberately designed to be simple, and uses only 15 'elements' – title, creator, publisher, subject, description, source, language, relation, coverage, date, type, format, identifier, contributor and rights. It is also intended to be generic, and goes beyond the type of objects found in libraries to include museums, art galleries etc – in effect it can be used to provide a description of any information object. For example, rather than 'author' it uses the concept of 'creator': 'the person or organisation primarily responsible for the intellectual content of the resource'. Dublin Core can be mapped to MARC. The Warwick Framework provides a conceptual framework for implementing Dublin Core and other metadata 'packages' to enable interoperability across a variety of domains.

It is also possible to use what is known as 'Qualified Dublin Core', in which an element value is associated with an externally defined scheme, although this clearly requires agreement among the user communities involved to be effective.

Dublin Core, while being probably the best-developed approach to a metadata structure for electronic and especially HTML-encoded information objects, will require very considerable development if it is to succeed. Among the issues that librarians and other players must resolve are:

- The lack of consistency in content as opposed to structure (note again that the RDF approach will enable much greater sophistication in structure). For example, there is little agreement on terminology. There may therefore be a need to develop agreed thesauri for different subject domains – where these do not already exist – and possibly a high-level thesaurus to try to enable interoperability between domains. A combination of existing general schemes, such as Library of Congress Subject Headings (LCSH), Dewey Decimal Classification (DDC) and Conspectus, might contribute to this role.
- Incompatibility between Dublin Core and the dominant systems, such as MARC or the Government Information Locator Service (GILS) system.
- Lack of take-up by the majority of information providers, including the majority of web page creators but more crucially by commercial information

providers. This is of course a classic chicken-and-egg situation: until there is a reasonable level of Dublin Core metadata available, system suppliers are reluctant to expend effort exploiting it so that content suppliers don't create it since there are insufficient systems which can use it.

Despite these problems there is every possibility that Dublin Core will become established, not least because no significant generalized alternatives are available. It might also be seen as the metadata scheme of choice where there is significant interchange *between* communities. Greenstein (1999) describes it as a possible 'lynchpin of cross-domain resource discovery'.

## Subject classification

Classification, along with cataloguing, is core territory for the professional librarian. It is important when considering the technologies of the library of the future to acknowledge the groundwork done by librarians and others in establishing the principles and application of subject classification. The description of content in the sense of its meaning, rather than in terms of more mechanistic attributes, is crucial to successful retrieval for many purposes, whenever a known item search is impossible because the user does not know which items might satisfy an enquiry. The simplest but crudest way to handle this requirement is to use keyword-based retrieval, but the limitations of this approach are well known. Improving subject-based retrieval using various techniques is a major research area and, incidentally, has provided one of the major foci for both the eLib and DLI programmes.

The problems that need to be solved in this area revolve around the systematic description of either the whole of knowledge (as with the Dewey Decimal Classification or the Library of Congress Classification) or a specific domain within it. Achieving interoperability through the use of standard terminology is a major area of research and development effort. Indeed, it could be argued that vocabulary control, or the use of thesauri both to guide subject description (indexing thesauri) and to permit cross-interpretation within and between domains (search thesauri), is one of the next, crucial issues to be tackled within the networked domain. Existing standard schemes, such as the Library of Congress Subject Headings (LCSH), may provide the basis for this work although there are syntactic variations that have appeared over time and cause significant problems. Equally, as librarians know, the necessity to update classification schemes from time to time results in the subject descriptions of older material being incompatible with newer material. As yet, this problem has not been addressed successfully in the digital environment, but it could be an area in which librarians could make a crucial contribution.

## Rights metadata

Efforts are being made to develop standard ways of associating rights information with information objects. The leading contender in this field is the INDECS project (**http://www.indecs.org**) which has the backing of most of the key representative bodies including CISAC and BIEM (representing copyright societies), IFPI (the recording industry), IFRRP (recording rights), ICMP (music publishing) and IPA and STM (book publishers). It also has the support of the International DOI Foundation.

The basis of INDECS lies in the recognition of three types of entity:

* people, including legal 'persons' as well as individuals
* stuff – information objects in the broadest sense
* deals – agreements between people about the use of stuff.

This leads to a triangular series of relationships that is captured in a rubric: *People make stuff; People use stuff; People do deals about stuff.*

It became apparent during 1998 (Bearman et al, 1999) that while there was much commonality between the Dublin Core and INDECS approaches, a considerable amount of work would be needed to make the approaches compatible. At the same time this would provide the opportunity to work towards resolution of some of the problems identified with Dublin Core – for example, the concept of 'creator' was far too simplistic to be useful in a rights negotiation context. A common approach was developed by building on a third metadata model, that produced under the auspices of IFLA and known as the Functional Requirements for the Bibliographic Record (FRBR) – see **http://www.ifla.org/VII/s13/frbr/frbr.pdf/**. This suggests that an information object (or 'information resource' in IFLA's terminology) can exist in four distinct states:

* a *work*, which is the original conception and is produced by a *creator*; this state is an abstraction
* an *expression*, which is a realization of a work – for example with a play two or more directors may produce the same work
* a *manifestation*, which is the embodiment of an expression, as when a printed script and a video of a performance are produced
* an *item*, which is the individual copy of the manifestation and may of course occur in many thousands or even millions of instances for each manifestation.

It will be readily seen that the rights associated with each of these states can be very different and that rights metadata must be capable of distinguishing between them. In other words, the attractive simplicity of Dublin Core must be developed to represent a greater level of metadata complexity. RDF, as described above, has been chosen to provide the necessary complexity of syntax that will enable these relationships to be expressed, and work is continuing on developing a common approach through the Schema Harmonization Working Group. It is perhaps worth noting that the flexibility of Dublin Core and RDF is such that it should be possible for rights metadata to be embedded in such a way that software that needs to use it can do so but other software will still be able to identify and use non-rights metadata. As described above, XML provides the functionality for any community to declare sets of elements that are recognizable within that community and thus to provide the extensibility required without undermining the basic expression.

## Content labelling

Labelling provides a tag or rating to websites or pages (and can in principle be extended to other information objects) that can then be used by software to judge the likely nature of the content. It has been most widely implemented in connection with 'blocking' software designed to screen out undesirable (eg pornographic) Internet content. Labels are applied on the basis of human judgment and in accordance with a standard scheme.

The dominant scheme is the Platform for Internet Content Selection (PICS) (**http://www.w3.org/PICS/#Introduction**), which is being developed by the World Wide Web Consortium (W3C). Essentially, PICS provides a structured language for labelling of Internet content. Labels may be embedded in an HTML document (within the META tag), or may be associated with a document, or may be available as a separate entity referenced through a source document's URL from a 'label bureau'. It is possible for labels to be applied to individual documents or to sites (ie the label can apply to all documents whose URL starts with a specified string of characters). It is also possible to provide both generic and specific labels so that a site can have a more open rating than specific pages within it: obviously, the more specific label should always override the generic ones. Applied properly, labels should always relate to the specific document or site itself, never to documents referenced by it.

Each label consists of three parts:

- a *service identifier*, which is the URL embedded in the label which enables any user to identify and find information on the rating agency
- *label options*, which provide information about the label, such as the date and time it was created
- a *rating*, which is a set of 'attribute pairs', giving the category of the rating and its value: eg category: *violence*; value: *6,* where '6' is defined by the rat-

ing agency as 'graphic' – this example is taken from *SafeSurf*'s system (**http://wwwsafesurf.com/**).

Each document has an associated 'label list': technically this is always the case even if the number of labels is one. Multiple labels can be used to rate different aspects, eg sexual content, violence, and so on.

A serious problem lies in the question of who creates the metadata – if the page designer creates it (unlike in the library parallel where the librarian creates the authoritative metadata, not the publisher) then what guarantee is there of its validity? Apparently, a favourite ploy of certain sex sites is to include terms like 'Ferrari' or 'Lamborghini' so as to broaden their catchment! Deliberate falsification of metadata is likely to be a major problem in open networked information spaces, pointing again to the potential role for libraries in providing quality assurance. While they may be able to do little about messages containing computer viruses described as 'love letters', they will need to find ways to act as effective filters for much published digital content.

Libraries in the USA have been heavily involved in the debate over content labelling because of its implications for the right to freedom of expression contained in the First Amendment to the Constitution, and one of the major issues has been who determines label values. In the UK the argument has been somewhat reversed, with the main concern apparently being to avoid legal action being taken against libraries for permitting access to illegal content. The issues were examined in the Extremism and the Internet (EMAIN) study at the Centre for Research in Library and Information Management (CERLIM) at the Manchester Metropolitan University (Brophy, Craven and Fisher, 1999).

## Directories

Directory approaches are important for managing collections of information about both information objects and the users of information. Typical current applications include holding addressing information, providing very fast lookup because of their hierarchical structure, but they have much wider significance. The major standards are:

- X.500, which provides a universal hierarchical structure; applications are distributed and the aim is to put a global system in place
- *Lightweight Directory Access Protocol* (LDAP), which provides a simpler means of accessing and querying X.500 directories as well as facilities for addressing non-X.500 directories

- WHOIS++, a separate distributed directory system that is falling in popularity as X.500 and LDAP become dominant; it is, however, used by the UK higher-education subject gateways.

The EC-funded People and Resources Identification for Distributed Environments (PRIDE) project is currently exploring the application of directory services using X.500 and LDAP to library services. A distributed directory would contain both service descriptions and personal user profiles, the latter enabling one-stop declaration of personal identification and credit data. The service descriptions would enable the identification of suitable services, including terms and conditions and would thus support authentication and authorization across very large numbers of widely distributed services. User profiles would enable 'push' or selective dissemination of information (SDI) services to be delivered. Since it is likely that in the real world of library services, each library will wish to provide access to literally thousands if not tens or hundreds of thousands of data services, to large numbers of individuals, efficient distributed directory services – which are proven to be scalable – seem likely to provide the best way to manage services to end-users in the long-term. It is likely that the first major application of the PRIDE approach will be in Australia.

## Managing objects and metadata
### Associating objects, identifiers, metadata and locations

It will be clear from the above discussion that one of the major challenges facing libraries – indeed facing the networked information world as a whole – will be associating each object with its identifier, with metadata describing it and with locations where the object may be retrieved. It is worth noting that there are a number of different mechanisms available to achieve this. The RDF model, to take one pertinent example, suggests that metadata can be associated with objects in at least four different ways:

- by embedding it within the object, as in HTML where the metadata tag forms part of the HTML page
- by holding the metadata separately from the object but delivering it with the object when that is requested – as with the HTTP GET or HEAD commands
- by holding the metadata separately from the object and requiring a separate request for it – for example, using an HTTP GET request to a service bureau

- by embedding the object within the metadata, known as 'wrapping'; an example of this is provided for within RDF itself.

A particular complexity is that for any given object use may be made of more than one of these methods, and each can be used more than once. So, for example, there may be metadata held by more than one service bureau as well as embedded metadata. An interesting development is the use of metadata within the DOI system, with the bibliographic sector as the pilot implementation (International DOI Foundation, 1999).

## Collection description

A particular issue in the electronic environment is to find standard ways in which *collections* can be described. As the number of searchable resources (library catalogues, websites, other datasets, and so on) expands, it is no longer feasible to rely on the user selecting particular collections to search manually. Nor is it a scalable approach for librarians to list resources of possible interest on a web page. What is needed are ways of describing collections so that software can handle selection, at least within parameters set by the user. Collection descriptions will need to provide for subject, level, scope, geographical location, access policy and a whole range of other attributes and will need to cover collections of analogue, digital and hybrid resources.

At the time of writing considerable work was underway on defining models and schemas for collection description. In the UK the Research Support Libraries Programme (RSLP) has funded a project to take this issue forward with involvement from UKOLN and Oxford University Library Services (**http://www.ukoln.ac.uk/metadata/rslp/**).

## Searching for and retrieving digital objects

The problem of identifying the existence of an appropriate digital object remains at the core of information access and thus at the heart of many library services. It is beyond the scope of this book to go into the detail of information retrieval systems, although it must be noted that highly sophisticated approaches to text, image, audio, multimedia and other objects are being developed. For example, shape recognition technologies, drawing in part from work on satellite-based earth observation, are maturing to the extent that they have become practical approaches to the retrieval of images from large databases.

The scale of the world wide web is such that it is not feasible to carry out real-time searches in response to user queries. Instead search engines index the content of the web and it is these, very partial, indexes that are searched.

Various approaches to index building are adopted. Some search engines rely entirely on software-based algorithms while others use human indexers to sift through pages that may be submitted to them or may be culled by their systems, using web crawlers, knowbots and harvesters.

## Z39.50

The main communications standard used between library systems is now Z39.50 (an American NISO standard but now with international acceptance), which assumes the use of a client–server (in Z39.50 parlance an origin–target) model. In essence the client (eg the user PC or local library system) requests a service from the server (eg a remote library catalogue system). The server performs functions on behalf of the client, as specified in the request, and returns a result set – this will then be interpreted by the client software and turned into, for example, a display of catalogue records. The client only needs to 'understand' the Z39.50 syntax in order to query any compliant server anywhere in the world. For distributed systems this is of course essential.

It is important to note that the client does not have to be an end-user, but can be another piece of software. Provided both client and server are Z39.50 compliant it should in theory be possible for any client to query any server and receive back an interpretable set of results. In practice it has proved difficult to achieve this, partly because of different implementations of the standard by software suppliers, and partly because of incompatibilities in the internal structure and content of records returned by the server.

In order to address these issues, systems suppliers and librarians have agreed a number of 'profiles' that specify an agreed way to implement Z39.50. The 'Bath Profile' (The Bath Group, 2000) is a recent attempt to provide a specification that can gain wide acceptance and is already proving effective (see **http://www.ukoln.ac.uk/interop-focus/bath**). It has been recognized by ISO as an Internationally Registered Profile – the National Library of Canada is acting as the maintenance agency.

Much more work remains to be done to overcome the implementation problems of Z39.50, however, and partly for this reason it still has limited acceptance outside the library arena – most practical experience of it is with public domain library catalogues. Its limitations include:

- Lack of agreed structure for the representation of local holdings and availability data, which is crucial to the completion of most end-user searches, ie a user wants to know not that a remote library has a copy of a given item in its catalogue but whether the item itself is available and at which location (eg branch). For example, while there has been agreement on how to return holdings information from a target, the availability field is defined as text – it could be represented as 'on loan' or 'due back . . .' or in many other ways that cannot readily be interpreted and manipulated.

- Loss of branding, so that the originator cannot be guaranteed acknowledgment on the end-user's display. This could make the Z39.50 approach unacceptable to some commercial companies.
- Complexity and thus high overheads for use.

A number of players, particularly publishers, are using HTTP/XML as a viable, pragmatic alternative. The problem here, of course, could be proliferation of 'standards' and schemas which, while it can be handled at the client end, may not be optimal for content producers and aggregators.

An interesting issue that has yet to be resolved is the efficiency of a distributed search of multiple targets as against the building of union catalogues (ie databases combining records from a range of service providers) to enable direct searching, albeit of a surrogate. Web search engines, as mentioned earlier, use the union catalogue approach by building their own databases of references and locators since it would clearly be impossible to search every web server every time a user issued a query. The problem with this approach is that the union catalogue is never up to date – hence the broken links so often encountered during an Internet search. More work is needed to enable the most effective mix of real-time distributed searching with union catalogues to be determined, but the issue is clearly of the utmost importance for the design of future library systems. It is considered further in the next chapter.

## The ILL protocol

The international standard interlibrary loan protocol, ISO 10160/1 (International Organization for Standardization, 1997) has been agreed as the protocol for the handling of document requests, using three sets of parameters (essentially, who is making the request (library and end-user), what is being requested, and where the item is to be sent). Although not yet widely implemented, most of the library system vendors and major interlibrary lending agencies (including the British Library) are at least in theory committed to supporting it, so that it stands some chance of becoming widespread. However, it has come in for considerable criticism because of its complexity and the systems, communications and management overhead it imposes. At present the major implementations are in Canada (see **http://www.nlc-bnc.ca/iso/ ill/main.htm/**).

## E-business

The discussion in this chapter has largely concentrated on specific technologies of significance for libraries, but it is also useful to place it in a broader context of electronic business. The concepts of e-business and e-commerce are essentially about how individuals and companies can conduct business across the networks, which clearly impacts considerably on intermediaries like libraries. Although a lot of press coverage is concerned with the security of individuals' credit card details, a much more profound revolution is happening in the way that business-to-business commerce is carried out. Individual authentication and authorization will be discussed in Chapter 10, but libraries are increasingly involved in using electronic data interchange (EDI) systems.

Such systems are capable of direct interchange of trading information from computer to computer without human intervention. Early implementations concentrated on order processing, and typical library use would be in the area of acquisitions with orders and reports being transmitted between the library and its supplier automatically. EDI could also be used for added-value services such as notification of new titles. However, early EDI systems used proprietary message formats, making it difficult to generalize approaches or to switch between systems. These have been replaced or updated and most systems now conform to the EDIFACT standards or to a national standard (such as TRADACOMMS in the UK or BISAC in the USA) that is converging with them. It seems likely that the standards used in the future will be XML based as business-to-business e-commerce shifts towards XML for all its applications.

EDI, in whatever form it becomes stable, will become of increasing importance to libraries as a means of structuring trading and other exchanges of data in electronic networked environments. The book sector more generally is heavily committed to the EDIFACT standards and there have been interesting experiments including the development of an EDI module within the PICA library system, which is widely implemented in the Netherlands and Germany (see **http://www.harninger.com/resource/edifact/**).

## Conclusion

This brief survey of the enabling technologies that are likely to impinge on libraries in the opening years of the 21st century has provided only an indication of the range of challenges to be faced. In the next two chapters the discussion is broadened to contextualize these issues and to consider the wider opportunities for new types and levels of library service that are opening up. In the meantime it is worth posing the question as to the extent to which librarians have been, and should be, involved in moving forward the enabling technologies that have been described.

# 9

# The information universe

Information is more useful than money.                    (Esther Dyson, 1997)
A library is thought in cold storage.          (Attributed to Herbert Samuel)

## Introduction

The idea of an 'information universe' was introduced in Chapter 7, as a way of referring to the sum totality of all the information sources available throughout the world, in whatever format. Overlaying this universe of information there are a wide variety of structures, including:

- the structuring of data into information objects, as discussed in the last chapter
- the aggregation of information objects into collections; traditionally, most objects – or at least their surrogates – were represented in more than one collection
- descriptive information, itself part of the information universe, which imposes meaning on the object and collection spaces
- data and structures related to rights, including commercial information such as pricing data, intellectual property rights such as copyright, etc
- services of very many different types based on underlying objects, collections and aggregates of collections, and including search, retrieve and delivery services
- governmental, legal and commercial structures, which relate to the acquisition, possession and retransmission of classes of information objects defined in various ways, for example by commercial interests and national security.

Libraries are heavily involved in this structuring process. In the past their involvement was centred on the selection of a sub-set of the objects available, providing description and structure to the ensuing collection, and taking steps to make it available to a defined user population. However, once libraries shift their focus away from collection building (in the sense of building collections of physical artefacts) towards a role as intermediaries that provide their users with access to remote sources, then their interests must also shift. Libraries cannot remain neutral while others design the systems and services on which they will rely. As a result, libraries must now take a very real and close interest in their regional, national and international information environments. It is the role of libraries in building these broader information environments that is the subject of this chapter. It begins however, by considering the broad policy context as evidenced by the development of national information policies.

## Global and national information policies and infrastructures

In the emerging and rapidly evolving information society it is becoming apparent that failure to plan strategically at international and national level could be disastrous. The interests of societies and their governments intermesh with a strong information sector, and even if market economics play a major role, governments cannot simply stand by and hope that appropriate structures emerge. The idea of a Global Information Society, with a Global Information Infrastructure (GII), has occupied meetings of the G-7 nations since the mid-1990s. In 1995 eight principles were agreed as the basis for work to develop the GII (G-7 Information Society Conference, 1995):

- promoting dynamic competition
- encouraging private investment
- defining appropriate regulatory frameworks
- providing open access to networks.

while

- ensuring universal provision of and access to services
- promoting equality of opportunity to the citizen
- promoting diversity of content including cultural and linguistic diversity
- recognising the necessity of worldwide cooperation with particular attention to less-developed nations.

International goodwill and good intentions are not enough however. To make matters more complex the interrelationships between sectors and information providers mean that there are an enormous number of stakeholders to consider. Users frequently cross neat boundaries, shifting from being a citizen looking for, say, government information, to being a consumer of entertainment, to being a student within an online learning environment to being a researcher seeking current survey data. Furthermore, users may become producers – by putting up web pages, or perhaps by creating an artistic object. And as produters their interests may conflict with those they have as consumers. Into this confusing mix of roles have to be added the interests of major corporate producers – publishers, film producers, newspaper proprietors and others, many of them operating across national boundaries. Yet another group of stakeholders consists of the 'information transport' agencies: broadcasters, Internet Service Providers (ISPs), cable companies and telecommunications companies.

In addition to these technological considerations, the legislative frameworks that nations put in place need to recognize the realities of this complex web of relationships. There are few guiding principles. Freedom of access to information is a fine banner, until it trips over confidentiality, privacy or the use of information as a valuable commodity – and if the last is denied, the whole basis of the new information society is removed. Among the better-articulated principles are those set out by US Vice-President Al Gore in 1994 (Kranich, 1996), which were clearly influential on the G-7 conference in 1995:

(1)    Encouragement of commercial investment;
(2)    Provision and protection of competition;
(3)    Provision of open access to the network;
(4)    Action to avoid creating a society of information haves and have nots; and
(5)    Encouragement of flexible and responsive government action.

Moore (1997) draws attention to the fact that these approaches have a great deal of commonality across the world – they are not just the stuff of G-7 meetings:

> The hopes and aspirations of Bill Clinton and Al Gore in the USA are, when it comes down to the development of an Information Society, uncannily like those of Jiang Zemin and Li Peng in China. They are a set of aims that are shared by the G7 nations, by developing countries like Thailand, by newly industrialized countries like South Africa and by small but mature economies like Belgium or Finland.

Among key policy concerns, then, are the encouragement of an advanced information and communications infrastructure, improved competitiveness including improved productivity, the development of appropriate legal and regulatory frameworks, societal and political development, social inclusion, personal well-being and lifelong learning. The last of these will be considered in the next chapter, but some comment on the others is appropriate here.

## Encouraging ICT infrastructure

A coherent national policy is needed to ensure that a modern telecommunications network is developed and made pervasive, that there is sufficient bandwidth to enable new and increasingly multimedia businesses to exploit it and that pricing is balanced to ensure wide take-up across all sectors of society coupled with sufficient return on capital to encourage investment. In addition most governments are taking steps to encourage advanced research and development in information technologies, taking the USA's Silicon Valley as the model. In the UK, for instance, high technology research, development and exploitation have been concentrated in the Cambridge area (sometimes called Silicon Fen), the Thames Valley and in the Glasgow area (Silicon Glen) – although it is an interesting question as to whether this has been assisted by any explicit government policies. While developments in Scotland have certainly been helped by some regional aid packages, the Cambridge concentration owes more to the proximity of a world-class university and that in the Thames Valley to its closeness to Heathrow Airport.

## Competitiveness

There is no doubt that the global economy is a reality, with individual governments less and less able to influence events on the world stage and even the economic environments within their own nations. National economies are simply players on a single global stage: exchange rates are in effect set by the markets with governments, or independent national banks, acting at arms-length on their behalf, setting base rates in response to global pressures. Multinational corporations have enormous power to influence national prosperity, recent upheavals in the automobile manufacturing sector being a particularly graphic case in point for UK citizens.

Governments are not entirely powerless in the face of these pressures, of course, but they must increasingly act in response to competition from other nations. Multinationals look keenly at the costs of production and distribution, and the factors they take into account include local wage rates, including social security costs, taxation, the costs of compliance with environmental and other regulations, the availability of a skilled workforce and ease of distribution – increasingly using technology. Factors of less importance include costs of raw materials, since these can be imported, the value of in-place manufacturing plant and national or local allegiance.

Although much information provision is global, there is still competitive advantage to be gained from possessing a strong national, regional or local information infrastructure. This may be seen as comprising the networks themselves, with good connectivity, adequate bandwidth, high reliability and so on;

the content, so that, for example, information on legislative frameworks or on local suppliers is readily available and is reliable; a suitable legislative framework to enable e-commerce to flourish and protect intellectual property; nodes or portals which provide structure and suitable mediated access; and a trained, ICT-aware workforce. It is also worth noting that a strong *local* infrastructure encourages innovative local businesses with the potential for expansion. For example, a small start-up company that can engage in e-commerce locally is in a good position to expand beyond its locality and address a regional, national or international market. Garage-based set-ups in the USA provide an interesting and much-talked-about role model.

## Legal and regulatory frameworks

It is still not clear what changes are needed in legal and regulatory provisions to enable the information society to flourish, but the following are some of the areas that need attention:

- information content: issues relate to intellectual property rights including patent rights, trademarks and copyright, and to rights of ownership and use – especially what it means to transfer ownership of a copy of a digital object
- e-commerce: a vast range of issues ranging from contract law and accounting procedures through authentication and non-repudiation to financial regulation and taxation
- infrastructure: pricing and access issues related to information and communications technology infrastructure, including such issues as the impacts of licensing of bandwidth for mobile communications and terrestrial broadcasting
- personal rights: freedom of information, copyright exemptions, data protection and privacy are just a few of the issues.

A major concern is how to regulate cross-border transactions, one of the reasons that the trend is towards larger trading blocks, such as the North American Free Trade Area and the European Union, where it is possible to harmonize regulations.

## Societal and political development

Government clearly has to take account of the fact that information and communication technologies are not limited in scope to business and private spheres but impact in a wide variety of ways on society, on governance and on political activity. Moore (1997) suggests that 'rising levels of crime, unemployment and social deviancy worry politicians and they see the creation of an Information Society as a means of halting the slide into chaos'.

A feature of information policy development is the extent to which governments see it as a way of transforming governance, perhaps through strengthened freedom of information legislation coupled with efforts to deliver government online or through such measures as e-voting. To date progress in these directions has been limited, but there is an open question as to whether in the future we will see the relationship between government and citizens changing through use of technology. Far more frequent e-referenda would be one possibility, for example.

An intriguing issue is the extent to which we should regard the concept of 'local community' as embracing cybercommunities. A particular concern is whether it is 'healthy' ( a loaded term!) to encourage individuals to pursue all their interpersonal relationships in virtual space. Without attempting to analyse the issues contained in the last short sentence, it is appropriate to note that cybercommunities do need their information portals, and that perhaps libraries could usefully analyse their possible roles as support mechanisms within such structures. The generic model of Chapter 7 would suggest that there is plenty of scope for such a role to be realized.

## Social inclusion

Exclusion from full participation in society can take many forms, some direct and some indirect. The UK's Department for Culture, Media and Sport (DCMS) has noted that while social exclusion is frequently experienced as an individual problem – a 'personal misfortune' – the evidence suggests that it is best tackled as a community issue. 'Successful policies for social inclusion must encourage people to take joint action on issues affecting their neighbourhood' (Department for Culture, Media and Sport, 1999). Furthermore it is noted that:

> . . . a key feature of a sustainable community is its connections. People living in affluent communities tend to have good road systems, trouble-free service from public utilities, access to quality education and health services, access to legal and financial services, access to leisure opportunities, access to political processes, and access to information and communication channels. By contrast, a feature of life in the least integrated communities is that such connections are not well-established.

Although these comments were made in the context of a policy paper on public libraries, their import is considerably broader.

## Personal well-being

Governments are becoming increasingly interested in how information and communication technologies can be used to enhance citizens' personal well-being. A focus of this activity at present is on health services, where the emphasis is shifting away from 'information for health' as the concern only of researchers and practitioners towards direct access by and delivery to the citizen. The UK's new National electronic Library for Health (NeLH) has as one of its basic principles that it will 'be equally open to patients and clinicians, the public and managers' and it will be constructed with a 'patient information floor':

> . . . many patients are better educated than the clinician. Furthermore, the patient may only have one problem whereas the clinician has to deal with hundreds, so the principle of giving patients always and only less information than clinicians is unsustainable for the 21st century. Furthermore, patients are already consulting the world wide web and bringing detailed . . . information to the consultation.
>
> (NHS Information Authority, 2000;
> http://www.guideline.gov/asp/splash2.asp?cp=t&ck=t)

It is interesting to compare this statement with that from the more litigious environment of the USA where the Agency for Health Care Policy and Research's *National Guideline Clearinghouse* has a specific message for patients accessing its site:

> If you are a patient and are accessing this site, you should understand that the information presented is intended and designed for the use of . . . expert audiences. . . . You should seek assistance from a health care professional in interpreting these materials and applying them in individual cases.

## Structure of information policies

There are very few 'command' economies left in the world and governments cannot readily develop master plans in any sector, let alone one as dynamic as information and communications, and expect them simply to be implemented. In thinking about national information policies it is useful, therefore, to consider them as consisting of a series of components that together contribute to a coherent whole. Rowlands (1997) suggests that it is useful to consider:

- *infrastructural policies*, which apply across the whole of society – these would include taxation policy, employment law, etc

- *horizontal information policies*, which apply across the information sector – an example would be the provision of public libraries
- *vertical information policies*, which are specific to a sector such as, perhaps, the health sector.

It is probably also useful to include in this taxonomy *sub-national policies*, such as those developed at regional or state (as opposed to federal) level since they also impact on the national policy. The national information policy then needs to be seen as the sum total of these various strands and the interplay between them.

## Libraries and national information policies

For all the above reasons, but also because individual information services are now being planned nationally – the National Grid for Learning (NGfL) and New Library: the People's Network being good examples in the UK – a series of issues has to be addressed by librarians that simply do not occur in traditional, localized libraries. There is a need to provide a 'managed environment' within which resources, both traditional and electronic, are provided by and to libraries and others in a coordinated fashion. The role of national libraries, which in the past have taken the main responsibility for developing collections of last resort, is unclear and will depend to a large extent on the leadership they choose to exercise. The UK's Library and Information Commission (nd) described the core issues in the following terms:

- *Content*: digitized text, images, sound and increasingly integrated multimedia packages held in personal, local, regional, national or international databases, together with indexes, catalogues and descriptions to enable the content to be located.
- *Connectivity*: the PCs, local networks, regional and national networks, international connections, together with the routers and software systems that send network traffic to the right destination.
- *Competences*: the skills – both of users and expert intermediaries – needed to provide and use networked information.

In a subsequent publication (Library and Information Commission Research Committee, 1998) two further research themes were added, the *value and impact of library and information services in the information society*, recognizing the need to demonstrate that libraries do add value and that their services have real impacts on people's lives; and, *the economics of library and information services in the information society*, looking both at the investment needed by government to maintain a healthy library and information sector and the 'multiplier' effect of such investment on national, regional and local regeneration and development.

In the context of the US National Information Infrastructure (NII) initiative, American librarians agreed their own set of principles (Kranich, 1996):

> Access to the NII should be available to all regardless of age, religion, disability, sexual orientation, social and political views, national origin, economic status, location, information literacy, etc.
>
> Privacy must be carefully protected and extended.
>
> The intellectual property system should ensure a fair and equitable balance between rights of creators and other copyright owners and the needs of users.
>
> Access must be available everywhere.
>
> The NII should support and encourage a diversity of providers in order to guarantee an open, fair, and competitive marketplace, with a full range of viewpoints.
>
> The design of the NII should facilitate two-way, audio, video and data communication from anyone to anyone easily and effectively.

In the UK, the development of national information policies has had a rather chequered history. Although professionals have lobbied for action for many years, it is only recently that government has appeared to show sympathy for the approach. In March 2000, one of the final acts of the Library and Information Commission, before it was merged into a new organization called Resource: The Council for Museums, Archives and Libraries, was to issue a publication entitled *Keystone for the information age: a national information policy for the UK* (Library and Information Commission, 2000). Using the triumvirate of connectivity, content and competencies as a baseline it suggested that the national policy should address:

- the creation of information networks, including the government's approach to regulation
- how universal access, which would ensure that no one was excluded from access, would be assured
- how interoperability between networks and services would be assured
- the policy for creating content that was primarily intended for the public good
- the effective delivery of content to ensure that it reaches citizens who have an interest in it
- the protection of the citizen and the preservation of electronic content
- a firm commitment to free access to core content, including the rights of individuals to access information about themselves

- the development of universal information literacy (an issue discussed further in the next chapter)
- measures to ensure that the supply of information specialists is adequate
- a framework within which organizations, including all publicly funded bodies, can develop their own information strategies.

In the remainder of this chapter, the focus shifts from the overall policy to the information and communications infrastructures that enable the information universe to be accessed and delivered and the structures within which content is stored, organized and from which it is delivered. In the following chapter the issue of competencies will be addressed.

## The infrastructure of the information universe

The infrastructures that make it possible for libraries to provide access to the information universe are of course varied and complex. The Internet itself is not a network but an interconnected network of networks that exchange data using internationally agreed standards like the Internet Protocol (IP). It uses packet-switching technologies so that data can be routed in many different ways to reach its destination, thus avoiding bottlenecks and system failures. Its design has proved tremendously resilient.

The growth of traffic on the Internet has inevitably led to problems with limited bandwidth and congestion at peak times as well as concerns over security and privacy. Government, universities and private companies have overcome some of these problems by building private networks, such as the Joint Academic Network (JANET and more recently SuperJANET), to which all UK universities are linked, NHSNet linking UK hospitals, and Internet2 in the USA. Currently there is considerable debate as to how widespread access to these networks should be – for example the public library network in the UK will initially use the public networks but is exploring the use of JANET or other options for the future. Public telecommunications networks carry considerable traffic, for example from home users, while the use of mobile networks is expected to mushroom, especially in Europe. It is also important to consider the internal infrastructure of organizations that allow the networking of workstations and the provision of content and applications based on intranets and extranets.

It is difficult to keep pace with the growth and development of information and communications infrastructure. End-user hardware is of course far more powerful than even the largest computers were a quarter of a century ago. Computing power doubles every 18 months or so in accordance with Moore's Law (named after the co-founder of Intel) and the pace shows no real sign of slackening. Storage capacities have increased to the extent that cost is rarely now an issue except for very large applications, so the local storage of information is not usually constrained by available digital space. Graphical user interfaces and applications software have developed to the stage where little additional training is needed to manipulate most kinds of digital information resource, and much of the underlying technology can in any case be hidden from the user. Access to computers is widespread, in the office, in the home, through cybercafés, through public libraries, in educational institutions and via laptops and personal digital assistants. Most are capable of acting as Internet clients and it has become virtually impossible – and fairly meaningless – to calculate the total number in use. Actual use may be a better indicator. The best estimates for Internet use (defined somewhat variably, but most surveys appear to use a definition of 'have used the Internet at least once in the last month') put the Internet population at 242 million world-wide in 1999 (CommerceNet Research Center, 2000) with a projection that by the end of 2005 there will be over 765 million users. The largest concentration of use is in the USA which in 1999 had 92 million users. The UK had 12.5 million, or about 27% of its population. According to a separate report (CommerceNet Research Center, 1999), in the UK 72% of users access the web for work-related activities, 49% have used it to check on the price of goods and services and 27% have used it to make a purchase.

## Content

The digital content available in the world is organized in many different ways and has to be accessed through a variety of mechanisms. It is simplest for descriptive purposes to divide content into that available freely, such as most websites, and that subject to some kind of restriction, such as many electronic journals and databases. In this section the emphasis is on the organization of 'restricted' content since that raises the most significant issues for libraries. Issues related to the description of all kinds of content were covered in Chapter 8.

Taking the UK academic sector as an example, digital content acquisition (including in that term the acquisition of access rights, ie ignoring the question as to whether the data is hosted locally or remotely) has gone through considerable evolution. It began with access to remote, usually bibliographic, data services such as MEDLINE – some libraries acquired tapes of records and ran them on a local machine as an alternative to accessing the remote server. During the 1980s the common pattern was for mediated online searching, the overriding issue being one of constraining costs – charged on some kind of usage basis – and the end result being very little use. Aston University Library pioneered the wide-scale use of full text with the ADONIS biomedical periodical service, installed in 1992-93 using a CD-ROM jukebox. CD-ROM datasets rapidly achieved wide penetration initially in standalone mode, but later being networked using jukeboxes or tower systems. The breakthrough that CD-ROMs delivered was not so much the technology as the shift in economic model – for almost the first time access to digital resources was not constrained by per use charges. It was this concept of 'free at the point of use' that was to prove crucial in the next stage.

The first major higher education data service in the UK was established at Bath University in the early 1990s. Bath Information and Data Services (BIDS) was offering, by mid-2000, the following services:

- the INSPEC data services from the Institute of Electrical Engineers, which provide abstracts of over 4000 journals in the field
- the Royal Society of Chemistry (RSC) data services, which include business and health and safety data as well as the core research information
- the *International Bibliography of the Social Sciences* (IBSS)
- EMBASE, a biomedical information service with coverage that complements that of MEDLINE
- education resources, including ERIC and the *British Education Index*
- the British Library's *Inside Information* service, which indexes every paper from the BL Document Supply Centre's 20,000 most requested titles – this amounts to about 1 million articles a year; it is possible to order articles directly, although this is a commercial service and the costs are considerably higher than with standard interlibrary loan
- *ingentaJournals*, a full-text document delivery service covering about 2000 journals and offering access to well over a quarter of a million full-text articles; publishers participating in *ingentaJournals* include Academic Press, Blackwell Science, Elsevier Science, Oxford University Press and Wiley.

Two other UK academic data centres have been established – EDINA in Edinburgh and MIMAS in Manchester. The above portfolio of services, however, is typical of a UK HE data centre at the present time. Services are selected by the Joint Information Systems Committee (JISC) Committee for Electronic Information (JCEI) Content Working Group, which has developed a collections policy that 'articulates a vision for a distributed national collection of digital information resources including a wide range of information types and delivery modes; serving a very wide range of user constituencies; and supporting learning, teaching, and research' (JISC, 1999b).

The range of data sets supported can be seen to be very wide. They include, for example, bibliographic resources, statistical data sets, mapping data and full-text resources. The economic model underlying these services is first that acquisition of the data set will involve a mix of 'top-sliced' funding from JISC and annual subscriptions from institutions and secondly that the dataset will be free at the point of use. This carries on the model referred to above and developed over a decade ago for CD-ROM datasets. This principle lies at the heart of UK higher education dataset provision, and means that the end-user does not have to constrain use in any way and can explore resources at leisure. Without it, it is doubtful if anything like as much progress would have been made.

The three data centres do not, of course, have a monopoly on data services. Other national services include the Arts and Humanities Data Service (AHDS), mentioned in Chapter 8, the Data Archive at the University of Essex, the National Electronic Site Licensing Service (NESLI) and the UK Mirror Service, which hosts copies of mainly US data services. In addition, institutions continue to have access to the full range of other commercial services, including those delivered on CD-ROM or other media.

## Delivering the content

The range of services, including in this category the free services that do not need to be subject to negotiated licences, is now so large that it is clear that added-value services will be needed to enable users to cope with the plethora of provision. One of the major successes of the Electronic Libraries Programme (eLib) has been the subject gateways like EEVL (engineering – **http://www.eevl.ac.uk/**), Biz/ed (business and economics – **http://www.bized.ac.uk/**) and SOSIG (social sciences – **http://sosig.ac.uk/**). These provide quality-assured web-based collections of electronic resource pointers in specific academic disciplines. Each resource represented has been quality-checked by an experienced professional (librarian or subject expert) and professionally catalogued. The ROADS software package, developed by UKOLN, provides the software base for these services (**http://www.ukoln.ac.uk/roads/**) and includes management facilities, for example to enable link checking.

One of the major benefits of these gateways is that they remove the need for individual libraries to assess and catalogue the electronic resources in each subject area. Instead a national service provides an authoritative resource that can be linked from each library's own website. In effect they are a mechanism for resource sharing at the national (and possibly, given current discussions with the USA) international level.

Early gateway developments are now leading to more sophisticated services and it is useful to distinguish, as far as is possible, between the different types. Although terminology tends to be used rather loosely, and not everyone would agree with these categorizations, the following have been suggested in discussions on JISC's forward programme of research and development:

- A *gateway* should be regarded as a virtual place that provides signposts to resources. The user enters the gateway, is assisted to select the most useful pointers and then follows them to locate the resources themselves. Typically, a gateway would consist of an ordered list of URLs; when the user clicks on a URL he moves to the site where the resource itself is to be found. The user is a temporary visitor to the gateway, moving rapidly on – but of course quite possibly returning again and again to find more, useful resources.
- A *portal* is a more sophisticated resource. The user sends a query to the portal, which examines it, reformats it and uses it to query a series of other resources that may contain content of relevance. The results from these searches are then concatenated and otherwise processed by the portal (eg to remove duplicates) before being presented back to the user. In essence the user, having entered the portal, never leaves – the portal goes out into the information universe on his or her behalf.

A concept that is starting to take shape is that of 'information fusion', which in essence is a way of describing the service a portal would offer in intelligently drawing together data from different sources and 'fusing' it for presentation as an integrated result set to the end-user.

Rowley (2000), although defining portals in a different way, points out that an organization that provides a successful portal gains four distinct advantages:

1  Strong visibility in cyberspace, coupled with a more high-tech image.
2  The opportunity to create a community of consumers who identify with the portal.
3  Control in strategic alliances with partners to whose sites links are made; mutual links might represent a collaborative arrangement, but organisations without such ready access to an online consumer community may be at a disadvantage in strategic alliances in virtual business networks.
4  They can . . . collect data about consumer choices, search paths, and interests. . . . This allows them to create a profile of their community . . . which . . . relates to elements of their behaviour as consumers.

Becoming the portal of choice is therefore of considerable importance. The danger is that there will be a process of 'portal proliferation', as libraries of all types, Internet Service Providers, national subject portals (perhaps funded by national government initiatives like the UK's National Grid for Learning), departments in universities, local government, commercial bodies, learned societies and others jockey for position and for market share. This proliferation is forcing providers to look carefully at how they target their potential audiences – one outcome is the 'vertical portal' or 'vortal' that some publishers are favouring to target their readership in a particular subject domain and to provide added-value services. A second outcome is the 'portal of portals'. The *Pinakes* service at Heriot-Watt University (**http://www.hw.ac.uk/libWWW/irn/ pinakes/pinakes.html**), which describes itself as 'a subject launchpad', might be regarded as a move in this direction although at present it is perhaps better described as a 'gateway to portals' or even 'gateway to gateways'. In its present form it is not scalable to the level required.

A further issue that deserves consideration is that of 'branding'. This becomes apparent when the scenario of a portal reaching into underlying resources is considered from the perspective of the resource supplier. The question is how the 'brand' of the underlying resource can be preserved and drawn to the attention of the end user. For example, if data is retrieved by the portal from, say, a geographic mapping service and then combined with medical data from another service and possibly demographic data from elsewhere, how is due acknowledgment to be given to each supplier? Workstation screens will soon run out of space to display any useful data if everyone's logo has to be incorporated, but at the same time suppliers wish to assert their rights to recognition for obvious commercial reasons. As yet it is unclear how this requirement can be met.

## New developments in content production

Most of the services referred to above rely heavily on long-established publishing paradigms, albeit transferred to the digital environment and with many enhanced features. For example, electronic journals have to date largely appeared as electronic 'copies' of paper-based journals, retaining many of the same editorial and production processes. There are signs, however, that this approach may be starting to break down, at least in the research arena, with the arrival of electronic replacements for the scholarly journal.

Because these new journals display all the characteristics of digital objects (such as speed of initial production, easy production of copies, amenability to distributed storage, accessibility from 'any PC, anywhere') one of their impacts is to break down the economic model on which journal publishing has been based. Instead of charging an annual fee in exchange for transfer of ownership rights to a paper copy of a journal, publishers and agents are testing out alternatives. These include:

- *Licensing* of access to the individual journal, often for a limited time (once the licence expires access, even to older material, is withdrawn) and often with conditions attached – such as limitations on who may view it.
- *Licensing* of access to a set of journals, defined by publisher, which are delivered from the publisher's server as a group. Similar conditions apply.
- *Joint preservation* of access to older material, digitized for the purpose, as for example in the JSTOR project described later in this chapter.
- *Cooperative agreements* for the delivery of journals to a group of libraries, as with the UK JISC data services. Delivery may be from publishers' servers or from mirrors.
- *Commercial aggregators* who bring together electronic journals from a number of publishers and offer access to the group. Examples include *ingenta* and OCLC. Aggregators often provide added-value services, such as enhanced search and retrieval systems.
- *Individual article supply*, which in essence breaks down the journals into their components and charges for each delivery of each part.
- *Electronic interlibrary loan*, a variant of individual article supply, which is based on the idea that libraries should be able to request articles from electronic journals in the same way, and on much the same terms, as traditional interlibrary loan. In particular, a flat fee would be paid for each article. The attraction to publishers would be that they would receive a percentage of the fee, which of course is not the case with traditional, print-based interlibrary loan. At the time of writing JISC and the Publishers Association are collaborating on a pilot 'electronic interlibrary loan' service called EASY (Electronic Article SupplY).

One of the implications of these changes is that libraries will need to move the focus of their attention, in terms of the legal underpinning of their activities, from copyright to contract law – a very significant shift.

Even more fundamentally, the above variants all assume that the established publication chain stays largely intact. However, this assumption is now being challenged widely. As Lyman and Chodorow (1998) remark, 'the system of scholarly communication governing the flow of information and knowledge within the academic community . . . has become unstable'. The same authors draw attention to the difficulty, in a digital, networked environment, of defining a 'publication': 'the electronic format encourages constant change – addition, subtraction, alteration – and its organization is fundamentally different from the one used in printed materials.'

One approach to change in scholarly communication is being led by consortia of libraries and research institutions. For example, the Scholarly Publishing and Academic Resources Coalition (SPARC) in the USA is creating new library–publisher alliances to counter the steep and ever-rising prices being charged by commercial publishers. A SPARC initiative, BioOne, is drawing in learned societies in the biosciences area, thus returning the scholarly journal to its roots. Johnson (2000) claims that this model will 'enable leading non-profit journals self-published by learned societies to remain viable, and offers them a cost-effective alternative to commercial publishers' digital aggregations'.

Stevan Harnad, Director of the Cognitive Sciences Centre at the University of Southampton, is a leading proponent of a new system of scholarly communication under which authors would simply make their papers available freely on the web, making expensive academic journals a thing of the past (Harnad, 2000):

> In the PostGutenberg era of global digital networks . . . there is at last an alternative, and not only researchers, but research itself, and hence all of society, would be the losers if we failed to take full advantage of it. For now we no longer have to rely on the expensive, inefficient and access-limiting technology of print on paper to disseminate research findings. They can be *self-archived* by their authors in public online archives . . . and thereby made accessible to one and all without any financial firewalls.

Ginsparg (1997) describes the development in these terms:

> hep-th@xxx.lanl.gov, the e-mail address for the first of a series of automated archives for electronic communication of research information, went online in August 1991. This 'e-print archive' began as an experimental means of circumventing recognized inadequacies of research journals but unexpectedly became within a very short period the primary means of communicating ongoing research information in formal areas of high-energy particle theory. . . . This system provides a paradigm for recent changes in world-wide, discipline-wide scientific information exchange. It also serves as a model for how the next generation of electronic data highways can provide for electronic transmission of research and other information as access to high-speed computer networks becomes universally available.

The high-energy physics archive, set up at the Los Alamos Laboratory in 1991, now contains in excess of 100,000 articles (**http://xxx.lanl.gov/**). Papers are initially submitted as pre-prints so as to alert the scientific community to research findings as quickly as possible and are then peer reviewed, with the peer-reviewed paper also being archived. More recently a proposal emerged to create a biomedical archiving service, similar to the Los Alamos service, under the title PubMed Central (it had originally been called E-biomed) and this went live at the start of 2000. However, it has come in for considerable criticism and is in any case only accepting peer-reviewed papers from established journals (partly as a reaction to this criticism). This episode is instructive, because it has served to draw attention to a number of issues that need to be resolved in this emerging field (see also Day, 1999):

- There is concern that, without some form of peer review, archives of this type will be filled with inaccurate and misleading information, making the whole enterprise worthless. Particular concerns have been expressed at the effects that this could have in a sensitive area like medical research, an issue that can be linked back to the prominence now given to evidence-based medicine as described in Chapter 2.
- Criticism has come from publishers that in effect the electronic archives will undermine the revenue streams of prestigious and valuable journals before any proven alternative has been put in place and could lead to the collapse of the scholarly publishing process.
- A counter-suggestion to the loss of income is that journals should charge a fee to authors to have their work published and thus maintain low prices or even free access from publishers' servers to enable widespread dissemination. In effect this would simply shift charges from libraries to authors.
- Authors have complained that publishers are being deliberately obstructive by insisting on what appear to the authors to be draconian copyright restrictions preventing a copy of a paper – even before it has been accepted – being deposited and thus threatening exclusion from prestigious journals.
- There is a risk of monopolistic actions (or inaction) by the owners and sponsors of the archives. If an electronic archive becomes an effective monopoly in its subject domain, could it place undue restrictions such as excluding minority subjects or imposing cultural views, or neglect its duties for long-term preservation?
- There is no clear economic model to underpin the long-term activity of e-print archives. Will universities and research institutes be willing to underwrite them in perpetuity, especially in minority subjects?

These issues remain under debate, but for libraries they offer tantalizing glimpses of possible futures. An international grouping, under the title of the Open Archives Initiative (OAI), has been established to encourage development of self-archiving initiatives – its goal is to contribute to the transformation of scholarly communication, and its mission is:

> to create a forum to discuss and solve matters of interoperability between author self-archiving solutions (also commonly referred to as e-print systems), as a way to promote their global acceptance.          (Ginsparg, Luce and Van de Sompel, 1999)

To achieve this it is developing specifications and principles for such archives under the generic title of the Sante Fe Convention, after the meeting-place of the initial founding group (Van de Sompel and Lagoze, 2000). The model adopted uses a three-tiered model of interoperability:

- *document models*, which is a specification for document structure in a repository
- *metadata harvesting*, which allows for the extraction of descriptive metadata
- *mediator services*, which describes the services that use and add value to the information in an archive.

It remains very unclear as to whether this approach will in fact prove attractive across disciplines – since different scholarly communities are constructed very differently – although it is perfectly possible that it could change the face of scholarly publishing. Libraries would potentially save subscription and shelving costs. Perhaps the most intriguing question is how the traditional library's bibliographic functions, including the provision of adequate metadata, of resource discovery mechanisms and of long-term preservation facilities, would be handled. Even more fundamentally, the question would undoubtedly be asked as to whether libraries still had a role to play.

Similar questions might be asked about the library's role in providing access to monographs if either electronic books or wide-scale book production on demand were to take off. These were outlined in Chapter 1 and there is little to add to that description here, except to ask whether libraries could position themselves to provide added-value services, via quality assurance, wide access arrangements and the like, so that they become the access point of choice.

## Cooperation

In many countries, consortium approaches to content organization and access, for both analogue and digital formats, are popular and appear to be operating with renewed vigour: 'consortia are experiencing renewed energy and stronger ties through the cooperative licensing of electronic products' (Forsman, 1998). Various levels of cooperation exist: for example, in the UK the major consortium is national (led by the higher education sector through JISC) while in Germany the approach tends to be based on the Länder and in the USA at state level.

Although cooperative collection development seems to offer an obvious way forward, with each library gaining by specializing in its own areas of interest and being able to rely on others for subjects more peripheral to its, or its parent institution's, interests, such agreements are extremely difficult to put in place and even more difficult to maintain. The problem is twofold. First, budgets are such that libraries tend to purchase only those items of immediate interest to their own users anyway, so there is little slack for, say, additional investment in a particular subject so as to build up national or even international strength. Secondly, because there has been a long period of cutbacks, it is precisely the less common titles – the ones that are best shared – which have disappeared altogether. As Wolf (1998) observes,

> . . . academic library collections, falling back on the retention of 'core' titles, have become more and more mirror-images of each other. This trend, combined with the difficulty of predicting budget cuts and forced cancellations, makes the coordination of any cooperative collection development plan that involves rationalization of holdings a challenge.

## The UK's Distributed National Electronic Resource

Although the organization of the delivery of major resources into data services, as described above, addresses a number of technical and contractual issues, it is fairly clear that further organization is needed if libraries are to be able to provide access to the growing mass of services on offer, if issues of interoperability are to be tackled systematically and if, nationally, maximum efficiency is to be obtained from investment. For this reason attention has turned in a number of countries to the management and organization of distributed resources. One example would be Denmark's Electronic Research Library (DEF), which Kvaerndrup (2000) describes as a 'large, coherent, electronic library structure providing integrated information services'. Another, discussed in greater detail here, is the UK's emerging Distributed National Electronic Resource (DNER).

The DNER, a concept now led by JISC but emerging originally from European-Commission-funded activity and refined in the UKOLN MODELS Workshops (see **http://www.ukoln.ac.uk/dlis/models**), recognizes that information content is provided from many different sources and that there can be no single national depository that can exercise control or impose itself on suppliers. However, JISC has been at pains to point out that, 'The distributed nature of the electronic resource does not imply that the collection will be unmanaged as a whole. The JISC will endeavour to develop it in a coherent, unified way; will promote the use of appropriate standards and will support a national resource discovery agency to ensure unified integrated access to all forms and sources of the material.' (JISC, 1998). The DNER was later described as 'a managed environment for accessing quality assured information resources on the Internet which are available from many sources' (JISC, 1999a).

The collection management policy for the DNER reveals its scope (JISC, 1998):

- Selection decisions will aim to develop a set of complementary and integrated resources in each discipline which include the full range of appropriate types of data and information. . . . A major objective will be to build a critical mass of information in individual disciplines.
- In managing the acquisition of content [JISC] will take a very broad perspective on the material it selects.
- Material selected for collection might have been developed either in digital or analogue form (such as microfilm and print).
- The resources will not be restricted to such traditional resources as scholarly journals, monographs and textbooks, but will extend to manuscripts, maps, and music scores. . . . It will include such categories of material as moving and still images, sound, and textual resources.
- Increasingly there will be needs for the digitisation of sound recordings, diagrams, photographs and slides for use by disciplines ranging from medicine to computational linguistics, and the content creation and acquisition programme will aim to address these requirements.
- Resources will be included which meet teaching and learning needs, and others will support research work.
- At all levels, in addition to primary data, material will be sought which provides added value through synthesis, analysis and commentary. This material would serve both to signpost a set of resources as well as to open them up to ensure their most appropriate use by the academic community.

A new programme of development, including the integration of DNER services with learning and teaching environments, was launched by JISC in mid-2000.

## Securing rights and delivery on demand

Libraries have long been in the business of protecting intellectual property rights, both by acting as part of a carefully controlled distribution chain and by enforcing restrictions on their users – to a greater or lesser extent. The personal signature required on a copyright declaration before a library will obtain a photocopy for a user is one example of this function, although publishers and other rights holders have long complained that open-access photocopiers allow users to flout the law. The emergence of copyright licensing agencies is in part a response to this perception and most UK libraries now hold licences for a variety of media – although not, usually, for electronic documents which have to be cleared individually.

An interesting strand of the UK eLib Programme was concerned with the development of 'on-demand publishing', which in the context of higher education was interpreted as the creation of electronic anthologies of core texts that could be printed as and when users made requests for them. Such systems would offer the benefits of continuous and simultaneous electronic access, and fast, flexible delivery of core material, without requiring libraries to expend resources on first acquiring many multiple copies of conventionally published texts. Potentially there would be advantages for publishers in avoiding up-front production and distribution costs.

The aim of these projects was to address a model with the following features:

- close involvement with publishers and/or book suppliers
- simple and effective mechanisms for copyright control and payment
- appropriate standards for storage and delivery
- adaptation to the UK university requirement
- approaches to encouraging a cultural change in the way texts were used in institutions.

Although the initial projects were not particularly successful, largely because the business model and the problem of copyright control proved much bigger problems to resolve than first anticipated, the issue was of sufficient importance, and the chances of success sufficiently high, for eLib in its final phase of projects to fund a single new service development. Known as Higher Education Resources ON-demand (HERON – **http://www.stir.ac.uk/infos-erv/heron/project.htm**) and administered jointly by the University of Stirling and Napier University, Edinburgh, it is intended to provide a national service that will take advantage of the potential economies of scale and of experience in negotiating rights clearance. Thus HERON will:

- develop a national database and resource bank of electronic texts that will widen access to course materials; the database will provide pointers to other collections as well as holdings, the latter including published book chapters and journal articles
- collaborate with rights-holders and representative bodies to remove blockages in copyright clearance and to determine appropriate conditions, including fees
- offer opportunities to universities to market their own resources.

Although this example is significant in the context of higher education, the safeguarding of intellectual property rights for electronic information objects is a subject of far wider concern since it underpins efforts to develop e-commerce.

The rights metadata work described in Chapter 8 forms part of the work needed to address this area as does work on authentication and authorization which will be discussed in Chapter 10, but of equal significance are efforts to find hardware and software solutions to prevent unauthorized copying and re-use of digital objects. There are a number of approaches that may become significant in the future:

- Technical blocks of one kind or another, which prevent access to the object unless the user has the key. These are familiar with software delivered, say, on CD-ROM where the user has to key in a code to load the software. Unfortunately they provide limited security against copying while also preventing some legitimate access.
- Digital watermarks, which may be perceptible or imperceptible to the end-user.
- The use of cryptography to prevent 'leakage' of objects between the supplier and end-user.
- The use of formats from which it is difficult to extract data, such as bitmaps for page images rather than text strings.
- The development of the concept of 'protected resources', which consist of databases of digital objects together with software-based resource managers that prevent unauthorized access. This is a typical library approach, but suffers from lack of control on forward copying unless coupled with another technology.

One of the problems that has not yet been successfully addressed is that approaches must be both scaleable and administratively inexpensive. Collections of tens of thousands of objects cannot be protected if some kind of individual attention has to be given to each object. This would suggest that for most library-type applications, although possibly not across the broader information e-commerce field, an approach based on authentication and authorization of users, coupled with resource protection, may provide the best, at least interim, solution. It is worth noting that in many sectors the delivery of an unprotected information object to an end-user is unlikely to result in significant loss to the rights holder – very few academics would set up their own onward supply operation for such objects on any significant scale and in any case they would be fairly easily detected if they tried to do so. The existing copyright licensing arrangements for paper-based resources, whereby regular surveys gather data on usage that then informs both blanket licensing and the distribution of royalty payments to rights holders, would seem to offer much practical advantage at the present time.

## Intelligent agents and push services

The development of intelligent agents, sometimes called 'bots' (and in the information industry, 'knowbots') is of interest in terms of document access and delivery although the territory is relatively unexplored. Agents take a query from a user and act on his or her behalf to find a solution – they may thus be part of the portal's service infrastructure. Typical of these is the 'shopping bot', which uses a customer's stated requirement for a product to visit a range of e-shopping sites, collecting data on price, availability etc. The results are sorted and presented to the user, who may then issue a 'buy' order. The application of this to information products is not yet well established.

A second area, that of push services, has been mentioned earlier but poses some interesting issues for libraries that wish to deliver such services. In particular the management of content within the source database, of data feeds into it and of user profiles all pose significant challenges.

## Parallel and serial searching across heterogeneous resources

Since search, retrieval and delivery processes are at the core of library systems, there is a major issue to be addressed concerning the management of these processes in the broad information space of national and international resources. Because of the problem of searching across hundreds of databases, it is in many cases essential that software is able to take a query from a user and search a selection of databases before returning results to the user in a sensible form (for example, removing duplicate entries) – hence the development of portals. So, if a user presents a query about a particular author, for example, the software should query a series of catalogues and present the results as a single result set, perhaps displaying the database originating each result or some other indicator of location and/or origin. The user does not want a scrolling display of what the software has found, line by line, as results come in. For this reason, considerable effort (not least in the eLib Phase 3, hybrid library and clump projects) is being expended on 'parallel' searching.

However, there are many occasions when the user in fact wants the software to perform a mix of parallel and serial searches. For example, he or she may want to query the local library catalogue first, then, if that does not produce a satisfactory result, other library catalogues in the vicinity, and only if there is still no result, perform a parallel search of a wide number of catalogues to try to identify a copy that might be available on interlibrary loan. A similar scenario could be painted for a subject search.

Interworking between heterogeneous services is a complex issue that needs to take account of a series of potential pitfalls and in particular the interoperability issues (technical, semantic, political/human, inter-community, international, accessibility) described in Chapter 8. There is still a long way to go in securing standardized implementation of standards and protocols, interworking of terminologies across different application domains, and communication of data, such as authentication statements, between heterogeneous applications.

Partly as a result of the difficulties of searching multiple data sets, there is currently renewed interest in union catalogues, as mentioned in the last chapter – see also Dovey (2000) where four different models of the union catalogue are described. Lynch (1997) set out the issues clearly:

> From a technical point of view, it seems clear that both centralized union catalogs and systems that can support intelligent distributed search offer important benefits to users, and that they can be used together in a complementary fashion to great advantage. Centralized catalogs are still the best way to support high volume searching against fixed collections that reflect explicit consortia or other resource-sharing arrangements, and which users will want to search regularly with high precision and performance. Indeed, centralized union catalogs can stand as visible symbols of such resource sharing arrangements. Distributed search can be used to provide a way of delivering on the promise that the networked information environment offers for enabling user to define arbitrary virtual information collections that span organizational and geographical boundaries. Both approaches continue to be relevant as we consider the broader environment of catalogs, abstracting and indexing databases, and primary content proliferating in a distributed network environment.

For those responsible for building services which provide access to multiple collections, the issues are thus complex and require careful consideration of the advantages of each model and the most cost-effective blend of approaches. Terminology is also somewhat confused: 'union catalogue' is sometimes used to include the searching of multiple targets, as in a clump, but sometimes restricted to mean only those catalogues which are physically combined in one dataset – the sense in which Lynch uses the term. The point at which maintenance of a union catalogue, in this latter sense, becomes more cost-effective than searching multiple targets is unclear. In the UK a feasibility study into a UK-wide National Union Catalogue (UKNUC), led by Sheffield University, was launched in Spring 2000 and will no doubt be addressing these issues.

## Preservation

The long-term preservation of information objects has in the past been a responsibility not only of libraries but also of other kinds of 'memory institution' – museums, art galleries, archives and others. While not all libraries and information services have played a significant part in this activity in the past, some seeing their role only in terms of the provision of access to current literature, the need for long-term preservation is widely recognized.

The 1998 European Parliament Green Paper on *The role of libraries in the modern world* (Rynänen, 1998) saw this preservation role as fundamental (although omitting to mention the role of other memory institutions):

> The unique function of libraries is to acquire, organize, offer for use and preserve publicly available material . . . in such a way that, when it is needed, it can be found and put to use. No other institution carries out this long-term, systematic work.

It is interesting that in the Parliament's debate on the Green Paper the issue of preservation – although, oddly, frequently expressed as a need to make use of 'permanent paper' – was prominent in the contributions from many MEPs.

The problem is of course not limited to the preservation of paper-based and other traditional media. Digital material is also subject to deterioration and loss, although the rate of loss in different digital media is as yet unclear. There are a number of problems that need to be addressed:

- Physical deterioration of the medium on which the data is stored. For example, there is still considerable uncertainty about the expected shelf-life of CD-ROMs.
- Technological change, which makes reading equipment obsolete and thus may make archives virtually inaccessible. For example, it is highly unlikely that CD-ROM players will still be widely available in ten or 20 years' time.
- Dynamic content, since digital content may change rapidly. An example would be a website offering a range of goods for sale, where updating of each page results in the loss of earlier versions. (In fact the pages would probably be created dynamically from a database, itself dynamic and almost certainly unpreserved.)
- Non-persistent identifiers, which mean that if a web page or other object is moved to another site, or re-addressed within a site, it becomes effectively lost.
- Security, especially loss by fire or water damage of materials where only one master copy is held.

- Responsibility, since it is by no means obvious that the archival functions of libraries with traditional media can be carried over into the electronic era. For example, few websites are currently archived in any systematic way.

A number of useful experiments and projects are being carried out into how digital preservation can be achieved, including the eLib CEDARS (CURL Exemplars in Digital ARrchiveS – **http://www.curl.ac.uk/cedarsinfo.shtml/**) project based at the London School of Economics and the *Internet Archive* (**http://www.archive.org/**), which has been archiving the web since 1986 and currently holds over a billion web pages acquired by taking snapshots of sites (see Kahle, 1997). It is important to note that in this context, 'digital preservation' is a term used to describe the preservation of digital objects: there are separate issues concerned with the use of digital technologies to preserve traditional objects, for example by creating page images of manuscripts – this is the approach of the important JSTOR (Journal STORage) project (**http://www.jstor.org/** – there is a UK mirror at **http://www.jstor.ac.uk/**). This initiative has developed a digital archive of over 100 scholarly journals, including some of the earliest scientific journals such as the *Philosophical Transactions of the Royal Society of London*. For each journal the archive begins with the first published issues and covers material up to a 'moving wall' set at between one and eight years before the current volume. JSTOR originated in the USA, being funded initially by the Andrew W Mellon Foundation, but has become an independent, not-for-profit organization generating revenue through access charges that are deliberately set at a level below the cost of storing paper copies of backruns. Because the operation concentrates on older material it avoids competition with publishers, who have generally been willing to negotiate contracts with JSTOR. At present 15 subject fields are covered, mainly in the humanities and social sciences.

Feeney (1999) reports on a national strategy being developed in the UK under the auspices of the Digital Archiving Working Group. This Group has surveyed the preservation issues of the major stakeholder groups, and suggests that it is helpful to consider the issues from two major perspectives, those of:

- players involved in the electronic publication cycle, from authors through publishers and distributors to libraries
- those involved in the use of electronic publications, primarily the research community, although noting that the research community also contains the originators of much electronic material – indeed this could be regarded as a kind of alternative publication cycle, following the electronic archive developments described earlier in this chapter.

This analysis has led to the identification of a number of issues, going well beyond the purely technical, that need to be addressed in this area:

1  The issue of intellectual property rights. Publishers are particularly concerned about the timing of electronic material deposit and how this might affect their commercial interests. This reiterates the concern that a single 'free' copy available on a network could destroy the market and thus the publishers' income stream. At the same time the view has been expressed that while an item retains commercial value it is in the publisher's or distributor's own interests to ensure its preservation.

2  The question of how integrity of information objects can be guaranteed over long periods of time. For example, one use of watermarking is to provide evidence of integrity, but without a persistent standard this could simply lead to the inaccessibility of older items.

3  Whether 'accidental' preservation could solve much of the problem. The argument here is that there is a kind of natural selection at work, whereby items that are most useful tend to be preserved anyway. It is worth remembering that archives are traditionally highly selective in the material they keep, so that a possible way forward is a kind of 'enhanced natural selection' – for example, peer-reviewed electronic journals would always be preserved but more general websites might be treated rather differently. There seems to be some consensus that the amount of electronic material being produced makes any attempt at comprehensive archiving impossible.

4  It may be helpful to separate the 'access' and 'preservation' roles when planning for preservation, so that the creation of an archival copy is a distinct process.

5  There is a need for the research community to have access to authoritative advice, guidance and standards, perhaps through a centre or network of centres. It is worth noting under this heading the work of the Arts and Humanities Data Service (**http://www.ahds.ac.uk**) and a useful report on digital preservation guidelines prepared for the European Commission (Fresko and Tombs, 1998).

A number of different methods of digital preservation are available, which can helpfully be considered as: *migration* – where an information object is transferred from its native technological base to another; *emulation* – where software is provided to enable the old format to be interpreted in a new technological framework; and *technology preservation*, which involves maintaining the old hardware/software platform as well as the content. Each of these approaches has its problems. Migration may destroy or alter part of the original structure and content, is expensive if there are large numbers of objects and if it has to be repeated, and is less and less feasible as objects become increasingly complex. Emulation is difficult because digital environments are inherently complex and becoming more so (trying to emulate pre-DOS environments in Windows 2000 is no easy matter, for example) so that the emulation may lose or alter features of the original, or simply not work with all objects. Technology preservation is unscalable as the number of platforms used historically increases and in any case maintaining hardware – such as, for example, a CD-ROM drive – for tens or hundreds of years is fraught with difficulty.

As yet there is no agreement on the most appropriate approach, although in practice a combination of all three seems the most likely way forward.

Steenbakkers (1999) reports on the innovative electronic publications depository established in the Netherlands. The aims of this development are given as:

- to conserve the cultural heritage of the Netherlands
- to foster the availability of electronic publications by acquiring, describing and promoting them via the national bibliography
- to create a last resort for electronic publications produced in the Netherlands.

The depository has developed criteria for the inclusion of materials, which are divided into offline products such as CD-ROMs and online objects such as databanks and electronic journals. Numbers of items are as yet quite small – in the former category, 370 items in 1997 and 1017 in 1998 – and items are simply housed on bookshelves. Online publications are stored in an IBM 'Digital Library' system and by 1999 this contained around 400 journal titles comprising nearly a quarter of a million articles occupying 150Gb.

In the UK ongoing work by the National Preservation Office, part of the British Library, in concert with JISC-funded initiatives like CEDARS and the Research Support Library Programme (RSLP) are likely to result in a series of actions to address the issues of digital preservation. Fresko and Tombs (1998) suggest that the areas that will need particular attention are:

- metadata, in terms of both schemas and management
- processes for acquiring and assimilating new objects into archives ('ingestion')
- ongoing management approaches, designed to facilitate ongoing access
- preservation of complex objects, including multimedia, hypermedia and dynamic objects.

As noted above, to these must be added issues to do with intellectual property rights and the management of preservation within emerging publication cycles.

There is also one further issue that is worth exploring, namely that while information objects need to be preserved and there needs to be some form of certification of their integrity, associated metadata is subject to change. There is a rather nice example of this in the archives of the Scottish Cultural Resources Access Network (SCRAN) in Edinburgh, where some old film footage of the world's last sea-going paddle-steamer, *Waverley*, shows the ship progressing down the Clyde. After a while the image cuts to a young singer playing guitar. The original metadata identifies the item by the location and name of the ship. Only later, when the singer had made his reputation as the comedian Billy Connelly, would the description be enhanced to identify him as a subject. The object itself has not changed, but its significance has. How can metadata be updated to reflect such changes in the vast range of electronic resources that will be preserved?

## Conclusion

The information universe is far more than a random agglomeration of data and requires a massive effort to enable its effective exploitation. National, and indeed international, policy frameworks are needed to enable society to ensure that access is both pervasive and efficient, and that legitimate e-commerce can flourish. Long-term strategies are required to develop the organizational infrastructure needed to create a new kind of national and global resource. Libraries have a role to play in this endeavour, not only as intermediaries in the information access process but as architects and builders of the structured information universe itself.

# 10

# The user universe

On autumnal afternoons we played a version of *What's My Line?* in which two students played a reference librarian and a reader, the object being to find out what the reader wanted to know through a gentle form of interrogation.

'Morning, sir, how can I help you?'

'Do you have any books on houses?'

'I'm sure we do. Do you have any particular kind of house in mind?'

'Semi-detached.'

Thus the exchange proceeded until the reader finally revealed that what he wanted was to have a bat removed from his loft. (Taylor, 1993)

## Introduction

Libraries have always maintained 'profiles' of their users, although the term has more commonly been used by industrial and commercial information services. A profile is simply a set of information about a user, and the traditional approach has been to collect it as part of granting membership, often limiting the data to name, address and, in higher education, status (ie student, staff, external etc). At this stage the individual has also been identified as a legitimate library user. These records are then used to authorize individual transactions, typically when a request to borrow is made, when the material 'conditions' are compared with the 'user' conditions. So, for example, a 'normal' loan book is matched with a 'staff' status to determine the appropriate loan period.

However, it should be clear from the discussion in earlier chapters that the user community that a library serves, or that forms a potential audience and market for its services, requires much greater attention in the Information Age – at least as much as is given to the information universe on which it draws for its products. In a hybrid environment with its vast array of heterogeneous services and the competitive stance of many potential suppliers, whether intra- or extra-organizational, a clear focus on users is essential if quality services are to be delivered. As discussed in Chapter 6, quality management is based on the idea that every service and every product must be focused on 'fitness for purpose' and 'conformance to requirements', the purposes and requirements being those of the customers or users. As Brophy and Coulling (1996) remark:

> Before we can legitimately give the tag 'quality' to anything we have first to have thought through what it is that the product or service is to be used for . . . quality for one person is not necessarily quality for another. . . . The concept of choice, the freedom we all have in democratic societies to decide what it is that suits our purposes, our predispositions, our concerns, our preferences is another side of the same basic idea about the word 'quality': so it becomes, when used properly, a statement that the essential *product–customer–purpose* linkage has been established. Fundamentally, quality is concerned with meeting the wants and needs of customers.

It follows that detailed knowledge and understanding of the needs, preferences and reactions of users is utterly fundamental to the future library. The closer the library can get to its users as individuals the more likely it is to find a place in the portfolio of services they choose to use. If libraries get this right, they can become the portal of choice for their users.

## Personalization

It is becoming increasingly clear that the trend in the service sector as a whole is towards personalization, whereby systems are designed to recognize the individual user's preferences and to respond accordingly. The motor industry provides an interesting example, where over a long period of time provision has shifted from the apocryphal 'any colour as long as it's black' of the Model T Ford, through mass production of an ever-increasing series of pre-defined models, to emerging services where the purchaser can specify the exact model, colour etc he or she requires *before* the car is built, with the details selected at a dealership and downloaded direct to the factory. An example of direct application in the information service sector is the use of cookies in web environments, enabling service providers to collect user data once and then to re-use it each time the same user (actually very often a user at the same workstation, which is not quite the same thing) accesses the service.

In the networked environment, as was described in Chapter 7, user 'intelligence' is particularly important since it offers the key to a range of added-value services. For example, sophisticated user intelligence provides the prospect of making the 'view' of information resources that each user sees (in MODELS terms the 'information landscape') personal – the library may know what type of material that particular user has accessed in the past and may tune the initial interface screens to highlight similar, new resources. Profiles also hold the key to a dynamic 'information population', since each user can be given a set of electronic privileges as part of membership – users of one type (say, those signed up with an educational provider) may be offered information sources not available to others. Perhaps most important of all, user profiles hold out the prospect of automated electronic commerce. For example, a charged service can be offered automatically if the user profile can be queried to provide the necessary credit rating. For these reasons 'personalization' is likely to prove essential for the future.

However, personalization is not simply a matter of the service provider or broker collecting user data. It is also concerned with the provision of tools to enable users to personalize their own workspaces. Bookmark files in web browsers are an obvious, though rather crude, example. In effect the user is creating metadata concerning objects and collections. In the case of bookmarks these are usually little more than ordered lists, but more powerful facilities are starting to emerge that will enable more sophisticated approaches to be used. A series of 'MyLibrary' services (akin to the personalized services of some search engines such as *MyYahoo* or *MyExcite*) have been developed in recent years. These offer the individual user the opportunity to personalize the library interface and are seen by some as an answer to the problem of information overload – see for example Morgan (2000).

A further type of personalization occurs with 'push' services. A development of this approach funded within the UK eLib programme, NewsAgent (**http://www.sbu.ac.uk/~litc/newsagent/**), demonstrated the delivery of 'alerts' to professionals in the library and information management area. Each user could access the project website to set up and refine a profile, and alerts were distributed by e-mail at user-selected intervals.

The management of personalized workspaces, including push services, is likely to become a major issue both for users and for suppliers of end-user services, not least because it is difficult to support spaces that are not pre-defined – enquiries to a help desk first have to explore the individual set-up before the immediate problem can be examined. There are dangers that unfettered personalization by users can simply lead them into a personal maze of dead ends, making it difficult for inexperienced users to navigate effectively – to borrow the web analogy, they can end up surfing down a narrow canal rather than across an ocean. There is a delicate balance to be maintained between providing workspaces carefully and professionally designed to meet the requirements of a particular group of users, and enabling users to redesign their own workspaces from the supplied components. Again, however, this depends a lot on knowledge of the users. Thus, in higher education, while most research staff should be capable of coping with and exploiting a large range of self-design possibilities, first-year undergraduates could simply be overwhelmed and might be better served by a standard desktop.

A further development under the heading of personalization is portability. This refers to the ability of users, having created their own personal workspaces, to take them with them wherever they go. So, the familiar workspace created in the office or home environment becomes transferable to a cybercafé, to a public library workstation or on to a laptop. There is currently considerable interest in applying this concept to accessibility to enable disabled users to set up a suitable workspace, including accessibility tools such as voice output software or a text browser. Portability could be achieved by holding the workspace profile on a floppy disk although a more sustainable approach would be to hold such profiles in distributed data warehouses from which they would be retrieved and loaded as required.

The library role, or that of any other information broker, may thus be seen as a series of services:

- automatic personalization by using gathered intelligence to present individually designed services
- provision of tools to enable users to personalize their own workspaces and create their own metadata
- management of workspaces to prevent users becoming lost in a personal maze
- support of workspace portability by providing the software and hardware shells into which personal workspaces may be inserted.

## Authentication and authorization

Authentication and authorization are the processes of checking the users' identities and rights so that they are able to use a service or particular parts of it. In essence authentication processes ensure that the user is who he or she claims to be, while authorization checks that the authenticated user has the necessary rights (or, possibly, has made the necessary payments) to use the service requested. In the simplest case, it involves a set of processes – usually after the user has made a request and after the availability of the requested item has been checked – to ensure that the user is authorized to use that particular item. Authentication may also be applied at the collection level – for example, the BIDS system performs an authentication (password) check before allowing users to access its databases, but they may then search and retrieve items without further authorization.

A particular issue is that with many hundreds of services available, there is a danger that users will have to be issued with a password for each: password proliferation. To avoid this, generalized authentication schemes are being introduced – of which the ATHENS system in UK higher education provides one example.

The advantages of a common, widely implemented and well-designed authentication/authorization system are numerous:

- For users there is only one password to remember.
- Within any one session the user needs to be challenged only once – the user's system should then be able to handle challenges from each underlying source system.
- Because the user has only one password to remember it is less likely to be lost or forgotten, or accidentally revealed to others (or as happens all too frequently, written on a piece of paper and stuck to the PC!), so improving security and reducing the management overhead.
- A well-designed system should be scalable across a very wide range of services so that the addition of a new service does not impose any kind of additional requirement on the user.

In order to keep the administrative burden to a minimum it is desirable that the authentication system should enable users to be treated as members of groups. In higher education, for example, it should be possible to set up and vary privileges for, say, all undergraduates – having to change settings for each individual would clearly be an administrative nightmare. It is also desirable that the system should move away from what is at present a common approach, namely IP addressing. This has been popular because each PC (strictly speaking each Internet connection) has an Internet (IP) address. A university can thus simply declare the range of addresses it uses and a supplier can be sure that the service is only being used at that site. However, IP addressing has serious drawbacks: the major problem for users is that if they want to use the service off-campus they are unable to do so. Since, increasingly, people want services accessible at home or via mobile connections IP addressing is unsatisfactory.

Common authentication systems that address the needs of a wide community have a number of additional benefits for various stakeholders. Wiseman (1998) reports, for example, that the implementation of the ATHENS system has brought significant benefits to service providers, including opportunities for marketing their products and a reduction in their overhead costs since they no longer need to support their own proprietary access-control mechanisms. Institutions that use the system have opportunities for monitoring patterns of use of different services and thus for managing subscriptions.

More advanced systems which incorporate electronic commerce capabilities are being developed by banks, credit card companies and others. Work on digital signatures and other strong encryption techniques is also of considerable significance in this field. Some libraries – for example in the Netherlands – are investigating smart card technologies for these purposes.

## Data protection and privacy

Data protection legislation has been in force in the UK since 1984 and in some other countries, notably in Scandinavia, for some time before that. The concern behind this legislation is that individuals' personal information should only be used in appropriate circumstances and for legitimate purposes, and that each individual has a right to expect organizations to take all reasonable care to ensure that this happens. Initially restricted to data held in computer systems, the provisions are being extended to all media. The key requirements of the relevant legislation are that all personal data that is held by organizations or individuals should:

- only be obtained fairly and legally
- be held only for purposes declared by the organization
- be used or disclosed to others only in accordance with the organization's declaration
- be limited to data that is adequate for, relevant to and not excessive for the declared purposes
- be accurate and be kept up to date
- be kept no longer than necessary
- be copied to the subject of the data on request
- be properly protected against unauthorized disclosure.

In networked environments the opportunities for compromising individuals' privacy are manifold and it is essential that organizations wishing to offer services are able to assure and preferably demonstrate to potential customers that data submitted will not be misused. Libraries may have additional strength as 'trusted intermediaries', provided they maintain the highest standards of care in this regard and ensure that personal data is not passed on, even inadvertently, to other parties. This issue has implications for authentication and authorization services, especially as these become organized on a wider-area basis.

## Information use

There is a considerable body of research evidence, from a number of sectors, concerning the ways in which information is used. Again this is a vast field, but it is clearly important for the design of future libraries that there is better understanding of *how* information is used.

Formal investigations of information use have perhaps been most notable in conjunction with information retrieval system evaluation and there has been a broadening of interest towards the study of more general *information behaviour* in recent years. For example, Bawden and Robinson (1997) have investigated information behaviour in midwifery, noting that even within specialisms there are distinct differences:

> Midwives are confirmed as clearly distinct from other nurses, in their information needs and information-seeking behaviour. They have a wider range of information needs, employ a wider range of sources and require a range of specialist resources in addition to more general sources. In this respect, and particularly in their increasing community orientation, with consequent need for multidisciplinary information, they may be showing the pattern of the future for this kind of professional.

Recently, investigators have realized that some of the most important variables are *task* (Saracevic et al, 1988), *behavioural characteristics of the user* (Wilson, 1981; Ellis, 1989) and *cultural background* (Steinwachs, 1999). This suggests that library services themselves need to be designed within this kind of typology – considering the type of task being performed, the behavioural characteristics of the users (of which more is said below) and the cultural environment. The last of these has certainly engaged public librarians in recent years, but the first two merit at least equal attention.

## Learning

Coupled with understanding of information behaviour it is useful to be aware of people's different approaches to learning. Again there is a vast literature on this subject, but since one of the major roles of libraries across all sectors is in facilitating learning it is as well to consider the issue. It is particularly important that as libraries start to deliver services through multifaceted delivery vehicles – such as the learning environment which combines teaching, learning by exploration, information resource support, tutorial support and assessment in one 'package' – they recognize that the 'one size fits all' approach will not work. Furthermore, the paradigm that seems to dominate much online education at present runs counter to modern understandings of effective pedagogy. Wilkinson (1997) has observed that:

> Most recent developments in information technology . . . seem to ignore the direction in which educational reform is moving. Courseware seems stuck in the old world of rote memorization and 'learning as reproduction' – as if software developers and educational innovators live on separate planets.

What Wilkinson is referring to is the trend in educational theory, design and practice towards *constructive* pedagogies, as opposed to 'objectivist' approaches. Objectivism sees the world as an ordered structure of entities that have their existence quite apart from the observer – learning becomes a process of trying to reach a complete or 'correct' understanding of this world. It has proved a reasonable basis on which to teach much of the basics of science and technology, but it is a poor basis on which to apprehend a complex world of multiple frames of reference or to reach understanding of the social sphere. Objectivism also tends towards a didactic approach in which the learning is teacher-centred.

Constructivism, on the other hand, builds on the learner's own internal representation of the world, on personal interpretation of experiences, with the tutor assisting rather than imposing a system of their own. The representation each individual construct is open to continuous change in the light of new experiences. Bednar et al (1993) write:

> Learning is an active process in which meaning is developed on the basis of experience. This view of knowledge does not necessarily deny the existence of the real world . . . but contends that all we know of the world are human interpretations of our experience of the world . . . learning must be situated in a rich context, reflective of real world contexts for this constructive process to occur.

The essence of the constructivist approach is that it encourages conceptual understanding rather than learning by rote, and because of this it should produce learners who are flexible enough to take on new situations and deal with them in ways that have been learnt. In an age of rapidly changing knowledge, such learning is invaluable.

Coupled with this shift towards constructivism is renewed interest in learning or cognitive styles and learning models, the classic work being that of Pask (1976, 1988) and of Kolb (1984). Pask showed that individuals take one of two basic approaches to learning: 'holists' tend to look at the relationships between topics so as to build up a conceptual overview into which details can be fitted later. 'Serialists' take things in sequence, analysing one thing at a time so as to build up an overall picture in small steps. Ford (2000) links these ideas with ideas about 'deep' and 'surface' learning and field dependent/independent cognitive styles (Witkin et al, 1977) to examine information system use in virtual environments, including hypertext navigation and database searching.

The importance of this work lies in the suggestion that it is not enough to address the user population as an undifferentiated whole. Rather it is essential to recognize the differences in the ways in which people use information and undertake learning and to reflect these in the ways in which information sources are offered and presented. Software that can adapt to different styles is starting to emerge and there is considerable scope for taking such approaches to the building of personal information landscapes.

## Lifelong learning

One of the reasons that it is important to concentrate attention on learning itself is that the role of libraries in the future may start to be predicated much more on the support of lifelong learning, which is showing signs of being *the* national and global agenda issue of the decade and possibly of the century. Brophy, Craven and Fisher (1998) define the concept as follows:

> Lifelong learning is a deliberate progression throughout the life of an individual, where the initial acquisition of knowledge and skills is reviewed and upgraded continuously, to meet challenges set by an ever changing society.

There is also a growing consensus around the idea that not only should steps be taken to encourage learning that is lifelong, but that lifelong learning should be an aspiration for all citizens. Jean-Claude Paye, Secretary-General of the OECD, put it in this way (Paye, 1995):

> Continuing to expand education and training systems that rely upon learning opportunities limited to early life . . . will not suffice as a strategy for meeting today's challenges. . . . Much has been said over the years about lifelong learning but, in truth, it is still a reality for only a tiny segment of the populations of OECD countries. The huge task now facing OECD Governments is to make it a reality for a progressively expanding part of the population, so that it eventually becomes a reality for all.

There seems to be general acceptance that libraries have considerable potential to assist in the achievement of these visions. Furthermore, this would appear to be an area where the onward march of technology may be somewhat slowed by the expectations and expressed preferences of learners, especially those from the more disadvantaged sections of society. Libraries therefore need to approach assessment of the needs of lifelong learners with considerable care. As Brophy and MacDougall (2000) have commented:

> In considering the role of libraries it is important to reiterate that lifelong learning is a much wider concept than networked learning. The issue for libraries will be to provide a range of services which support lifelong learners who choose to learn in any one of many modes, and probably in a personal mix of all those available. The term 'hybrid', coming into common use to describe the types of media (traditional

and electronic) with which libraries will deal, may equally be applied to the learning processes which they support.

It is important, therefore, that libraries do not approach the issue of lifelong learning support as though it were entirely revolutionary and heralded the total demise of traditional services. Libraries have a strong tradition of support on which they can build, from the public library offering myriad opportunities for informal learning to the university library supporting leading-edge research – itself a form of lifelong learning. It is also worth remembering that "it is the basic, 'bread and butter' services such as access to books and study space that learners themselves regard as the highest priority" (Brophy, Craven and Fisher, 1998). . . . However, neither is there room for complacency.

## Networked learning

The term 'networked learning' can be used to describe all those methods of delivering learning that rely on information and communications technologies. The term is in widespread use although there is some ambiguity in its application, since a traditional, on-campus student who makes use of an electronic information resource in the university library could be regarded as a 'networked learner'. Usually, however, the term implies some measure of online interaction as part of the learning event.

Although enormous claims are made for networked learning the evidence for its efficacy is as yet mixed. In their evocatively titled paper, *Students' distress with a web-based distance education course*, Hara and Klung (2000) suggest that 'we need more student-centred studies of distance education that are designed to teach us how the appropriate use of technology and pedagogy could make distance education more beneficial for more students'.

A distinction needs to be made between synchronous and asynchronous learning, the former requiring all students to be available at the same time (as, for example, with a videoconference) and the latter allowing students to contribute at their own time (as, for example, with e-mail). This distinction is quite crucial in evaluating some of the claims made for networked learning – for example, students cannot learn at the place, pace and time of their choosing if synchronous techniques are in use.

Educational researchers suggest that networked learning has both strengths and limitations. Work by the CSALT team at Lancaster University (Centre for Studies in Advanced Learning Technology (CSALT), 2000), by Sproull and Kiesler (1991), Levy (1998) and others suggests that some of the strengths of networked learning may be the following:

- It promotes interactivity while providing flexibility in terms of time and place.
- It promotes active engagement by all learners.
- It encourages openness and reduces the inhibition of talking and/or pre-senting face-to-face which can be a major disincentive to some learners.
- It promotes reflective learning by requiring learners to consider what others in the group are saying.
- It can automatically create a permanent record of discussions to which tutors, and possibly students, can refer.
- It provides new opportunities for group learning, especially for part-time students and those with other responsibilities, such as students with families who live off-campus.
- It promotes social interaction as a side-benefit, for example through the use of e-mail to establish social as well as learning relationships.
- It gives easy access to the global resources of the web and other digital infor-mation.
- It provides better access for some under-represented groups.
- It changes relationships in learning: the tutor changes from being the 'sage on the stage' to the 'guide on the side' or, more appropriately, to a carefully selected mix of both roles.

And the limitations:

- It lacks what is known as 'expressive richness' in contributions: typed text lacks the nuances of the face-to-face spoken word.
- It lacks immediacy, especially for asynchronous communications, so that a contributor can be left wondering how others are reacting.
- It risks excessive immediacy, especially for synchronous communications, where impulsive messaging may adversely affect the discourse and some may be more impulsive than others.
- It reduces barriers to confrontational behaviour – it is easier for individuals to be domineering without immediate challenge.
- Synchronous 'conversation' may proceed too quickly for some students – an issue noted by Hara and Klung (2000) – and too slowly for others.
- Groups may take a long time to achieve consensus on a decision since tem-poral cues, such as the end of a scheduled meeting, may be missing.
- It requires access to equipment and network connections and some compe-tence in their use, neither of which can be assumed.
- Its style of communication – predominantly through short text messages – does not suit everyone even after long practice; there is a learning styles issue here which is currently under-researched.

- There may be differing and possibly conflicting styles of communication within a discourse, which some participants may find difficult.
- The lack of visual and other cues may make communication impersonal and may make it difficult to understand underlying 'messages' that are not explicit. In extreme cases this can result in students 'disconnecting' from the class.
- The lack of the sort of timetabling that traditional learning supplies may make it more difficult to gain the commitment needed from all participants where activity is predominantly asynchronous.
- Management of networked learning can be extremely onerous – how, for example, should a tutor deal with e-mail arriving from literally hundreds or even thousands of online students at all hours of the day and night?
- Feedback to students may be inadequate, especially where negative comments need to be given within the ambit of pastoral concern.

The CSALT team suggest that it is 'rather dangerous to make any strong claims about the strengths and limitations of networked learning . . . these are "claims in principle" rather than guarantees'. However, with so many issues to consider, the design of appropriate library services for lifelong learners will quite clearly need considerable research and development effort.

## Information literacy

Users cannot operate within networked environments without some basic skills. Literacy is the first of these, for without the ability to read – an issue noted in Chapter 2 in relation to the public library's role – no one can participate meaningfully in the information society. But literacy must go well beyond the simple ability to read. As Balsamo (1998) puts it:

> The construction of meaning is a complex behavior that is dependent on the embodied knowledge of individuals – in short, embodied literacy. . . . Literacy is the ability to make significant connections, to form interpretations, to evaluate situations, and to provide context.

It is now generally accepted that literacy must go well beyond basic reading, writing and numeracy skills. 'Functional literacy' refers to the ability to function in an advanced society – the OECD has used a threefold definition (Organization for Economic Cooperation and Development, 1995):

- *Prose literacy* – the knowledge and skills needed to understand and use information from texts including editorials, news stories, poems and fiction

- *Document literacy* – the knowledge and skills required to locate and use information contained in various formats, including job applications, payroll forms, transportation schedules, maps, tables and graphics
- *Quantitative literacy* – the knowledge and skills required to apply arithmetic operations, either alone or sequentially, to numbers embedded in printed materials, such as balancing a chequebook, figuring out a tip, completing an order form or determining the amount of interest on a loan from an advertisement.

The second of these sets of skills, termed 'document literacy' by the OECD, comes closest to the information literacy that many observers have suggested needs to be a focus of attention in the information age, although a considerably wider definition would be required to be able to function fully in the ICT-intensive world of developed countries today. Such literacy underpins the ability to participate in many activities, not least in lifelong learning.

## Information skills

Libraries have long had a role in helping their users to acquire skills, often under the title of 'user education' – a term that, incidentally, reveals a somewhat objectivist and teacher-centred view of learning. Academic libraries have traditionally provided a conducted tour for new students, usually at the start of the academic year, and then followed up with more targeted instruction (the term is chosen deliberately) later in the year. While attempts have been made to target students' particular interests, not least by ensuring that subject librarians have opportunities to demonstrate information resources to those within the departments for which they are responsible, such sessions have usually been attended by a minority. The reasons for this are not hard to find and centre round the issue of immediate relevance. Students are motivated in many ways, but principally by their assessments. If user education programmes are seen to provide worthwhile assistance in completing assignments they will be attended. Even better, if completion of this training leads to a grade that counts towards the final award, students will be even more highly motivated.

Burge and Snow (2000) point to the problem that librarians have in making the connection with users:

When some adult learners know that they lack information literacy skills, or even don't know such skills exist but know they have some kind of information problem, they feel reluctant to approach a librarian (especially one behind a big desk), and admit their need for help. After all, their sense of adulthood is bound up with feeling and being seen to be competent. It takes courage to ask for help from a stranger, and it takes time to develop confidence and skills as a learner. Why not instead go the convenience route?: ask the teacher or a nearby classmate, then get whatever is printable from an online database, and failing all those, a librarian.

These issues have led to a debate about 'embedding' such teaching within the curriculum. The 1997 Dearing Review of higher education in the UK reviewed the 'key skills' that graduates should possess and came down in favour of embedding rather than separating out key skills teaching. Recently, Levy (2000) concluded that 'the proportion of academic departments which include information skills training as an integral element of their programmes has increased recently in many institutions, especially in relation to postgraduate and distance learning courses'.

But just what are 'information skills'? Clearly they need to be defined much more broadly than IT skills. In an educational context, for example, Williams and Zald (1997) suggest that the essence of librarians' concerns should be to ensure that students:

- know when they need information;
- identify what information will address a particular problem;
- find the needed information;
- evaluate the information;
- organise the information;
- use the information effectively in addressing the problem.

The UK Standing Conference of National and University Libraries (SCONUL) recently produced its own definition of information skills, drawing attention to the need to distinguish between skills required by students to enable them to study effectively – sometimes called 'study skills' – and those required to enable them to function effectively in the real world where information itself is increasingly the dominant resource – in other words skills related to a high level of functional literacy (Standing Conference of National and University Libraries, 1999). For this latter set of skills the term 'information literacy' is perhaps more appropriate. SCONUL argues that to a large extent the difference between study skills and information literacy is one of degree. For example, while basic IT skills are essential for study, advanced IT skills contribute to information literacy and both are 'information skills'.

Seven 'headline' information skills were identified, as follows:

1 The ability to recognise a need for information.
2 The ability to distinguish ways in which the information 'gap' may be addressed.
    - Knowledge of appropriate kinds of resources, both print and non-print.

- Selection of resources with 'best fit' for task at hand.
- The ability to understand the issues affecting accessibility of sources.

3  The ability to construct strategies for locating information.
- To articulate information need to match against resources.
- To develop a systematic method appropriate for the need.
- To understand the principles of construction and generation of databases.

4  The ability to locate and access information.
- To develop appropriate searching techniques (e.g. use of Boolean searching).
- To use communication and information technologies, including international academic networks.
- To use abstracting and indexing services, citation indexes and databases.
- To use current awareness methods to keep up to date.

5  The ability to compare and evaluate information obtained from different sources.
- Awareness of bias and authority issues.
- Awareness of the peer review process of scholarly publishing.
- Appropriate extraction of information matching the information need.

6  The ability to organise, apply and communicate information to others in ways appropriate to the situation.
- To cite bibliographic references in project reports and theses.
- To construct a personal bibliographic system.
- To apply information to the problem at hand.
- To communicate effectively using the appropriate medium.
- To understand issues of copyright and plagiarism.
- The ability to synthesise and build upon existing information, contributing to the creation of new knowledge.

It will be seen that the need to assist users to develop skills that will make them effective within the information society provides a major challenge, especially as changes in technology and applications will almost certainly mean that skills will have to be updated regularly. Libraries, which will have to develop a high level of expertise simply to design and deliver information services in the future, should be well placed to provide the learning opportunities that their users will need if they are to develop such skills.

## Conclusion

Consideration of the user universe leads rapidly from purely technical considerations concerned with authentication and authorization and the development of factual intelligence about users to broader consideration of information usage and learning itself. Those, such as libraries, who make services available as intermediaries, need to be concerned to a much greater degree than hitherto with the processes of information usage in its many contexts. The knowledge of and expertise in the information universe that librarians must develop must also be accompanied by equal efforts to develop deep knowledge and understanding of users themselves.

# 11

# Into the future

One must never lose time in vainly regretting the past nor in complaining about the changes which cause us discomfort, for change is the very essence of life.
(Attributed to Anatole France)

## Introduction

The core of library and information services is to be found, this book has suggested, in the intermediary role between users and the information universe. At first glance, this seems a fragile position to occupy when individuals are more and more able to access information for themselves directly. When the world wide web was in its infancy, it was common to hear the comment that it spelt the end for all manner of intermediaries and brokers, and especially for those involved in the old-fashioned, convoluted publishing industry. After all, if anyone can publish anything for themselves, why pay publishing companies to do the job? Cut out the middlemen and both author and end-user would benefit – wouldn't they? Prices would fall and everyone – except of course the much lambasted middlemen – would benefit.

It hasn't turned out quite like that. Indeed, quite the opposite seems to have occurred. Far from destroying the intermediary role the web has actually encouraged it. Most of the recent dot.com start-ups are in fact intermediaries. Lastminute.com, to take one example, is not a producer of anything, but simply takes other companies' products and markets them in a coordinated way that saves the customer having to trawl round thousands of separate websites.

Web search engines, themselves intermediaries between the content providers and the customers, are becoming subject to higher levels of intermediation. inferenceFind (**http://www.infind.com**), for example, takes the user's search terms and uses them to search AltaVista, Excite, InfoSeek, Lycos, Web Crawler and Yahoo! simultaneously and clusters the results before presenting them. All kinds of intermediary software products are emerging. An example is 'direct hit' (**http://www.directhit.com**) which monitors a user's searching and builds up a ranked profile of sites, so that the most often visited are automatically listed first.

Could it be that the intermediary is actually in the strongest position? That in a fast-changing, confusing, information-overloaded world, what people want most is someone or some organization that will help them to make sense of the mass of information that threatens to overload them? That a *good* intermediary, able to adjust to new content streams and new technologies, and able to deliver quality (ie meeting the user's requirements), will prosper? And why shouldn't libraries be those intermediaries?

## The library as learning enabler

One of the remarkable linking themes that emerged from the discussion in Chapter 2 on libraries across the sectors was that almost always libraries see their contribution to society in educational terms. Panizzi was at pains to stress this regarding the national library in Britain. It formed the underlying theme of the academic libraries' Follett Report, where on the very first page there is the statement, 'it is impossible to imagine any university or college functioning effectively without a good library service'. School libraries have emerged from the, often warm, shelter of the English Department to become 'a tangible expression of the school's ethos and values, its approaches to equality of opportunity, the moral and spiritual development of children and young people and its educational purposes' (Tilke, 1998). Workplace libraries are placing increasing emphasis on their role in enabling employees to *learn* – this is, after all, the whole point of knowledge management and the underlying assumption of evidence-based practice. If, as suggested in the last chapter, lifelong learning is set to become *the* policy agenda for all nations in the 21st century, libraries should be well placed to develop a firm place within society, within corporations and within educational and other institutions – in fact across the whole organizational, societal and personal landscape. That place will be secured not solely by their role as information intermediaries, but by becoming 'learning centres' and perhaps 'centres of learning'.

But learning is not passive. It has impacts on individuals and on societies, and part of learning is learning how to share, to go beyond the educational consumer into membership of what might be called a 'learning network'. Such networks – characterized by interactions between people, regardless of the technology used – complete the information chain and turn it into a virtuous circle where publishing reinforces learning and learning becomes shared experience. Individuals become publishers – maybe only within their own small network, maybe growing in confidence to publish within their own local or domain communities, maybe contributing across a wider stage. The community information intermediary would seem ideally placed to provide not just infrastructure – for anyone can publish on the web – but authority (which may be localized), descriptive metadata, security, privacy and preservation.

## The library as place

While technology steals the headlines, people still live in real places and use real objects. Consider this comment on the UK *New Library* proposals:

> The vision projected in *New Library: the people's network* . . . was of public libraries 'at the hub of the community' and 'nurturing social cohesion', while a national survey carried out as a contribution to [the UK's] National Libraries Week 1997 found that over half of the responding authorities were involved in community development at a strategic level, with many of the initiatives aimed at children. The case studies showed public libraries as safe places where children learn a sense of ownership, one of the few public places where they are free from commercial pressures, and at times the only welcoming social space in a desolate landscape.
>
> (Heeks, 1998)

When Heeks speaks of 'place' she does not, one suspects, mean 'virtual space'. It is easy, in the excitement of cyberspace, to lose sight of the fact that physical places remain important and are where people actually live out their lives. In academic institutions, the library – centrally situated on the campus – often becomes the meeting place for staff and students. The public library is, as a physical place, hugely important to its local community. At its best it does more than offer books for borrowing and somewhere to read the newspapers – it inspires citizens. As Waite (2000) writes of one of the newest public libraries in Britain:

> The Peckham Library and Information Centre, one of the most distinctive new buildings in Britain and one that aims to draw a broad public back to reading and researching in the age of video shops and burger joints . . . is a bit of a show-off building, as it was intended to be. Its purpose, in a smaller way, and at a 20th of the cost, is to do for this poor area of inner London what, say, Frank Gehry's Guggenheim Museum has done for Bilbao: draw attention, attract visitors and investment, cheer people up and let them know that, far from being forgotten, they have one of the most exciting new public buildings in Europe.

This value of the library as place, and as a symbol of something much greater than the role of information intermediary might suggest, can be found everywhere. The exterior of the new British Library building at St Pancras symbolizes, albeit somewhat contentiously, the ship of knowledge. Inside the scale and quality of the building shine through as symbols of its role in preserving the nation's intellectual heritage. On a much smaller scale the Ruskin Library at Lancaster University, built at the top of a hill as the entrance road reveals the university, makes a statement of the enduring value that the library represents:

> The linear arrangement is deliberately church-like with entrance, treasury and read-ing room standing for narthex, choir and sanctuary. The public have access from a double height entrance to the first floor gallery which is arranged as two spaces con-nected through the treasury by a glass bridge. . . . Lighting will be kept to a mini-mum to preserve the archive . . . the only sunlight allowed into the building will be at sunset which will illuminate the metal soffit running through the centre of the building.                                    (MacCormac Jamieson Prichard, 1995)

Libraries say something important about the communities that build them. Until human beings disappear entirely into cyberspace, it seems likely that this role will remain.

## Conclusion

There are many, highly valued, roles that libraries can fill in the 21st century, but the most powerful will be the 'community information intermediary', a body that understands and has empathy with its community of users, has deep understanding of the information universe and its organization, and actively develops and promotes the mechanisms that link the two together. But, while this book has attempted to demonstrate the commonality that underpins all libraries, and to elucidate the complex technology-rich world in which they must now operate, it has not demonstrated that there is any inevitability about these roles. The ability to see possibilities, and even to point to exemplars, does not mean that libraries will of necessity occupy a central place in future society. That place has to be earned. It is librarians who must earn it.

# Bibliography

Abram, S (1998) Post information age positioning for special librarians: is knowledge management the answer? In *Knowledge management: a new competitive asset*, Economist Intelligence Unit.

American Library Association (1996) *Library Bill of Rights*, available at http://www.ala.org/work/freedom/lbr.html

American Library Association (2000a) *ALA interests and activities*, available at http://www.ala.org/work/

American Library Association (2000b) *Diversity in collection development: an interpretation of the 'Library Bill of Rights'*, available at http://www.ala.org/alaorg/oif/div_coll.html

American Library Association (2000c) *Evaluating library collections: an interpretation of the 'Library Bill of Rights'*, available at http://www.ala.org/alaorg/oif/eval_lib.html

American Library Association (2000d) *Interpretations of the 'Library Bill of Rights'*, available at http://www.ala.org/work/freedom/interprt.html

Appiah, A (1997) Realizing the virtual library. In Dowler, L (ed) *Gateways to knowledge: the role of academic libraries in teaching, learning, and research*, MIT Press.

Arms, C R (1996) Historical collections for the National Digital Library: lessons and challenges at the Library of Congress, *D-Lib Magazine*, (April), available at
http://www.dlib.org/dlib/april96/loc/04c-arms.html and
http://www.dlib.org/dlib/may96/loc/05c-arms.html

Arms, W Y (1995) Key concepts in the architecture of the digital library, *D-Lib Magazine*, (July), available at
http://www.dlib.org/dlib/July95/07arms.html

Arms, W Y, Blanchi, C and Overly, E A (1997) An architecture for information in digital libraries, *D-Lib Magazine*, (February), available at http://www.dlib.org/dlib/february97/cnri/02arms1.html

Atkinson, R (1996) Library functions, scholarly communication, and the foundation of the digital library: laying claim to the control zone, *Library Quarterly*, **66** (3), 239–65.

Audit Commission (1997) *Due for renewal: a report on the library service*, Audit Commission.

Balsamo, A (1998) Myths of information: the cultural impact of new information technologies. In Porter, A L and Read, W H (eds) *The information revolution: current and future consequences*, Ablex.

Bath Group, The (2000) *The Bath profile: an international Z39.50 specification for library applications and resource discovery: release 1.1*, UKOLN, available at
**http://www.ukoln.ac.uk/interop-focus/bath/1.1/**

Battin, P (1998) Leadership in a transformational age. In Hawkins, B L and Battin, P (eds) *The mirage of continuity: reconfiguring academic information resources for the 21st century*, Council on Library and Information Resources.

Bawden, D and Robinson, K (1997) Information behaviour in nursing specialities: a case study of midwifery, *Journal of Information Science*, **23** (6), 407–21.

Bawden, D and Rowlands, I (1999a) Digital libraries: assumptions and concepts, *Libri*, **49** (4), 181–91.

Bawden, D and Rowlands, I (1999b) *Understanding digital libraries: a conceptual framework*, British Library Research and Innovation Report 170, British Library Research and Innovation Centre.

Bearman, D et al (1999) A common model to support interoperable metadata, *D-Lib Magazine*, **5** (1), available at
**http://www.dlib.org/dlib/january99/bearman/01bearman.html**

Bednar, A et al (1993) Theory into practice: how do we link? In Duffy, T and Jonassen, D (eds) *Constructivism and the technology of instruction*, Lawrence Erlbaum Associates.

Bell, D (1973) *The coming of the post-industrial society*, Basic Books.

Berners-Lee, T (1999) *Weaving the web*, Orion Business Books.

Bertot, J, McClure, C R and Ryan, J (1999) *Developing statistics and performance measures for the networked environment: interim report*, available at
**http://www.albany.edu/~imlsstat**

*Borrowed time: the future of public libraries in the UK* (1993), Comedia.

Brack, V (1999) Service developments at the RIDING Z39.50 gateway, *The New Review of Information and Library Research*, **5**, 135–44.

Branin, J J (1998) Cooperative collection development: significant trends and issues, *Collection Management,* **23** (4), 1–17.

British Medical Journal (1996) Evidence-based medicine, *British Medical Journal*, **312**, 71–2.

Brockman, J et al (1997) *Quality management and benchmarking in the information sector: results of recent research*, Bowker-Saur.

Brophy, P (1991) The mission of the academic library, *British Journal of Academic Librarianship*, **6** (3), 135–47.

Brophy, P (1993) What's in a name? *Library Management*, **94** (1108), 27–9.

Brophy, P (1998a) It may be electronic but is it any good? Measuring the performance of electronic services. In *Robots to Knowbots: the wider automation agenda. Proceedings of the Victorian Association for Library Automation 9th Biennial Conference, January 28–30 1998*, VALA.

Brophy, P (1998b) Overview: management information for the electronic library. In Hanson, T and Day, J (eds) *Managing the electronic library: a practical guide for information professionals*, Bowker-Saur.

Brophy, P (1999) *Digital library research review*, Library and Information Commission, available at
**http://www.lic.gov.uk/**

Brophy, P (2000) Towards a generic model of information and library services in the information age, *Journal of Documentation*, **56** (2), 161–84.

Brophy P and Coulling, K (1996) *Quality management for information and library managers*, Gower.

Brophy, P and Craven, J (1999) *The integrated, accessible library: a model of service development for the 21st century: the final report of the REVIEL (Resources for Visually Impaired Users of the Electronic Library) project*, British Library Research and Innovation Report 168, Centre for Research in Library and Information Management, Manchester Metropolitan University.

Brophy, P, Craven, J and Fisher, S (1998) *The development of UK academic library services in the context of lifelong learning: final report*, Library Information Technology Centre, South Bank University on behalf of JISC.

Brophy, P, Craven, J and Fisher, S (1999) *Extremism and the Internet*, British Library Research and Innovation Report 145, Centre for Research in Library and Information Management, Manchester Metropolitan University.

Brophy, P and Fisher, S (1998) The hybrid library, *The New Review of Information and Library Research*, **5**, 135–44.

Brophy, P and MacDougall, A (2000) Lifelong learning and libraries, *The New Review of Libraries and Lifelong Learning*, **1**, 3–17.

Brophy, P and Wynne, P M (1997) *Management information systems and performance measurement for the electronic library*, Library Information Technology Centre on behalf of the Higher Education Funding Councils' Joint Information Systems Committee.

Brophy, P et al (1997a) *EQLIPSE: Evaluation and quality in library performance: system for Europe: final report and final functional specification*, Centre for Research in Library and Information Management, Manchester Metropolitan University.

Brophy, P et al (1997b) *Self-service systems in libraries: final report*, Centre for Research in Library and Information Management, University of Central Lancashire.

Buckland, M K (1988) *Library services in theory and context*, 2nd edn, Pergamon Press.

Burge, E J and Snow, J E (2000) Candles, corks and contracts: essential relationships between learners and librarians, *The New Review of Libraries and Lifelong Learning*, **1**, 19–34.

Bury, L (2000) Phantom sales menace for DK, *The Bookseller*, **4908**, (28 January), 6.

Caplan, P (1995) You call it corn, we call it syntax: independent metadata for document-like objects, *The Public-Access Computer Systems Review*, **6** (4), 19–23, available at
**http://info.lib.uh.edu/pacsrev.html/**

Castels, M (1998) *The information age: economy, society and culture*, Blackwell.

Centre for Studies in Advanced Learning Technology (CSALT) (2000) *Effective networked learning in higher education: notes and guidelines*, Lancaster University, available at
**http://csalt.lancs.ac.uk/jisc/**

Childers, T and Van House, N A (1989) The grail of goodness: the effective public library, *Library Journal*, **114** (16), 44–9.

Chodorow, S and Lyman, P (1998) The responsibilities of universities. In Hawkins, B L and Battin, P (eds) *The mirage of continuity: reconfiguring academic information resources for the 21st century*, Council on Library and Information Resources and Association of American Universities.

Chowdhury, G G and Chowdhury, S (1999) Digital library research: major issues and trends, *Journal of Documentation*, **55** (4), 409–48.

Clapp, V W (1964) *The future of research libraries*, University of Illinois Press.

Clarke, Z (1999) The EQUINOX project and the development of performance indicators for the electronic library. In *Proceedings of the 3rd International Conference on Performance Measurement in Libraries and Information Services held at Longhirst Management and Training Centre, Longhirst Hall, Northumberland, England, 27–31 August 1999*, Information North.

Cochrane, P (1999) What is the future of man, woman and machine?, *RSA Journal*, **2** (4), 64–9.

CommerceNet Research Center (1999) *Ecommerce survey shows 27% of British adults now use the Internet on a regular basis*, available at
**http://www.commerce.net/research/news/press/102799.html**

CommerceNet Research Center (2000) *Worldwide Internet population*, available at
**http://www.commerce.net/research/stats/wwstats.html**

Committee on Higher Education (1963) *Higher education: report of the committee appointed by the Prime Minister under the chairmanship of Lord Robbins 1961–1963* (The Robbins Report), Cmnd 2154, HMSO.

Council of Chief State School Officers (1961) *Responsibilities of state departments of education for school library services: a policy statement*, Council of Chief State School Officers. Cited in Gaver, M V (1972) United States. In Lowrie, J E (ed) *School libraries: international developments*, Scarecrow Press.

Cowley, J (1985) Current management concerns. In Cowley, J (ed) *The management of polytechnic libraries*, Gower.

Crawford, W (1999) *Being analog: creating tomorrow's libraries*, American Library Association.

Cunningham, A (1997) New direction for the national bibliography, *Select: Newsletter of the National Bibliographic Service,* **21**, 1–2.

Day, M (1999) The scholarly journal in transition and the PubMed Central proposal, *Ariadne*, **21**, available at
**http://www.ariadne.ac.uk/issue21/pubmed/**

de Kerckhove, D (1997) *Connected intelligence: the arrival of the web society*, Somerville House.

Dempsey, L (1999) The library, the catalogue, the broker. In Criddle, S, Dempsey, L and Heseltine, R (eds) *Information landscapes for a learning society: networking and the future of libraries 3: an international conference held at the University of Bath, 29 June–1 July 1998*, Library Association Publishing.

Dempsey, L and Heery, R (1997) *DESIRE – Development of a European service for information on research and education: specification for resource description methods. Part 1. A review of metadata: a survey of current resource description formats*, Version 1.0, (19.3.97), UKOLN.

Dempsey, L, Russell, R and Murray, R (1999) Utopian place of criticism? Brokering access to network information, *Journal of Documentation,* **55** (1), 33–70.

Department for Culture, Media and Sport (1999) *Libraries for all: social inclusion in public libraries*, Department for Culture, Media and Sport.

Department for Culture, Media and Sport (2000) *Comprehensive and efficient: standards for modern public libraries: a consultation paper*, Department for Culture, Media and Sport.

Department of National Heritage (1997) *Legal deposit of publications: a consultation paper*, Department of National Heritage.

Department of National Heritage (1997) *Reading the future: public libraries review*, HMSO.

Dovey, M (2000) So you want to build a union catalogue? *Ariadne*, **23**, available at http://www.ariadne.ac.uk/issue23/dovey/intro.html

Drucker, P (1997) Interview, *Forbes Magazine*, (March 10), 126–7.

Duff, A S (1998) Daniel Bell's theory of the information society, *Journal of Information Science*, **24** (6), 373–93.

Dyson, E (1997) *Release 2.0: a design for living in the digital age*, Broadway.

Elkin, J (1998) Focus on the child: children's libraries in Portugal: report of a workshop held in Lisbon during the Festival of Public Libraries, *The New Review of Children's Literature and Librarianship*, **4**, 93–106. Quoted in Elkin, J and Kinnell, M (2000) Introduction: children's libraries for the next millennium. In Elkin, J and Kinnell, M (eds) *A place for children: public libraries as a major force in children's reading*, British Library Research and Innovation Report 117, Library Association Publishing.

Elkin, J (2000) Overview and summary of findings. In Elkin, J and Kinnell, M (eds) (2000) *A place for children: public libraries as a major force in children's reading*, British Library Research and Innovation Report 117, Library Association Publishing.

Ellis, D (1989) A behavioural approach to information retrieval system design, *Journal of Documentation*, **45** (3), 171–212.

ESYS Limited (2000) *Summative evaluation of phases 1 and 2 of the eLib initiative: final report*, ESYS, available at
http://www.ukoln.ac.uk/services/elib/info-projects/phase-1-and-2-evaluation/elib-fr-v1-2.pdf

Feeney, M (1999) Towards a national strategy for archiving digital materials, *Alexandria*, **11** (2), 107–21.

Fidel, R (1984) On-line searching styles: a case-study-based model of searching behavior, *Journal of the American Society for Information Science*, **35** (4), 211–21.

Fidel, R (1984) Searchers' selection of search keys: III. Searching styles, *Journal of the American Society for Information Science*, **42** (7), 515–27.

Fonfa, R (1998) From faculty to librarian materials selection: an element in the professionalization of librarianship. In Mech, T F and McCabe, G B (eds) *Leadership and academic libraries*, Greenwood Press.

Ford, N (2000) Cognitive styles and virtual environments, *Journal of the American Society for Information Science*, **51** (6), 543–57.

Forsman, R B (1998) Managing the electronic resources transforming research libraries. In Lynden, F C and Chapman, E A (eds) *Advances in Librarianship*, **22**, Academic Press.

Fresko, M and Tombs, K (1998) *Digital preservation guidelines: the state of the art in libraries, museums and archives*, European Commission DGXIII/E-4.

Frye, B E (1997) Universities in transition: implications for libraries. In Dowler, L (ed) *Gateways to knowledge: the role of academic libraries in teaching, learning, and research*, MIT Press.

G-7 Information Society Conference (1995) *Chair's conclusions*, available at **http://www.ispo.cec.be/g7/keydocs/G7en.html**

Garfield, E (2000) *Inaugural address: ASIS Mid-Year Conference 2000*, available at **http://www.asis.org/garfield.html**

Garvin, D A (1988) *Managing quality*, Free Press.

Gaver, M V (1972) United States. In Lowrie, J E (ed) *School Libraries: International developments*, Scarecrow Press.

Ginsparg, P (1997) First steps in electronic research communication. In Dowler, L (ed) *Gateways to knowledge: the role of academic libraries in teaching, learning, and research*, MIT Press.

Ginsparg, P, Luce, R and Van de Sompel, H (1999) *The Open Archives Initiative*, available at **http://www.openarchives.org/**

Goodall, D and Brophy, P (1997) *A comparable experience? Library support for franchised courses in higher education*, British Library Research and Innovation Report 33, Centre for Research in Library and Information Management, University of Central Lancashire.

Greenberg, D (1998) Camel drivers and gatecrashers. In Hawkins, B L and Battin, P (eds) *The mirage of continuity: reconfiguring academic information resources for the 21st century*, Council on Library and Information Resources and Association of American Universities.

Greenstein, D (1999) Discovering resources across the humanities: an application of the Dublin Core and the Z39.50 network application protocol. In Criddle, S, Dempsey, L and Heseltine, R (eds) *Information landscapes for a learning society: networking and the future of libraries 3: an international conference held at the University of Bath, 29 June–1 July 1998*, Library Association Publishing.

Grimes, D J (1998) *Academic library centrality: user success through service, access and tradition*, American Library Association.

Hara, N and Klung, R (2000) Students' distress with a web-based distance education course, available at **http://www.slis.indiana.edu/CSI/wp00-01.html/**

Hardesty, L (2000) The age of information, the age of foolishness, *College & Research Libraries,* **61** (1), 6–8.

Hardison, O B Jr (1989) *Disappearing through the skylight: culture and technology in the twentieth century*, Viking Penguin.

Harnad, S (2000) E-knowledge: freeing the refereed journal corpus online, *Computer Law and Security Report*, **16** (2), 78–87, available at **http://www.cogsci.soton.ac.uk/~harnad/Papers/Harnad/harnad00. scinejm.htm**

Harris, M H and Hanna, S A (1993) *Into the future: the foundations of library and information services in the post-industrial era*, Ablex.

Hawgood, J and Morley, R (1969) *Project for evaluating the benefits from university libraries*, OSTI Report 5056, University of Durham.

Hawkins, B L (1998) The unsustainability of the traditional library. In Hawkins, B L and Battin, P, *The mirage of continuity: reconfiguring academic information resources for the 21st century*, Council on Library and Information Resources and Association of American Universities.

Heeks, P (1998) A place for children: reflections on a project, *The New Review of Children's Literature and Librarianship*, **4**, 81–91.

Higham, N (1980) *The library in the university: observations on a service*, Deutsch.

Higher Education Funding Council for England (1995a) *The effective academic library: a framework for evaluating the performance of UK academic libraries: a consultative report to HEFC(E), SHEFC, HEFC(W) and DENI by the Joint Funding Council's Ad Hoc Group on performance indicators for libraries*, Higher Education Funding Council for England.

Higher Education Funding Council for England (1995b) *Report of the group on a national/regional strategy for library provision for researchers*, The Anderson Report, Higher Education Funding Council for England, available at **http://www.ukoln.ac.uk/services/elib/papers/other/anderson/**

Higher Education Funding Council for England, Scottish Higher Education Funding Council, Higher Education Funding Council for Wales and the Department of Education for Northern Ireland (1993) *Joint Funding Councils' Libraries Review Group: report* (The Follett Report), Higher Education Funding Council for England.

Holdsworth, M (2000) Demands of on-demand, *The Bookseller,* **4908**, (28 January), 30–1.

House of Commons (2000) *Culture, media and sport: Sixth report*, House of Commons, available at **http://www.publications.parliament.uk/pa/cm199900/cmselect/ cmcumeds/241/24102.htm**

House of Commons, Select Committee on Public Libraries (1849) *Report, together with the proceedings of the committee, minutes of evidence and appendix*, The Stationery Office.

Hutton, R S (1945) The origin and history of Aslib, *Journal of Documentation*, **1** (1), 6–20. Quoted in Meadows, A J (1987) Introduction. In Meadows, A J (ed) *The origins of information science*, Taylor-Graham.

IFLA (1995) *UNESCO Public library manifesto*, IFLA.

Institute of Information Scientists (1998) *Criteria for information science*, available at
**http://www.iis.org.uk/membership/Criteria.html**

Institute of Information Scientists and The Library Association (1999) *Our professional future: revised proposals for a new organisation for the library and information profession*, Institute of Information Scientists and The Library Association, available at
**http://www.la-hq.org.uk/directory/prof-issues/opf.html**

International DOI Foundation (1999) *DOI metadata principles*, available at
**http://www.doi.org/META-PRIN.PDF**

International Organization for Standardization (1996) Information and documentation - format for information exchange, ISO 2709, International Organization for Standardization.

International Organization for Standardization (1997) Information and documentation – open systems interconnection – interlibrary loan application service definition, ISO 10160, (Amendment 1 acknowledges the National Library of Canada as the maintenance agency.) International Organization for Standardization.

International Organization for Standardization (1998) Information and documentation – library performance indicators ISO 11620, International Organization for Standardization.

Johnson, R K (2000) A question of access: SPARC, BioOne, and society-driven electronic publishing, *D-Lib Magazine*, **6** (5), available at
**http://www.dlib.org/dlib/may00/05johnson.html**

Joint Information Systems Committee (1998) *An integrated information environment for higher education: developing the Distributed, National Electronic Resource (DNER)*, Joint Information Systems Committee, available at
**http://www.jisc.ac.uk/dner_colpol.html**

Joint Information Systems Committee (1999a) *Adding value to the UK's learning, teaching and research resources: the distributed national electronic resource (DNER)*, Joint Information Systems Committee, available at
**http://www.jisc.ac.uk/dner_vision.html**

Joint Information Systems Committee (1999b) *Content Working Group (CWG) of the Committee for Electronic Information (CEI): Progress overview 1996–1999*, Joint Information Systems Committee, available at
**http://www.jisc.ac.uk/cwg_96_99.html**

Kahle, B (1997) Preserving the Internet, *Scientific American*, March 1997, available at
  **http://www.sciam.com/0397issue/0397kahle.html**
Kahn, R and Wilensky, R (1995) *A framework for distributed digital object services*, available at
  **http://www.cnri.reston.va.us/home/cstr/arch/k-w.html**
King Research Ltd (1990) *Keys to success: performance indicators for public libraries*, HMSO.
Kinnell, M (1992) *Learning resources in schools: Library Association guidelines for school libraries*, Library Association Publishing.
Kinnell, M and Sturges, P (1996) Introduction. In Kinnell, M and Sturges, P (eds) *Continuity and innovation in the public library: the development of a social institution*, Library Association Publishing.
Kohl, H (1997) [Speech by German Chancellor Kohl at the opening of Die Deutsche Bibliothek]. Quoted in McCormick, P and Scott, M, *National libraries*. In Line, M B (ed) (1999) *Librarianship and information work worldwide 1999*, Bowker-Saur.
Kolb, D A (1984) *Experiential learning: experience as the source of learning and development*, Prentice Hall.
Kranich, N C (1996) Staking a claim for public space in cyberspace. In Reed, S G (ed) *Creating the future: essays on librarianship in an age of great change*, McFarland.
Kuhlthau, C C (1991) Inside the search process: information seeking from the user's perspective, *Journal of the American Society for Information Science*, **42**, 361–71.
Kvaerndrup, H M (2000) Denmark's Electronic Research Library (DEF): A project changing concepts, values and priorities. In Brophy, P, Fisher, S and Clarke, Z (eds) *Libraries without walls 3*, Library Association Publishing.
Lagoze, C and Fielding, D (1998) Defining collections in distributed digital libraries, *D-Lib Magazine*, available at
  **http://www.mirrored.ukoln.ac.uk/lis-journal/dlib/november98/11lagoze.html**
Lancaster, F W (1983) Future librarianship: preparing for an unconventional career, *Wilson Library Bulletin*, **57**, 747–53.
Levy, P (1998) Perspectives on organisational network communities: a review paper for library and information service managers, *Program*, **32** (4), 343–58.
Levy, P (2000) Information specialists supporting learning in the networked environment: a review of trends and issues in higher education, *The New Review of Libraries and Lifelong Learning*, **1**, 35–64.

Levy, S (1999) Wired for the bottom line, *Newsweek*, **CXXXIII** (15), (11 October), 51–2, 54, 56, 58, 60.

Library and Information Commission (1997) *New Library: the people's network*, Library and Information Commission.

Library and Information Commission (2000) *Keystone for the information age: a national information policy for the UK*, Library and Information Commission.

Library and Information Commission (nd) *2020 vision*, Library and Information Commission.

Library and Information Commission Research Committee (1998) *Prospects: a strategy for action: library and information research, development and innovation in the United Kingdom*, Library and Information Commission.

Library and Information Services Council (1986) *School libraries: the foundations of the curriculum: report of the working party on school library services*, HMSO.

Library Association (1998) *Committed to excellence: a century of achievement; annual report 1998*, Library Association.

Library Association (2000a) *Professional issues*, available at **http://www.la-hq.org.uk/directory/prof_issues.html**

Library Association (2000b) *The Royal Charter of the Library Association*, available at **http://www.la-hq.org.uk/about/charter.html**

Library Association (2000c) *Who we are*, available at **http://www.la-hq.org.uk/directory/about.html**

Line, M B (1999) Making sure that national collections continue to be available, *Alexandria*, **11** (2), 81–3.

Line, M B (2000) The lifelong learner and the future library, *The New Review of Libraries and Lifelong Learning*, **1**, 65–80.

Lyman, P (1996) Access is the killer application, *Journal of Academic Librarianship*, **22** (5), 371–5.

Lyman, P (1997) The gateway library: teaching and research in the global reference room. In Dowler, L (ed) *Gateways to knowledge, the role of academic libraries in teaching, learning, and research*, MIT Press.

Lyman, P and Chodorow, S (1998) The future of scholarly communication. In Hawkins, B L and Battin, P *The mirage of continuity: reconfiguring academic information resources for the 21st century*, Council on Library and Information Resources and Association of American Universities.

Lynch, C (1997) Building the infrastructure of resource sharing: union catalogs, distributed search, and cross-database linkage, *Library Trends*, **45** (3), 448–61.

MacCormac Jamieson Prichard (1995) Lancaster University Library extension and the Ruskin Library. In Taylor, S (ed) *Building libraries for the information age*, Institute of Advanced Architectural Studies.

MacDougall, A (1998) Supporting learners at a distance, *Ariadne*, **16**, available at
http://www.ariadne.ac.uk/issue16/main/intro.html

Mainwood, H R (1972) School libraries in the United Kingdom. In Lowrie, J (ed) *School libraries: international developments*, Scarecrow Press.

Malhotra, Y (1999) *What is really knowledge management? Crossing the chasm of hype*, available at
http://www.brint.com/advisor/a092099.htm

Maxwell, M F (1989) *Handbook for AACR2 1988 revision*, American Library Association.

McClellan, A W (1973) *The reader, the library and the book*, Bingley.

McClure, C R and Lopata, C L (1996) *Assessing the academic networked environment: strategies and options*, Coalition for Networked Information.

McCullagh, D (1998) Library computers logged off, *Wired*, available at
http://www.wired.com/news/politics/0,1283,16481,00.html

McGonagle, J (1998) *SLA guidelines: promoting literacy through the primary school library*, School Library Association.

Miller, P (2000) Interoperability: what is it and why should I want it?, *Ariadne*, **24**, available at
http://www.ariadne.ac.uk/issue24/interoperability/

Milner, E, Kinnell, M and Usherwood, B (1994) Quality management: the public library debate, *Public Library Journal*, **9** (6), 151–7.

**MODELS**, available at
http://www.ukoln.ac.uk/dlis/models/

Moore, N (1997) Neo-liberal or dirigiste? Policies for an information society. In Rowlands, I (ed) *Understanding information policy: proceedings of a workshop held at Cumberland Lodge, Windsor Great Park, 22–24 July 1996*, Bowker-Saur.

Moore, P (1998) Primary school children's interaction with library media: information literacy in practice. In Shoham, S and Yitzhaki, M (eds) *Education for all; culture, reading and information*, International Association of School Librarianship.

Morgan, E L (2000) Personalized library interfaces, *Exploit Interactive*, 06, available at
http://www.exploit-lib.org/issue6/libraries/

Murison, W J (1971) *The public library: its origins, purpose and significance*, 2nd edn, Harrap.

National Committee of Inquiry into Higher Education (1997) *Higher education in the learning society* (The Dearing Report), HMSO.

National Library of Australia (1997) *Statement of principles: preservation of and long-term access to Australian digital objects*, available at
http://www.nla.gov.au/npo/natco/princ.html

Ober, J (1999) The California Digital Library, *D-Lib Magazine*, 5 (3), available at
http://www.dlib.org/dlib/march99/03ober.html/

Organization for Economic Co-operation and Development (1995) *Literacy, economy and society: results of the first international adult literacy survey*, OECD and Statistics Canada.

Orr, R H (1973) Measuring the goodness of library services: a general framework for considering quantitative measures, *Journal of Documentation*, 29 (3), 315–32.

Osburn, C B (1997) The research university and its library. In Schwartz, C A (ed) *Restructuring academic libraries: organizational development in the wake of technological change*, American Library Association.

Owen, J S M and Wiercx, A (1996) *Knowledge models for networked library services: final report*, Report PROLIB/KMS 16905, Office of Official Publications of the European Communities.

Oxbrow, N and Abell, A (1998) Putting knowledge to work: what skills and competencies are required? In *Knowledge management: a new competitive asset*, Economist Intelligence Unit.

Pask, G (1976) Styles and strategies of learning, *British Journal of Educational Psychology*, 46, 12–25.

Pask, G (1988) Learning strategies, teaching strategies, and conceptual or learning style. In Schmeck, R R (ed) *Learning strategies and learning style*, Plenum Press.

Paskin, N (1997) Information identifiers, *Learned Publishing*, 10 (2), 135–56.

Paskin, N (1999) *E-citations: actionable identifiers and scholarly referencing*, available at
http://www.doi.org/resources.html

Paye, J-C (1995) *Making lifelong learning a reality for all*, OECD.

Peek, R (2000) *ASIS summit 2000: defining information architecture*, available at
http://www.asis.org/peek.html

Pinfield, S and Hampson, A (1999) Partnership and customer service in the hybrid library, *The New Review of Information and Library Research*, 5, 107–19.

Powell, A (ed) (1998) *Collection description working group: work in progress*, UKOLN, available at
http://www.ukoln.ac.uk/metadata/cld/wg-report/intro.html/

Quality Assurance Agency for Higher Education (2000) *Librarianship and information management*, Subject Benchmark Statements, available at **http://www.qaa.ac.uk/benchmark/library.pdf**

Ranganathan, S R (1931) *Five laws of library science*, Madras Library Association.

Reid, E O F (1999) *The Internet and digital libraries: implications for libraries in the ASEAN region*, available at **http://www.apmforum.com/alf/diglibs.htm**

Revill, D (1985) The measurement of performance. In Cowley, J (ed) *The management of polytechnic libraries*, Gower. (The quotation by Charlton is found on p 132.)

Rider, F (1944) *The scholar and the future of research libraries*, Hadham Press.

Rowlands, I (1997) Understanding information policy: concepts, frameworks and research tools. In Rowlands, I (ed) *Understanding information policy: proceedings of a workshop held at Cumberland Lodge, Windsor Great Park, 22–24 July 1996*, Bowker-Saur.

Rowlands, I and Bawden, D (1999) Digital libraries: a conceptual framework, *Libri*, **49** (4), 192–202.

Rowley, J (2000) Portal power, *Managing Information*, **7** (1), 62, 64.

Royce, J (1998) More than surviving, thriving in the information age: reading as a basis for using information technology efficiently. In Shoham, S and Yitzhaki, M (eds) *Education for all; culture, reading and information*, International Association of School Librarianship.

Rusbridge, C (1998) Towards the hybrid library, *D-Lib Magazine*, (July–August), available at **http://mirrored.ukoln.ac.uk/lis-journals/dlib/dlib/dlib/july98/rusbridge/07rusbridge.html**

Rynänen, M (1998) *Report on the Green Paper on the role of libraries in the modern world*, European Parliament: Committee on Culture, Youth, Education and the Media, available at **http://www.lib.hel.fi/syke/english/publications/report.htm**

Sanderson, C (1999) Doing the grounds, *The Bookseller*, (24/31 December), **4904**, 24–6.

Saracevic, T et al (1988) A study of information seeking and retrieving, *Journal of the American Society for Information Science,* **39** (3), 161–76.

Schement, J R and Curtis, T (1995) *Tendencies and tensions of the information age: the production and distribution of information in the United States*, Transaction Publishers.

Shank, R (1983) Management information and the organization: homily from the experience of the data rich to the information poor. In Lancaster, F W (ed) *Library automation as a source of management information: papers pre-*

sented at the *1982 Clinic on Library Applications of Data Processing, April 25–28 1982*, University of Illinois.

Shuman, B A (1989) *The library of the future: alternative scenarios for the information profession*, Libraries Unlimited.

Smith, D (1980) *Systems thinking in library and information management*, Bingley.

Spreadbury, H and Spiller, D (1999) *Survey of secondary school library users*, LISU Occasional Paper 21, Library and Information Statistics Unit, Loughborough University.

Sproull, L and Kiesler, S L (1991) *Connections: new ways of working in the networked organization*, MIT Press.

Standing Conference of National and University Libraries (1999) *Information skills in higher education*, SCONUL.

Steele, V (1995) Producing value: a North American perspective on the future of higher education libraries. In Taylor, S (ed) *Building libraries for the information age*, Institute of Advanced Architectural Studies, University of York, quoting Sack, J R (1986) Open systems for open minds: building the library without walls, *College & Research Libraries,* **47** (6), (November), 538.

Steenbakkers, J F (1999) Developing the Netherlands depository of electronic publications, *Alexandria,* **11** (2), 93–105.

Steinwachs, S (1999) Information and culture: the impact of national culture on information processes, *Journal of Information Science*, **25** (3), 193–204.

Summers, R et al (1999) Information science in 2010: a Loughborough University view, *Journal of Documentation*, **50** (12), 1153–62.

Surridge, R (1984) The priorities for research in librarianship, *Library & Information Research News*, **7** (27 & 28), 11–16.

Syvestre, C (1987) *Guidelines for national libraries*, UNESCO.

Takeuchi, H (1998) Beyond knowledge management: lessons from Japan, available at
**http://www.sveiby.com.au/LessonsJapan.htm**

Taylor, A (1993) Introduction. In Taylor, A (ed) *Long overdue: a library reader*, Mainstream.

Taylor, D (2000) An e-future? It's academic, *The Bookseller*, **4921**, 32–4.

Tennant, R (1998) Strategies for building 21st century libraries and librarians. In *Robots to Knowbots: the wider automation agenda. Proceedings of the Victorian Association for Library Automation 9th Biennial Conference, January 28–30 1998*, VALA,.503–7.

Thompson, J (1977) *A history of the principles of librarianship*, Bingley.

Tilke, A (ed) (1998) *Library Association guidelines for secondary school libraries*, Library Association Publishing.

Toffler, A (1980) *The Third Wave*, Collins.

Underwood, P G (1996) *Soft systems analysis and the management of libraries, information services and resource centres*, Library Association Publishing.

University Grants Committee (1967) *Report of the committee on libraries* (The Parry Report), HMSO.

University Grants Committee (1976) *Report on capital provision for university libraries* (The Atkinson Report), HMSO.

Van de Sompel, H and Lagoze, C (2000) The Santa Fe Convention of the Open Archives Initiative, *D-Lib Magazine*, **6** (2), available at **http://www.dlib.org/dlib/february2000/vandesompel-oai/02vandesompel-oai.html**

Van House, N A, Weil, B T and McClure, C E (1990) *Measuring academic library performance: a practical approach*, American Library Association.

Waite, R (2000) Shelf life, *Guardian Weekend*, (4th March), 19–24.

Wiegan, W A (1999) The structure of librarianship: essay on an information profession, *Canadian Journal of Library and Information Science*, **24** (1), 17–37.

Wilkinson, J (1997) Homesteading on the electronic frontier. In Dowlin, L (ed) *Gateways to knowledge: the role of academic libraries in teaching, learning, and research*, MIT Press.

Williams, H and Zald, A (1997) Redefining roles: librarians as partners in information literacy education, *International Journal of Electronic Library Research*, **1** (3), 253–66.

Wilson, T (1999) Exploring models of information behaviour: the uncertainty project, *Information Processing and Management,* **35**, 839–49.

Wilson, T and Walsh, C (1996) *Information behaviour: an inter-disciplinary approach*, British Library Research & Innovation Report 10, Department of Information Studies, University of Sheffield, available at **http://www.shef.ac.uk/~is/publications/prelims.html/**

Wilson, T D (1981) On user studies and information needs, *Journal of Documentation*, **37** (1), 3–15.

Wilson, T D (1998) Redesigning the university library in the digital age, *Journal of Documentation,* **54** (1), 15–27.

Winograd, T (1997) From computing machinery to interaction design. In Denning, P and Metcalfe, R (eds) *Beyond calculation: the next fifty years of computing*, Springer Verlag, available at **http://hci.stanford.edu/~winograd/acm97.html**

Winston, I (1997) Lights, camera, action! Videos for legal deposit, *National Library News,* **29** (9), 3–4.

Wiseman, N (1998) Implementing a national access management system for electronic services: technology alone is not enough, *D-Lib Magazine*, (March), available at http://www.dlib.org/dlib/march98/wiseman/03wiseman.html

Witkin, HA et al (1977) Field-dependent and field-independent cognitive styles and their educational implications, *Review of Educational Research*, **47**, 1–64.

Wolf, M T (1998) Cooperative collection development: significant trends and issues, *Collection Management*, **23** (4), 59–93.

Wood, F et al (1997) Information skills for student centred learning: a computer-assisted learning approach, British Library Research and Innovation Report 37, British Library Research and Innovation Centre.

Wood, F E, Ford, N and Walsh, C (1992) The effect of postings on searching behaviour, *Journal of Information Science*, **20** (1), 29–40.

*World Book Encyclopedia* (1999) Dennis Publishing.

World Wide Web Consortium (2000) *Resource Description Framework Model and syntax specification*, available at
http://www.w3.org/TR/REC-rdf-syntax

Wusteman, J (1998) Formats for the electronic library. *Ariadne*, **8**, available at
http://www.ariadne.ac.uk/issue8/electronic-formats/intro.html

Wynne, P M and Brophy, P (1998) Performance measurement and management information for the electronic library. In *Northumbria International Conference on Performance Measurement in Libraries and Information Services, 7–11 September 1997*, Information North.

Xerox Palo Alto Research Center (1999) *Electronic paper*, available at
http://www.parc.xerox.com/dhl/projects/epaper/

Yates, J (1989) *Control through communication*, Johns Hopkins University Press.

# Glossary

| | |
|---|---|
| AACR | Anglo-American Cataloguing Rules |
| ADS | Archaeology Data Service – part of **AHDS** |
| AGORA | **eLib** Phase 3 'hybrid library' project |
| AHDS | Arts and Humanities Data Service |
| AIFF | Audio Interchange File Format |
| ALA | American Library Association |
| ANSI | American National Standards Institute |
| applet | Computer program that can be transmitted from a **server** and executed on a **client**, usually within a world wide web environment |
| ARL | Association of Research Libraries (USA) |
| ASCII | American Standard Code for Information Interchange (ISO 641) – widely used character set, using 7 bits per character; limited to 128 characters. |
| AVI | Audio–Video Interleaved – Microsoft video format |
| BICI | Book Item and Component Identifier |
| BIDS | Bath Information and Data Services – one of the UK higher education data centres |
| BIOME | Health and life sciences hub (one of the **RDN** hubs) |
| BL | British Library |
| BLDSC | British Library Document Supply Centre |
| BUILDER | Birmingham University Integrated Library Development and Electronic Resource (**eLib** Phase 3 'hybrid library' project) |
| cache | Temporary store for data to which a system or **client** is expected to require access |
| CAIRNS | Cooperative Academic Information Retrieval Network for Scotland (**eLib** Project) |
| CALIM | Consortium of Academic Libraries in Manchester |
| CDF | Channel Definition Format – an **XML** application, used mainly for 'push' services |
| CD-ROM | Compact Disc Read Only Memory – a format for physical media for digital content |
| CEDARS | CURL Exemplars in Digital ARchiveS (**eLib** project) |
| CERLIM | Centre for Research in Library and Information |

| | |
|---|---|
| | Management (Manchester Metropolitan University) |
| CGI | Common Gateway Interface – used to enable clients to access services other than standard world wide web servers |
| CIMI | Computer Interchange of Museum Information |
| CIT | Communication and Information Technologies (more usually **ICT**) |
| client | End-user workstation or other computer that requests services from a **server** |
| CMC | Computer-Mediated Communication |
| CNI | Coalition for Networked Information (USA) |
| CNRI | Corporation for National Research Initiatives (USA) |
| CORBA | Common Object Request Broker Architecture |
| CSS | Cascading Style Sheets – used to separate visual and other formatting of web pages from **HTML** content, providing greater control, efficiency of updating and personalization |
| CWIS | Campus Wide Information Service |
| DAISY | Digital Audio based Information SYstem – an emerging tagged digital audio standard, being implemented particularly for the use of blind and visually impaired people |
| DC | **Dublin Core** |
| DCMS | Department for Culture, Media and Sport (UK government department) |
| DDC | Dewey Decimal Classification |
| DES | Data Encryption Standard – used with private key encryption |
| DHTML | Dynamic Hypertext Mark-up Language – uses **CSS** and a scripting language to add dynamic functionality to **HTML** pages |
| DLI | Digital Libraries Initiative (USA) |
| DN | Distinguished Name (an object name in **X.500** or **LDAP** directories) |
| DNER | Distributed National Electronic Resource |
| DNS | Domain Name System |
| DOI | Digital Object Identifier |
| DSC | *see* BLDSC |
| DTD | Document Type Definition |
| Dublin Core | Metadata element set specifying a minimal (15) set of resource description elements, used mainly in world wide web environments but capable of much wider |

| | |
|---|---|
| | implementation |
| DVD | Digital Video Disk or Digital Versatile Disk |
| EAD | Encoding Archival Description – **SGML DTD** for archival documents |
| EARL | Electronic Access to Resources in Libraries |
| EC | European Commission |
| EDI | Electronic Data Interchange |
| EDINA | Edinburgh Data and INformation Access – one of the UK higher education data centres |
| EEVL | Edinburgh Engineering Virtual Library (one of the **eLib** subject gateways, now part of **EMC**) |
| eLib | Electronic Libraries Programme |
| ELJ | Electronic Law Journals (**eLib** project) |
| EMC | Engineering, Mathematics and Computing hub (one of the **RDN** hubs) |
| EU | European Union |
| FOI | Freedom of Information |
| FTP | File Transfer Protocol |
| GIF | Graphics Interchange Format |
| GII | Global Information Infrastructure |
| GILS | Government Information Locator Service |
| GIS | Geographic Information Systems |
| Gopher | Character-based document transfer protocol, now obsolescent and eclipsed by **HTML/HTTP** |
| GPRS | General Packet Radio Service |
| Handle system | A system of unique and persistent identifiers and for resolving them into locations |
| HCI | Human–Computer Interaction |
| HDS | History Data Service – part of **AHDS** |
| HEADLINE | Hybrid Electronic Access and Delivery in the Library Networked Environment. **eLib** Phase 3 'hybrid library' project |
| HEI | Higher Education Institution |
| HERON | Higher Education Resources ON-Demand (**eLib** project, now becoming a UK national service) |
| HTML | HyperText Mark-up Language |
| HTTP | HyperText Transfer Protocol |
| Humbul | Humanities hub (one of the **RDN** hubs) |
| HyLiFe | Hybrid Library of the Future (**eLib** Phase 3 'hybrid library' project) |
| IBD | International Bibliographic Description |

| | |
|---|---|
| ICT | Information and Communications Technologies |
| IEEE | Institute of Electrical and Electronic Engineers |
| IETF | Internet Engineering Task Force |
| IFLA | International Federation of Library Associations and Institutions |
| IIS | Institute of Information Scientists |
| ILEJ | Internet Library of Early Journals |
| ILL | Interlibrary Loan – may also refer to the ISO 10160/10161 interlibrary loan protocols |
| IMS | Instructional Management System |
| IP | Internet Protocol |
| IPR | Intellectual Property Rights |
| ISAAC | Information Seeker's Avenue to Authoritative Content (USA) – subject gateway/portal service |
| ISAD(G) | General International Standard Archival Description |
| ISBN | International Standard Book Number |
| ISO | International Organization for Standardization |
| ISO Latin 1 | Replacement character sets for **ASCII** that enable a series of 256 character sets to be accessed (using escape sequences) and so extend ASCII to a range of mainly European languages |
| ISP | Internet Service Provider |
| ISSN | International Standard Serial Number |
| ISWC | International Standard Work Code (for musical compositions) |
| JANET | Joint Academic NETwork – the UK universities' communications network |
| Java | Mobile, machine independent programming language, widely used for user interfaces |
| JISC | Joint Information Systems Committee (of the UK higher education funding councils; recently also expanded to provide services to the UK further education sector) |
| JPEG | Joint Photographic Expert Group – compression format for images |
| JSTOR | Journal STORage – service that digitizes and makes available back-runs of important journals |
| KM | Knowledge Management |
| LA | Library Association (of the UK) |
| LAN | Local-Area Network |
| LaTeX | A version of **TeX** |
| LC | Library of Congress |

| | |
|---|---|
| LCSH | Library of Congress Subject Headings |
| LDAP | Lightweight Directory Access Protocol |
| LIC | Library and Information Commission (from 1st April 2000 became part of Resource: the Council for Museums, Archives and Libraries) |
| LLL | LifeLong Learning |
| LMS | Library Management System |
| MALIBU | MAnaging the hybrid Library for the Benefit of Users (**eLib** Phase 3 'hybrid library' project) |
| MAN | Metropolitan Area Network |
| MARC | MAchine-Readable Cataloguing – formats based on ISO 2709 for the interchange of bibliographic information in machine-readable form |
| MeSH | Medical Subject Headings |
| MIA | **MODELS** Information Architecture |
| MIMAS | Manchester InforMation and Associated Services (formerly MIDAS) – one of the UK higher education data centres |
| MIME | Multi-purpose Internet Mail Extensions – adds additional functionality (eg attachments) to **SMTP** |
| MIS | Management Information System |
| MODELS | MOving to Distributed Environments for Library Services (**eLib** study, including a series of influential expert workshops) |
| MPEG | Moving Pictures Expert Group – popular compression standard for video |
| NCIP | North American Collection Inventory Project (USA) |
| NDLP | National Digital Library Program (of the Library of Congress) |
| NeLH | National electronic Library for Health |
| NESLI | National Electronic Site Licensing Initiative |
| NGfL | National Grid for Learning |
| NII | National Information Infrastructure |
| NISO | National Information Standards Organization (USA) |
| NISS | National Information Services and Systems |
| NSF | National Science Foundation (USA) – a major funder of digital library research |
| OCLC | Online Computer Library Center (USA) |
| OECD | Organisation for Economic Co-operation and Development |
| OPAC | Online Public Access Catalogue |

| | |
|---|---|
| OSI | Open Systems Interconnection – basic seven-layer architecture for network communications |
| OTA | Oxford Text Archive – part of **AHDS** |
| PADS | Performing Arts Data Service – part of **AHDS** |
| PDF | Portable Document Format – proprietary format owned by Adobe |
| PGP | Pretty Good Privacy |
| PI | Performance Indicator |
| PICS | Platform for Internet Content Selection – metadata set that provides the basis for Internet content filtering |
| PII | Publisher Item Identifier |
| PKCS | Public Key Cryptography Standards |
| PLN | Public Library Network |
| PostScript | Programming language that controls formatted printing (ie a page description language) |
| PSIgate | Physical Sciences hub (one of the **RDN** hubs) |
| PSLI | Pilot Site Licence Initiative – replaced by **NESLI** |
| PURL | Persistent Uniform Resource Locator |
| QTVR | QuickTime Virtual Reality – Apple's product to enable objects to be viewed through 360° |
| QuickTime | Apple's video compression format |
| RDF | Resource Description Framework – generalized method of specifying metadata syntax |
| RDN | Resource Discovery Network – part of the UK **DNER** (also Relative Distinguished Name in **X.500** and **LDAP**) |
| RDNC | Resource Discovery Network Centre – coordinates the **RDN** |
| RealAudio | Proprietary audio file format, widely used |
| RealVideo | Proprietary video file format, widely used |
| RLG | Research Libraries Group (USA) |
| ROADS | Resource Organisation And Discovery in Subject-based services – an **eLib** project that developed software for subject gateway services |
| RSLP | Research Support Libraries Programme |
| RTF | Rich Text Format – a portable exchange format for word-processed documents |
| SBIG | Subject-Based Information Gateway |
| SCONUL | Standing Conference of National and University Libraries |
| SDI | Selective Dissemination of Information |
| SEREN | Sharing of Educational Resources in an Electronic |

| | |
|---|---|
| | Network (**eLib** project) |
| server | Networked computer that stores data and/or programs |
| SET | Secure Electronic Transactions |
| SGML | Standard Generalized Mark-up Language |
| ShockWave | Multimedia standard from Macromedia; widely implemented and included in both Internet Explorer and Netscape Navigator |
| SICI | Serial Item and Contribution Identifier |
| SIG | Special Interest Group |
| SLA | Service Level Agreement |
| SLE | School of Library Economy (of Columbia University) – where Melvil Dewey inaugurated librarianship training |
| SME | Small and Medium-sized Enterprise |
| SMIL | Synchronized Multimedia Integration Language – used to ensure files within a multimedia package are displayed correctly |
| SMTP | Simple Mail Transfer Protocol – widely implemented e-mail standard |
| SOIF | Summary Object Interchange Format |
| SOSIG | Originally Social Science Information Gateway, now Social Sciences, Business and Law hub (one of the **RDN** hubs) |
| SPARC | Scholarly Publishing and Academic Resources Coalition (USA) |
| SQL | Structured Query Language – widely used for querying relational databases |
| SSL | Secure Socket Layer |
| SuperJANET | Enhanced **JANET**, providing greater bandwidth |
| tag | A standard sequence of characters that indicates structure within a document |
| TCP/IP | Transmission Control Protocol/Internet Protocol |
| TEI | Text Encoding Initiative |
| Telnet | Application that enables a user to log in to a remote server and access applications such as library catalogues; now superseded by world wide web-based interfaces using **CGI** scripts etc. |
| TeX | Encoding system that defines appearance precisely – widely used for mathematical notation |
| TIFF | Tagged Image File Format – a widely used image format |
| TQM | Total Quality Management |
| TREC | Text Retrieval Conferences – known especially for their |

|  | standard sets of documents against which retrieval systems are tested |
|---|---|
| UfI | Originally, University for Industry, now UfI (marketing its services as *learndirect*) |
| UGC | University Grants Committee |
| UNICODE | A 16-bit character coding system, intended to cover all the world's written languages; **XML** supports it although it is not yet widely implemented. |
| URC | Uniform Resource Characteristics (or Uniform Resource Citation) |
| URI | Uniform Resource Identifier – includes **URN**s, **URL**s and **URC**s |
| URL | Uniform Resource Locator – the standard addressing system for the world wide web |
| URN | Uniform Resource Name |
| VADS | Visual Arts Data Service – part of **AHDS** |
| VRML | Virtual Reality Modelling Language – public domain standard |
| W3C | World Wide Web Consortium |
| WAI | Web Accessibility Initiative (of **W3C**) |
| WAP | Wireless Application Protocol |
| Warwick Framework | A scheme for the interchange of metadata packages in containers, usually associated with the implementation of **Dublin Core** |
| watermark | A visible or invisible code that is bound into a document to indicate integrity or ownership |
| WAV | Microsoft audio file format |
| WHOIS++ | Directory search protocol, used by UK subject gateways |
| WML | Wireless Mark-up Language |
| WoPEc | Working Papers in Economics (**eLib** project) |
| X.500 | Standard for online directories |
| XLS | eXtensible Style Language – a style sheet (*see* CSS) system for use with **XML** |
| XML | eXtensible Markup Language |
| Z39.50 | Information retrieval protocol (ISO 23950) that specifies rules and procedures for searching server (target) databases by clients (origins) |

# Index

# The Academic Library

## PETER BROPHY

This authoritative and wide-ranging textbook provides a comprehensive overview of the changing functions of higher education libraries and the organizational cultures in which they operate. It offers an assessment of the impact of such changes on service delivery from both provider and user perspectives, and considers the future role of the academic library. Written in a readable and accessible style, the book focuses on:

- the library in the institution
- users of the academic library
- the impacts and opportunities of ICTs
- human resources
- management and organization of resources
- collection and access management
- library systems and networks
- specialist services
- management and professional issues.

This textbook is an indispensable introduction to the range of issues facing academic libraries. Invaluable for new information professionals and for students on information and library studies courses, it also makes stimulating reading for education administrators and academic library managers in both higher and further education. While the book considers emerging scenarios in the United Kingdom in depth, it also draws examples from institutions elsewhere in the world, and is of broad international interest.

## The Author

**Peter Brophy** BSc FLA FIInfSc FRSA is Professor of Information Management in the Department of Information and Communications at Manchester Metropolitan University, where he is also Director of the Centre for Research in Library and Information Management (CERLIM). He was formerly University Librarian of the University of Central Lancashire.

**2000; 224pp; paperback; ISBN 1-85604-374-6; £29.95**

# International Yearbook of Library and Information Management 2000–2001: Collection Management

## GENERAL EDITOR: G E GORMAN

About the series: *The International Yearbook* is essential reading for anyone who wants to keep up-to-date with recent developments in library science and information management on a global basis. Each thematic volume will include papers covering current issues, emergent debates, models of best practice and likely future developments, contributed by an internationally respected panel of researchers, practitioners and academics.

The first volume of this authoritative annual publication provides a timely and forward-looking focus on the theme of collection management. This broad subject area is examined from a range of perspectives in a series of historical, analytical, evaluative and provocative essays that tell us where we have been, where we are and where we seem to be going. The book is divided into five main sections:

- Part 1: People, Principles and Problems
- Part 2: Electronic Publications, Access and Acquisitions
- Part 3: Cooperative Collection Management and Storage Facilities
- Part 4: Evaluating and Weeding
- Part 5: Preservation and Archives.

The substantive chapters comprise a mix of research-based, practice-based or reflective scholarly studies of worldwide application and interest.

The series editor: **Dr G E Gorman** BA MDIV STB GRADDIPLIB MA THD FLA FRSA is senior lecturer in library and information science at Victoria University of Wellington in New Zealand. He has published extensively in the field of library and information work and he is a regular contributor to scholarly and professional journals. The Editorial Board of the International Yearbook series includes members from Australia, New Zealand, China, Vietnam, India, Uganda, South Africa, Singapore, UK and USA.

**2000; 464pp; hardback; 1-85604-366-5; £60.00**